Bantam/Britannica Books

**Unique, authoritative guides
to acquiring human knowledge**

What motivates people and nations? What
makes things work? What laws and history lie
behind the strivings and conflicts of
contemporary man?

One of mankind's greatest natural endowments
is the urge to learn. Bantam/Britannica books
were created to help make that goal a reality.
Distilled and edited from the vast Britannica
files, these compact introductory volumes offer
uniquely accessible summaries of human
knowledge. Oceanography, politics, natural
disasters, world events—just about everything
that the inquisitive person wants to know about
is fully explained and explored.

BANTAM/BRITANNICA BOOKS

The Arabs
People and Power

**Prepared by
the Editors of
Encyclopaedia
Britannica**

THE ARABS: PEOPLE AND POWER
Bantam edition/November 1978

*Bantam Books are published by Bantam Books, Inc. Its trademark,
consisting of the words "Bantam Books" and the portrayal
of a bantam, is registered in the United States Patent Office
and in other countries. Marca Registrada.
Bantam Books, Inc.,
666 Fifth Avenue, New York, New York 10019.*

Printed in the United States of America

Foreword:
Knowledge for Today's World

One of mankind's greatest natural endowments is the urge to learn. Whether we call it knowledge-seeking, intellectual curiosity, or plain nosiness, most people feel a need to get behind the newspaper page or the TV newscast and seek out the background events: What motivates people and nations? What makes things work? How is science explained? What laws and history lie behind the strivings and conflicts of contemporary man? Yet the very richness of information that bombards us daily often makes it hard to acquire such knowledge, given with authority, about the forces and factors influencing our lives.

The editors at Britannica have spent a great deal of time, over the years, pondering this problem. Their ultimate answer, the 15th Edition of the *Encyclopaedia Britannica*, has been lauded not merely as a vast, comprehensive collection of information but also as a unique, informed summary of human knowledge in an orderly and innovative form. Besides this work, they have also thought to produce a series of compact introductory volumes providing essential information about a wide variety of peoples and problems, cultures, crafts, and disciplines. Hence the birth of these Bantam/Britannica books.

The Bantam/Britannica books, prepared under the guidance of the Britannica's Board of Editors, have been distilled and edited from the vast repository of information in the Britannica archives. The editors have also used the mine of material in the 14th Edition, a great work in its own right, which is no longer being published because much of its material did not fit the design imposed by the 15th. In addition to these sources, current Britannica files and reports—including those for annual yearbooks and for publications in other languages—were made available for this new series.

All of the Bantam/Britannica books are prepared by Britannica editors in our Chicago headquarters with the assistance of specialized subject editors for some volumes. The Bantam/Britannica books cover the widest possible range of topics. They are current and contemporary as well as cultural and historical. They are designed to provide *knowledge for today*—for students anxious to grasp the essentials of a subject, for concerned citizens who want to know more about how their world works, for the intellectually curious who like good reading in concise form. They are a stepping-stone to the thirty-volume *Encyclopaedia Britannica*, not a substitute for it. That is why references to the 15th Edition, also known as *Britannica 3* because of its three distinct parts, are included in the bibliographies. While additional research is always recommended, these books are complete unto themselves. Just about everything that the inquisitive person needs to catch up on a subject is contained within their pages. They make good companions, as well as good teachers. Read them.

The Editors,
Encyclopaedia Britannica

Contents

Introduction:
The Arab World

Flying inland from the Persian Gulf, a jet airliner circles into its landing pattern and approaches Riyadh. Not far from some of the world's richest oil reserves, the new airport is scheduled for an expansion that will accommodate up to ten million passengers a year. It is striking evidence of the enormous leap that Saudi Arabia, like many of its Arab neighbors, has made from poverty to power in a single generation.

Aboard the plane one traveler in uniform is on his way to the military college. Another, a Saudi prince, is returning to his family mansion near the grounds of the royal palace. A German archaeologist carries a letter asking official approval to explore the interior deserts, which still preserve undisclosed secrets. A Mormon engineer seeks an answer from the central government about mining exploration. A graduate nurse is reporting to one of the new hospitals; a student, to Riyadh University. In traditional Muslim costume, a party of pilgrims plans to spend a few days in the capital before continuing on its way to Mecca and Medina, the holy cities of Islam. No Jews are on the passenger list.

Driving into the city from the airport, the foreign visitor sees little that is not new — Western-style buildings, new government ministries, and modern hospitals and hotels. Riyadh still displays picturesque houses with antique red balconies, but the young mayor has plans for parks and a civic center. The city has bought statuary by the British sculptor Henry Moore as well as recent works by French, Italian, and Saudi sculptors. In the largest city of Saudi Arabia the walls and houses of old Riyadh crumble everywhere amid the constant din of construction. Riyadh has already become a city of the present in a kingdom that is incessantly absorbed in its future.

For tomorrow's pilgrim a transpeninsular highway will run from Riyadh across the desert to Mecca near the shores of the Red Sea and from there to Jidda, the kingdom's chief port and commercial center. Under a master plan to be executed by West German and U.S. companies, Jidda will eventually have the world's biggest airport, larger than Manhattan island, with a huge plant to desalinate Red Sea water and with all its facilities air-conditioned — including a hospital, seven mosques, a one-hundred acre pilgrimage terminal, and a royal pavilion. In Jidda itself, traditionally known as the "Bride of the Red Sea," picturesque buildings have been replaced by blocks of concrete apartments, new shops, and modern hotels. Foreign embassies identify Jidda as the Saudi diplomatic capital, and the pilgrim quarantine station provides protection against epidemics.

Secular and Sacred

Leaving the modern novelties of Jidda, the traveler to Mecca begins a journey backward in time. The tarmac road follows an ancient camel track 45 miles across a sandy plain, over arid hills, then across the Hejaz range to a point where two pillars mark the boundaries of sacred soil. As Saudi officials make certain, no unbeliever may pass beyond these pillars, and the business of today must be set aside according to the pattern laid down by Mohammed himself. The use of jewelry, perfume, and other personal adornment—as well as sexual intercourse—is forbidden until the pilgrimage is completed. During the holy season at Mecca living creatures, excepting criminals who have been condemned to death by the Islamic court, may be killed only for food or sacrifice.

The three capitals—Riyadh and Jidda for business, diplomacy, and pleasure and Mecca for the Muslims of every country—are divided by the vastness of the Arabian Peninsula and yet are inseparable in the mind and life of "Arabdom." The line between the world of today and the religion and traditions of yesterday is often as elusive as a mirage. The banker in Riyadh or the ambassador in Jidda is surrounded by living witness to Allah and his Prophet, while pilgrims in Mecca, especially the more devout, find Muslim puritanism inevitably tempered by the sudden wealth of its Saudi custodians. (On the gulf coast the town of Jubayl will be transformed into an ultra-modern industrial complex at a cost to the Saudi treasury of $45 billion.) In the same way cities all over the Arab world, as they struggle to maintain tradition, are being revolutionized in different degrees by the oil economy and by the immeasurable impact of Western technology at every level.

Death of the Romantic Past

The old tribal life is no match for "progress." Around Riyadh the expansion is inexorable, proceeding without pity in every direction over uprooted date groves, past neglected and dying palms, into the desert. Abandoning the oasis in search of jobs and a share in the economic revolution, nomads themselves join the influx of newcomers from Syria, Lebanon, Egypt, and Yemen. Few of them recognize anything familiar in "the land of spices" that enchanted the audience of the ancient Greek historian Herodotus—an Arabia "where the whole country gives off a heavenly sweet aroma." Nor do they find many of the oriental splendors of *The Thousand and One Nights.*

Westerners have been intoxicated since the reign of King Midas by the fabled luxuries of the East and by the "noble savage" of the dunes, usually seen at one remove, however, through the eyes of eccentric European travelers. The desert horseman in his flowing cape now belongs more properly to the museum of folklore, beside the "Saracens" charging down on the Crusaders or the Rifi warriors making a last noble stand against the French Foreign Legion. Like the beckoning alleyways of forbidden casbahs, however, such figures still haunt the imagination and the motion picture screen. At times, the romantic Arab past even casts a lingering shadow across the landscape of reality.

The Sulubba, or Slebs, for example, by ancestral custom breed the white asses of Arabia. The men continue to be hunters and can guide even a Bedouin rider through an unfamiliar waste of sand. The Sulubba also practice the ancient craft of tinkering and allow the women to become prostitutes. Their trades have been handed down through unrecorded generations and, like all trades, are beneath the dignity of the Bedouins. Historically, the Sulubba belonged to the "ignoble" tribes—smiths, carpenters, copper workers and cattle watchers—who paid protection to the "noble" tribes of raiders and fighters and who were considered inviolate in battle. Nostalgia for "romantic Araby"—for the parched "fanatic Arabia" of the British explorers Charles Doughty and Sir Richard Burton—is a powerful but fading force, and the speed of modern communication is obliterating the stereotypes of nineteenth-century writers. The bearded patriarch is becoming the playboy sheikh.

The speed of change affects the best reality as well as the worst stereotype. The king's palace in the center of old Riyadh, once an exemplar of the latest in Arabian architecture, has been replaced by a large office building, oddly reminiscent of the cubist style. With a single, low minaret, the mud brick mosque that faced it was a more obvious anachronism. The new concrete mosque has two tall minarets equipped with loudspeakers so that the muezzin's call to prayer is not blurred in the bustle of the city. These new towers, in turn, have no guarantee against future aspirations and the assault of technology.

Race, Religion, and Language

Looking at this unstable mixture of mud and concrete, of East and West, hearing the pounding of jackhammers and the confusion of tongues, an observer might wonder if it is possible any longer to define the simple word *Arab*, to say nothing of the more complex and recent notion of "the Arab world." The answer is obviously more than a matter for demographers and anthropologists. Since World War II knowledge of this dynamic world has become essential to political and economic life everywhere. Knowledge of the Arab world daily becomes more essential as Arab men, and now Arab women, awaken to a renaissance of greater significance than historic Islam at its imperial zenith.

In its narrowest definition *Arab* is applied to certain Semitic-speaking tribesmen, the "pure Arabs" who originally inhabited the great peninsular deserts between Riyadh and Mecca. Over the centuries their language has become the official or colloquial idiom from the Spanish Sahara to the edge of the Iranian plateau, lands where native, often nomadic, populations are mixed with nearly every racial strain. Today these speakers of Arabic number more than one hundred million. The Muslim faith, first propagated among the pure Arabs and long since divided into many sects, is now shared by one-sixth of mankind. But the huge majority of contemporary Muslims around the globe, four out of five, speak no Arabic, and few can hope to make the pilgrimage to Mecca. They belong to the Islamic, not to the Arab, world.

The tall African Somali—so closely tied to Arabia by religion, history, and even geography—is nevertheless Muslim rather than Arab. As Muslims, Iranians and Turks have a preeminent role in the history and culture of Islam, but their heritage does not include a Semitic racial background or the Arabic language. Persian, the main language of Iran, belongs like English to the Indo-European family, but it has been written in a modified Arabic script since early Arab conquerors first converted Iranian natives. Turkish is considered a linguistic relative of Mongolian; but it too was written in Arabic script until 1928, when Turks adopted the Roman alphabet. Converts and then conquerors in their turn, the Ottoman Turks dominated the later history of Islam, but no Turk today would count his country as part of the Arab world.

Because the old Arabs recognized a kinsman according to descent in the male line only, ignoring the ethnic origin of the mother, race is an obsolete element in the definition of *Arab*. As a result, because of generations of interbreeding, both white Syrians and black Sudanese are among the heterogeneous "Arabs," although a Saudi might be reluctant to give this name to one whose descent from "the ancient Arab race of conquerors" is in doubt. Neither race nor faith will explain the Arabic-speaking Jews outside Israel who have called themselves Arab or the Muslims of Mauritania who speak Arabic but reject the name "Arab." Along the Nile and the Euphrates an "Arab" in local terminology means the desert Bedouin as opposed to a farmer of the river valley.

Shortly after President Anwar el-Sadat of Egypt launched his peace mission *vis à vis* Israel's Prime Minister Menahem Begin in November 1977, a worker in downtown Cairo commented in Arabic on the Libyans who denounced Sadat's action: "Arab, garab!" *Garab*, Arabic for "leprosy," indicated how strongly, for the moment at least, one Egyptian felt his identity to be purely pharaonic. In fact, there could hardly be a more graphic demonstration of the lack of connection between race and language than in the Arab world. As for racial purity, despite the surviving remnant of "pure" Bedouins in central Arabia, myths about characteristic "Semites" should be as discredited as those about "Aryans" or "Caucasians."

The Arab League

For a working definition of *Arab*, the countries of the Arab League are of more help today than are historical questions of race or linguistics. In March 1945, seven Arab states—Egypt, Syria, Lebanon, Iraq, Transjordan (now Jordan), Saudi Arabia, and northern Yemen—signed a covenant in Cairo, forming a loose confederation "to consider in general the affairs and interests of the Arab countries." As other Arab states gained independence, they were added to the League: Libya (1953); Sudan (1956); Tunisia and Morocco (1958); Kuwait (1961); Algeria (1962); southern Yemen (later the People's Democratic Republic of Yemen, 1968); Bahrain, Oman, Qatar, and the United Arab Emirates (all in 1971); Mauritania (1973); Somalia (1974); and Djibouti (1977). The

Palestine Liberation Organization was admitted in 1976.

After so many centuries of division and colonization, harmony in this miniature "United Nations of Arabs" could not be achieved at the stroke of a pen. Immediate differences were manifest in 1948 when the original members attempted to prevent the establishment of an Israeli state, but in economic problems related to oil and the boycott of Israel the league has proved more effective. The basic unity is much more religious and cultural than political. Indeed, political assassination and political terrorism, Muslim against Muslim, remain as cruel a fact of Arab life as they do in parts of the non-Muslim world.

Modern Conflicts

In the Arab community such open conflict is as old as the blood vengeance of tribal feuds. Oil now exacerbates jealousies even as it raises living standards. The presence of the West, too, can create religious and psychological tensions unknown to the past. Along the broad asphalt streets of Riyadh lined with shops selling Western goods, in the residential suburbs, and in hotels and hospitals, many of the puritan laws once central to orthodox Islam have been quietly relaxed. The Koran and the Saudi government forbid alcohol, but a cocktail can be found for the thirsty. In the ancient quarter smoking in public is officially discouraged and movie theaters entirely banned. Many Saudis smoke, however, and the richer ones can enjoy their movies in private on television cassettes. It seems to require the wisdom of the Prophet to reconcile Koranic law and Western luxury.

In no sphere is the psychological conflict more apparent than in the life of the Arab woman. The ordinary Arab can no longer afford, if he ever could, the four wives permitted by the Koran, and the wealthy no longer flaunt their concubines. In this comparative security the Arab wife finds it increasingly difficult to limit her activities to Koranic tradition while her husband or son is on a Los Angeles campus, at a United Nations conference, or on a mission of aid to a Third World country. Seeing Westerners in their own travels or entertaining Westerners at social functions in their homes, many wives today are no longer content with children and gossip, no matter how affectionate and close family life can be in Arab households. The veil, where worn, is a token.

The visible conflicts outside the seclusion of private life result in a variety of Arab responses to the Western "challenge" and to the new prosperity. The voices are many. An "oil sheikh" orders a new fleet of limousines; another, with far greater consequence, whispers to a colleague in a London boardroom. A flow of eloquence at a Geneva summit is counterpointed by the blast of a gun at an airport. The current renaissance of Arab poetry is often inaudible against the harangue of a radio demagogue. The thunder of threats against Israel is heard everywhere, and the brief oil embargo of 1973 has had repercussions everywhere. Whether it be Arab poetry or Arab power, the voice has a new ring that the world ignores at its peril. The Arab voice proclaims not only conflict but also aspiration. The poet's intellectual message may ultimately prove the more forceful, but meanwhile, in blunt economic terms, experts estimate that within a decade the banking reserves of Saudi Arabia alone will surpass the combined total of the United States and Japan.

The conflict between today's aspirations and Islamic tradition is not lost even as the devout pilgrim arrives at Mecca. The country in this area alone possesses perhaps twenty-five percent of the world's untapped oil. Aside from obvious changes in religious standards, the pilgrim sees this postwar Saudi boom as a mixed blessing. Airplanes and automobiles have speeded his travels but have added to his expenses. Water mains, electric lighting, paved streets, modern buildings, blocks of flats, and the fumes of traffic have all but obliterated the colorful way stations of the past. Such "amenities" may be a high price to pay for the loss of traditional Muslim simplicity.

Before the pipelines came, King ibn Sa'ud brought the robber tribes of the desert under control in 1925, making the pilgrimage safe and much more profitable to his treasury. He kept order and maintained a high moral standard, even as he raised the dues that pilgrims had to pay, all of which was achieved entirely in the name of Islamic tradition. Measured in billions of dollars, the wealth of oil does not spare the birthplace of the Prophet any more than the rest of the Arab world. Manners and morals tend to be westernized, and this conflict in tradition—more than disputes about weapons and politics—is both a threat and a tragedy to Muslim conservatives.

In the world outside higher stakes on the diplomatic and economic fronts have increased the pressures toward Arab unity. Since World War II political independence from the West has been fortified by the Arab position as a link between the industrial world and the Third World of undeveloped countries. But economic self-interest cannot, any more than the question of Israel, bring Arab unity out of such a broad diversity. In comparison, the European Common Market has only begun to achieve a sense of community, even though, compared to the variety of cultures in the Arab world, it is almost monolithic.

Arab Diversity and Identity

Unlike any other people, Arabs share a heritage that is part nomadic, part peasant, part European, and part Oriental. There is a bewildering range of subcultures sheltered within the Arab world. The non-Arab Kurds of Iraq, like Jews and Christians along the whole Mediterranean shore (there are no native Christians in Saudi Arabia), are highly volatile minorities. The Bedouins and Berbers of desert regions must trade with "foreign" cosmopolitans in the cities. The historic hostility between Moroccan Berbers of the countryside and Arab nationalists in the cities was not assuaged until after World War II in a common enmity toward the French.

Syria is typical of such disparate elements. Primarily of Arab-Semitic stock, Syrians speak an official Arabic, while the Assyrians speak Syriac. The Muslim majority in Syria includes five principal sects, and the Armenian Christians are split into Orthodox and Catholic. Jews practice their religion as they have done for centuries under Arab rule. The Syrian radio broadcasts in Arabic, French, and English with "foreign" programs in Hebrew, Spanish, and Portuguese.

Not surprisingly, polyglot Syria produced one of the most influential pan-Arabists of modern times. Seeking some common bond, the writer Sati al-Husri settled for language. "The Arab nation," as he saw it in the 1930s, "consists of all who speak Arabic as their mother-tongue, no more, no less." But this definition could not really satisfy Syria or any other Arab territory. At Brussels in 1938 a conference of Arab students expanded the definition to include "all who are Arab in their language, culture and loyalty (or national feeling)." Is religion a part of "culture"? The Arabs who led the literary renaissance of the nineteenth century and even the nationalist movement itself were largely Christian. And an Arabic-based language does not produce "Arab loyalty" among the inhabitants of Malta.

If today's Arab League shows us a kaleidoscope of cultures and Arab history, we are tempted to think of the Arab world as defined by its very diversity. Deep beneath this exasperating surface, however, lies a profound sense of a shared past, an invisible bond between all Arabs. Few other people embody living history as an Arab knows it. Modern Arabs can agree that their "great period" began after A.D. 632 when Muslim warriors overran the Persian, Byzantine, and Roman borders and that it ended as the Ottoman Turks arrived to rule Islam for four hundred years. No less vivid is the period of European domination at the hands of French, Italian, and British interests, a colonialism that ended only yesterday and still agitates passions today. In this checkered history was born a spirit of Arab pride and independence, a degree of racial tolerance, a certain psychological attitude toward the West, and an emerging sense of mutual destiny.

The Past and the Future

Whether this spirit will be strong enough to forge a practical sense of unity remains for the future to see. The bridge that history has built between Baghdad and Casablanca has often been raised on uneven stones. A young Algerian Muslim may prefer to think of himself as more French than Arab. The doctrine of Marxism joins the verses of the Koran as matter for student dispute. The "pure Arab" from Medina, listening to echoes in his tribal memory, is not astonished when Libya quarrels with Egypt. Arab unity was not aroused against Christian Crusaders or the Ottoman Turks and was only a faint protest against colonial Europeans. Israel, the most annoying symbol of the West, has not brought unity on the battlefield or at the bargaining table.

Westerners have an urgent interest in the stability of the Arab world. Today the press is dominated by the question of peace or war with Israel, by the problem of a Palestinian homeland, and by the possibility of negotiations between once irreconcilable Cairo and Jerusalem. Equally basic questions remain for the future. After the pipelines and tankers have gone, the Arabs alone will remain, with huge investments in the West and vast changes within their own sphere. It may prove a fruitful paradox that Westerners, so recently colonial enemies and oppressors, are now dependent on Arab oil for a large percentage of their supplies. It is also paradoxical that Arabs must open their doors to the Western ideas that slip in along with Western machines and that the Arabs must send back a substantial part of their oil profits to buy shares in the Western economy.

In 1932 oil was discovered in Bahrain, then in Kuwait and Qatar, then offshore in the Persian Gulf. Along the Red Sea coast the Saudi government, aided by the U.S. Geological Survey and the Arabian American Oil Company, searches for fresh mineral resources. Between the Persian Gulf and the Red Sea the shopkeeper of Riyadh can still turn back to the true heartland of Arabia and of Arab history—the deserts that stretch almost without break from the Great Nafud in the north downward to the Rub' al-Khali. About 1,500 years before Christ and 2,000 years before Mohammed, nomads of Semitic speech such as the Midianites and Amalekites of the Old Testament domesticated the wild camel and developed trade routes in these barren regions. They called themselves "Arabs," meaning, as some say, "those who speak clearly." Long after its soils have been exhausted of oil and minerals, their nomadic heartland will continue like the Koran itself to exert an ancestral and magnetic force upon "the Arab mind" and on the Arab world. To understand this Arab voice, we must return to where it was first heard.

1.
The Earliest Arabs

In the ancient wisdom of the Near East, Shem (or Sem) was the eldest of Noah's three sons. Old Testament genealogies rank Hebrews, Aramaeans, and Arabs among the descendants of Shem, from whose name we take the term *Semitic*. The term was first used in 1781 by A. L. Schlözer, a German scholar, to describe the large family of languages that includes Hebrew and Arabic. The word *Semite* was later corrupted by racial theorists on the misleading assumption that a linguistic connection presupposed a close genetic connection. The error was made all the more plausible by the strong cultural and linguistic ties that connected biblical Hebrews and Arabs. Their remote ancestors spoke a proto-Semitic tongue, and indeed one branch eventually gave its name to Jazirat al-Arab, the "Island of the Arabs," or the Arabian Peninsula.

The Arabian Peninsula and Its Archaeology

Extending southeast from the Syrian desert, the world's largest peninsula (about one million square miles) is surrounded by the Red Sea on the southwest, the Gulf of Aden and the Arabian Sea on the south, and by the Gulf of Oman and the Persian Gulf on the northeast. The peninsula has easy access to Africa and Asia along coasts where communities have been established since prehistoric times. Cut off from the sea by mountains on three sides, the interior of the great plateau is remarkable for its aridity and barrenness.

Archaeologists have not had an easy task in the Arabian Peninsula, especially since local rulers until recently have seldom been interested in digging up pre-Islamic sites. In the south and east, however, excavators have been able to reveal evidence of Paleolithic or Old Stone Age hunters. Flint tools and hand axes have been found in central Arabia, and desert travelers have reported seeing Neolithic and Bronze Age artifacts. The range of time indicated by these finds is highly speculative. A hand axe of Acheulean style may be 50,000 years old, while the early Bronze Age on Bahrain in the Persian Gulf can be dated from around 3000 B.C. Cairnlike mounds—stones loosely piled over a crude oblong burial space—have been reported from all over the mainland, but

Desert oases, such as the one at Khafs Daghrah, Saudi Arabia, have been centers of Arab life since pre-Islamic times.

only a few have been investigated. Some of these mounds can be dated to 6000 B.C. Present data, however, supply no ethnic link between the mound builders of the peninsula and the earliest Semitic populations.

By 10,000 B.C. villages and farms had begun to appear to the north of the barrens, stretching in the famous Fertile Crescent from the Euphrates Valley to Syria and Jerusalem and beyond. The villages were subject to constant raids from desert Bedouins ("outsiders" in Arabic). Such a pattern of incursion, from desert into village, has led to the theory that Arabia was the original home of the Semites and that villages of Semitic culture in the Fertile Crescent represented an "overspill" of desert nomads who chose to become settled.

Arab Origins and Early History

According to their ancient tradition, the nomads themselves were descended from two stocks. The first was believed to have originated in the southwest corner of Arabia, while the second, or northern group, was alleged to have been the descendants of Ishmael, the son of Abraham. Almost every Arab tribe today claims to originate from one or the other of these two stocks. The legends may be based on actual racial variants; but, if so, the distinguishing features of the two groups have long since been lost. The civilization that subsequently arose in southern Arabia, however, had such marked affinities with Fertile Crescent cultures to the north that a common Semitic origin seems certain.

Between about 1500 and 1200 B.C. nomads domesticated the dromedary camel, a beast whose milk is far sweeter than its disposition. A trade route, "the incense road," conveyed frankincense, gold, and other valuables from southern Arabia to the Mediterranean and to Europe. The Midianites and Amalekites, the camel raiders mentioned in the Old Testament's Judges, can be dated from this period. Other trade routes spanned the Indian Ocean and ran to Africa as well.

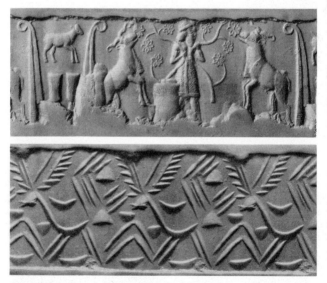

One of the characteristic artifacts of Sumerian civilization is the cylinder seal, a small stone cylinder used to make impressions on clay tablets. The designs were sometimes pictorial, like that of a man feeding a herd of animals with flowering branches (top), and sometimes more stylized and decorative, like the brocade-style horned animal motif (bottom).

Ramses II filled Egypt with colossal stone statues of himself. The most famous are these, at the entrance to a cliff temple at Abu Simbel, which were salvaged from the rising waters of the Aswan High Dam reservoir in the 1960s and moved to higher ground.

Trade linked all of the ancient civilizations whose historic dramas were enacted around the borders of the peninsula. The Sumerians, the first known settlers in Mesopotamia, appeared along the Tigris and Euphrates around 4000 B.C. A thousand years later Semitic cultures—Akkadians, Assyrians, and Babylonians, followed toward the end of the twelfth century by Aramaeans—appeared on the peninsula. By 2500 B.C. the Egyptians had already completed their pyramids, and by 1250 B.C. Ramses II the Great was defending his empire against the Indo-European Hittites. (This Ramses was very likely the Pharaoh in the story of Moses.) The first Persian empire rose to power in Iran with Cyrus the Great (550–530 B.C.) and dominated the people from Egypt to the Indus, much the same area that had been conquered by Alexander the Great before his death in 323 B.C. Long before Alexander, Greek colonists had penetrated everywhere along Mediterranean shores. When Alexander left his generals to fight over the spoils, Hellenistic culture had triumphed.

By the time of Christ, Rome had risen to power and had absorbed Greek culture. In A.D. 325 Constantine the Great made Christianity the dominant religion of the empire, which he divided between the western or Latin territories with the capital at Rome and the eastern territories with the capital at Byzantium (renamed Constantinople). Constantine's successors, the Byzantine emperors, soon had to face the threat of a revived Persian empire on their eastern borders. Coming as the climax of this long chronology, warfare between Byzantine and Persian armies was destined to have a decisive effect on Arab history. For most of these centuries the Arabian desert had felt little impact from Alexander's campaigns, from Hellenistic culture, or from the political genius of Rome. The "island" was vulnerable through the Fertile Crescent and along its coasts to outside arms and influences, but the interior preserved its own tribal and fragmented way of life. In fact, the barren deserts of inland Arabia have kept race and custom in protective isolation almost to this day.

The Name Arab

Islamic scholars have elaborated our knowledge of these ancient ways. According to their records of the two main Arab stocks, the southern Arabs—"true Arabs"—sprang from an ancient patriarch named Qahtan. Northerners—"Arabized Arabs"—were traced to the patriarch Adnan. Preserved orally by wandering tribes, these half-mythic genealogies reflect the innate conservatism of the desert. As his grandfathers did before him, the educated oil sheikh of Kuwait uses tribal genealogies to trace his pedigree to "pure" Arabs.

Another desert tradition, that the word *Arab* derives from a verb meaning "speak" or "enunciate," may be as open to question as the folklore of bloodlines. In modern Arabic, *Arab* is the collective name for a group of tents, which does indeed echo the preliterate past. When certain Arabs halted their flocks and tents and settled in village outposts of Semitic culture, they moved at last from the disputed mists of tradition into the pages of recorded history.

The first reference to Arabs is usually taken to be an Assyrian inscription marking the supposed victory of Shalmaneser III at the Battle of Qarqar on the Orontes River in 853 B.C. over a south Syrian alliance including Ben-Hadad of Aram-Damascus, Ahab of Israel, Cilicians, Egyptians, Arabs, Ammonites, and various Phoenician contingents, all under

Jarhuleni of Hamath. "Gindibu' the Arubu" (*gindibu* means "locust" in Arabic) is recorded as having contributed a thousand camels to the alliance. These Arubu left no identifiable records of their own and possessed a culture vastly inferior to their neighbors in the Fertile Crescent and in various kingdoms of the south. Among the latter, ancient writers refer to Minaeans, Qatabanians, Hadhramautites, and Himyarites as well as to the Sabaeans, who dominated pre-Islamic history in the southern peninsula.

The Sabaeans

The Sabaeans are mentioned in Assyrian annals on two occasions, the first in about 700 B.C. as having sent tribute to the king of Assyria. Seven hundred years later Pliny the Elder, a Roman writer, found the "wealthy" Sabaeans still flourishing in the Yemen coastline, the *Arabia Felix* or "Fertile Arabia" of the Romans where the Red Sea flows into the Arabian Sea. The huge mass of Sabaean inscriptions is difficult to date and interpret, but they indicate a Semitic culture sharing affinities with Semitic people of the north. Some scholars, therefore, have placed the original home of the Semites in northern Arabia, supposing that emigrants moved south to impose themselves on a pre-Semitic population. An ethnic mingling of this kind is hinted at by biblical genealogies that number the later Queen of Sheba (Saba) among the descendants of Shem. The magnificent queen reputedly visited King Solomon in Jerusalem, her legendary camel caravan loaded with gold, precious stones, and spices. The long history of the wars and alliances of her merchant kingdom is yet to be sorted out with any precision.

Ma'rib, the Sabaean capital, was located in the drainage basin of Wadi Adhana, where the river breaks through a rocky barrier before losing itself in the Rub' al-Khali desert. With the construction of an immense dam that turned the drainage basin into an area of farms and forests, the river valley of the Sabaeans became a fertile region. In about A.D. 600 the dam at Ma'rib burst beyond repair, and over time agriculture vanished as once fertile land was abandoned to the nomadic Bedouins. The collapse of the dam at Ma'rib was literally an historic watershed that marked the decline of agricultural communities in the realm of Saba.

In the middle period of their prosperity, perhaps around the time of Christ, Sabaean inscriptions first mention the word *Arab*, meaning a Bedouin nomad. The Sabaeans themselves were builders, especially at Ma'rib and Sirwah; and most of their great temples and monuments, including the dam at Ma'rib, date to their early period when Solomon is said to have received their queen. Like other people in southern Arabia the Sabaeans were polytheistic, and their cults had strong similarities with the northern Semitic religions. Of particular importance in their pantheon was a triad of deities. 'Athtar, god of the planet Venus, was worshiped along with a moon god and a sun goddess. The moon god seems to have been a national deity binding together smaller communities of the Sabaean state that had local cults and loyalties. Rahman the Merciful later became the sole lord of heaven until Jewish and Christian teachers introduced another deity. Some Himyarite kings who converted to Judaism continued to worship their deity under the name of Rahman, and pre-Islamic Himyarite inscriptions reveal the first concept of a holy war for the faith.

The Bedouins and Language

Viewed overall, the pre-Islamic history of southern Arabia is that of Sabaean expansion. Between Saba and the Fertile Crescent the Bedouin cultures were undeveloped. The region was a buffer between its richer neighbors but was open to influences from both. Yet during the "Age of Ignorance" before Islam, the desert nomads devised a Bedouin legacy of incomparable influence for all Arabs—the language and rhythms of Arabic poetry. The Arab may express deep feeling in music, in dancing, and in ceramics and other visual arts, but words and language remain the supreme aesthetic channel for his emotions. Arab song, now as then, can have a magical power over its audience, and the classic Arabic of the Koran is the enduring standard of excellence in speech.

For a language used over such an expanse of space and time, Arabic has developed the expected degree of variation. The colloquial speech of a Cairo politician does not remind us of a pre-Islamic poem. On the whole, however, Arabic has been as conservative and slow to change as the desert. The Semitic of ancient inscriptions—a relative of Ethiopic, Berber, and Hebrew—is dead writing, but the Arabic of the ancient Bedouin poet lives.

Bedouin Poetry

There were two main kinds of pre-Islamic poems. The earliest was the short occasional verse in praise of a tribe, animal, or person or a verse written as a call to war and revenge. Praise of kin and abuse of enemies were important themes. The nomad poet was a *sha'ir*, "one who knows," a name akin to *seer*, expressing the widespread belief that the poet was supernaturally inspired. A number of women poets became famous for short elegies and even for invective. (Even today Jewish women in Yemenite communities satirize topical events in Arabic verse.)

The longer form of pre-Islamic poem was the *qasidah*, an elaborate ode of between sixty and one hundred lines with a definite structure. It opened with a section called the *nasib*. The poet depicted himself as being on a journey with one or two companions. As they halted at a deserted encampment once occupied by his own or a friendly tribe, its ruins caused the poet to recall the happiness he had shared there with his beloved and his sorrow when they had to part. The mood is more elegiac than erotic.

The *nasib* ended with the separation of the lovers as their tribes went off in search of fresh grazing grounds. The poet and his companions continued their journey; and he then described, sometimes in detail, the horse or camel on which he rode, comparing its speed and endurance to that of a wild creature of the desert. This description led to a section often attractive to Western students—a vivid description of the natural life of the desert or of a hunting scene. Finally the main theme was introduced—praise of the poet's tribe and of his own gallantry, further description of a desert scene or tribal life, and possibly a panegyric to his patron.

Much of pre-Islamic poetry was lost or survives only in fragments scattered through later collections that included the work of Arabian Jews, whose verses sang with the same pagan spirit. Much poetry was preserved by oral transmission through a class of professional reciters (*rawis*) who attached themselves to particular poets and learned their works by heart. After such an apprenticeship, the reciter himself often became a famous poet. There were also "robber" or "outlaw" poets such as Ta'abbata Sharran, whose "Song of Revenge" has been one of the most frequently translated Arabic poems, and Shanfara, whose intense depiction of desert life reveals satiric resentment of tribal "security."

Doubt and speculation were present in religious poetry. Propaganda and sarcasm were circulated in topical verses that were passed from mouth to mouth and often dreaded by a local chief. "To cut off the poet's tongue" meant to pay him to keep quiet. (Mohammed himself, enraged at the bite and irony of three pagan poets of Medina, had his disciples actually kill them.)

Because sentences did not run on from verse to verse, each line of a poem usually contained a complete idea. As a result, in transmission or in later transcriptions, verses could be omitted or inserted without obvious injury to the sense as a whole. The oldest recorded poetry dates to the sixth century A.D. and shows an art fully developed over ages of recitation.

Bedouin Religion

The art of poetry helped give continuity to Bedouin life while the inhabitants of the Fertile Crescent and the merchants of the south saw kingdoms rise and fall. With his wandering camels, sheep, and goats, the nomad survived by tenacity. His loyalty was to his family and tribe, without awe for social or supernatural authority. The simple worship of desert Semites was directed toward the stones and springs of an oasis or toward sacred trees on which offerings were hung. At Mecca the well of Bi'r Zamzam near the Ka'ba, or "cube," was considered holy. The Ka'ba housed the Black Stone, probably a meteorite, and an array of other idols sacred to pilgrims. Here a stage of animism seems to have passed into polytheism without requiring a mythology for the many deities. Belief in spirits was common, filling the air with demonic *jinn,* the familiar "genies" of the *Thousand and One Nights.*

As the poetry indicates, however, pre-Islamic animism and polytheism had no primary hold on nomadic thought. Based on the agriculture of settled tribes, polytheism had little to do with the wanderings of desert people. The effective religion of the Bedouin was more likely to be focused on the nobility of the tribal stock and on clan membership, which provided an outlet for deeds of valor. Group honor was a dominant force for the individual, who would perish if left alone in the desert.

Bedouin Society

Within the group there were few, if any, class distinctions. Among both Arab and Hebrew nomads a slave was, like Abraham's servant Eliezer, a "son of the house." The Bedouin spoke to the head of his clan, or sheikh, as an equal. He was the master of his polygamous household, but an ill-treated wife could leave him. Brides were free to choose their husbands, and women were respected for what was considered the special fecund mystery inherent in their nature. (When a woman poet turned from elegiac verse to satire, her sting was more fearful because it came from a female.) Beyond members by descent, the tribe might also have women and children captured in fighting who, if not ransomed, could be bought and sold. A man needing protection could become the "client" (*mawla*) of a more powerful patron, and freed slaves also had this privilege.

All Bedouins looked down on settled societies. The farmer, tradesman, or merchant, even kings like Solomon and Hammurabi, were less than "foreigners." They were slaves to back-breaking toil, to a monotonous or devious trade, or to a rigid legal code. The libertarian code of the desert was "life for life, eye for eye, tooth for tooth." The manly business of the Arab was to raid the flocks of his neighbors. "Make raids on the enemy," said an early poet, "on our neighbor and on our own brother, in case we find none to raid but a brother." The fighting mood was chronic; and the *razzia* ("raid," from Arabic *ghazw*), which was aimed chiefly at driving off camels, has been justly called the Arab national sport. Because no Arab tribe wanted to destroy its rivals, intertribal differences might be referred to an arbiter (*hakam*), a man respected for his wisdom, tact, and knowledge of custom. Mohammed himself was later to play this role. Even then, immediate settlement was often postponed to give the contestants a chance to show prowess in the *razzia*.

The rules of the *razzia* usually precluded treachery and stealth, which might win victory but never glory. The time and place of a battle were often fixed in advance, and the sheikh's honor demanded that he lead the attack in person. In these maneuvers the key element was the camel; and indeed Arabic has as many names, about a thousand, for the breeds, shapes, and ages of the camel as it has for the sword. The celebrated Arabian horse, unexcelled in a short run, was a handicap across chains of sand dunes. In pre-Islamic days the horse was also a luxury requiring special diet and care. As isolated in breed as its master, the pure Arabian was remarkable for stamina, intelligence, and beauty; but no force of cavalry on horseback, as the Byzantines and Persians were to discover, could prevail in the desert.

Greek and Roman Influences

Like other novelties, whatever changes did take place in

weaponry or warfare had to come through contact with foreign kingdoms. The Bedouin chief might think that eloquence, archery, and horsemanship were skills sufficient to make the perfect man, but he was not totally cut off from other cultures and from the tide of history. To the north, people Hellenized by Alexander's conquests remained so under the dominion of Rome. Caravans going northward from the interior of Arabia passed through the lands of the Nabataeans, who had gained a monopoly of this rich trade. As the Hellenic kingdoms of Asia Minor weakened around 200 B.C., the prosperous Nabataeans extended their frontiers and later became allies of Rome. In 24 B.C. the Emperor Augustus sent Aelius Gallus with an expeditionary force south from Nabataea to Yemen. The Romans managed to penetrate far inland, but their one and only thrust into the Arabian heartland ended in retreat. Under Caligula and Nero, Nabataean dominion reached from the Sinai Peninsula well into the Arabian desert and brought the Hellenistic influence of their coinage, houses, and temples. In A.D. 248 an equestrian of Arab lineage was proclaimed emperor of Rome in a military coup, and the one-thousandth anniversary of the founding of Rome was thus celebrated by Philip the Arab.

Although by Philip's time Rome in the West had begun its decline, the empire was still united. Its power was evident to those Arabs who had mixed with Semitic Aramaeans in the population of Palmyra. This kingdom of the Syro-Arabian desert lay at the western end of the trade route from the Persian Gulf. By A.D. 250 the Palmyrans enjoyed some independence as a buffer between the eastern territories of Rome and Persia, which was once again a major power under its last native dynasty, the Sasanians. Palmyra itself was ruled by Odainath the Younger, also of Arab origin, and after his death by his widow, Zenobia. This "second Cleopatra" dared to proclaim her son as Caesar. Her rebellion was defeated by the Emperor Aurelian in A.D. 273, and Zenobia was brought to Rome to be exhibited in golden chains. Her Palmyran advisers, whom she blamed for her rashness, were executed, but Zenobia married a Roman senator and lived as a matron at Tivoli.

These colorful episodes had little real impact on the center of the Arab world. Far away in the West, Rome might hail the accession of Philip the Arab, but what was more important to the Arabian Peninsula was the persistence of Hellenic culture in the East and the rise of the Sasanians in Persia.

When Constantine made Christianity the supreme religion of the empire, it made no difference to Arabs. Much more important was the establishment of Constantinople as the capital of the future Byzantine Empire.

Byzantine and Persian Influences

A century after Zenobia, Christian Byzantines and pagan Persians were the great rivals north of the Fertile Crescent. In southern Arabia the power of Byzantium was felt early in the sixth century when a number of Christians at Najran were massacred by a local king said to have professed Judaism. The Byzantines were shocked by the massacre and persuaded the Christian ruler of Abyssinia to invade southern Arabia. The Abyssinians, perhaps equally interested in trade routes to India, made a successful invasion in A.D. 530. For more than a century Christian monarchs ruled Arabs in the south and maintained a precarious independence between Byzantium and Persia. The monarchs sent military expeditions deep into central Arabia and made repairs on the irrigation works at Ma'rib. When the dam at Ma'rib collapsed in about A.D. 600, southern Arabia became subject to Persian occupation.

The reign of a Persian ruler could be a precarious matter, but the Sasanians had managed to create a centralized new empire. At the death of Ormizd II, nobles of the Persian court had killed his eldest son, blinded the second, imprisoned the third, and in A.D. 310 brought the newborn Shapur II to the throne. In Shapur's infancy Persia was invaded by Arabs from Bahrain and Mesopotamia, but at the age of seventeen Shapur himself retaliated with terrible effect. In A.D. 363 his forces killed Julian the Apostate, the Byzantine emperor. Religious intolerance (Shapur hated all non-Zoroastrians) became a factor in power politics. After he at last had come to respect the freedom of Armenian Christians, Shapur himself was murdered by Roman treachery in A.D. 374.

The End of Isolation

Treachery, turmoil, and intolerance—the Near East hardly enjoyed to the full the blessings of a pax Romana. At the crossroads of East and West, the Arabian Peninsula unlike somnolent Egypt felt the currents sweeping along its borders. It was even producing some history of its own. Around the time of Shapur II a section of the Kinda tribe emigrated from southern Arabia to settle near Mecca. By the latter half of the fifth century the kings of Kinda had established their influence over most of central Arabia. Their heritage endures in Arab poetry, which under Kinda leadership developed a standard dialect and gave separate tribes a measure of cultural unity. The Kinda were eventually overthrown in a disastrous war with Arabs of the northeast kingdom of Hira near the Euphrates, where with Sasanian support Lakhmid rulers had become the mightiest of Bedouin monarchies. The defeated Kinda tribes were forced to return to their homeland. As Kinda control weakened, the Arabian Peninsula began to emerge further from its comparative isolation. By A.D. 500, Arabian tribes had started to flow outward to Syria and Persia, and in A.D. 604 rival Arabs entered the kingdom of Hira and overthrew its Persian "protectors."

The "island" of the Arabs, despite its sands and barrens, had begun to resemble a political and cultural patchwork. Trade and war brought the cultures of Persia and Byzantium. Jewish and Christian settlements were sources not only of new doctrines but also of Hellenistic and Aramaic influences. Long after the massacre at Najran the city remained an advanced Christian center, and Judaized Arabs were prominent in Yathrib, later to be named Medina. The fall of the kingdoms of Kinda and Hira around A.D. 600 left a confusion of petty states with no force to unify them.

In their disunity the Arabs—*Sarakenoi* (or Saracens) as Greek writers had begun to call them after an obscure Sinai tribe—seemed of small consequence to Persia and Byzantium, the two mighty adversaries of the time. These great states fought each other indecisively with imperial legions along endless frontiers, while nearer the throne the hand of a traitor or assassin often held the balance of power. The times seemed ripe for a new apocalypse, and many sects, including Jews and Christians, preached such an event. As the two empires struggled, devout souls throughout the Near East could agree that the world was approaching its final bloodbath.

Preparation for Mohammed

Sensational prophecy had long been current in the bazaars. Well situated between Byzantine borders and southern Arabia, Mecca was filled with the talk of traders and pilgrims. Merchants of many faiths assembled their caravans and conversed with the camel-breeding Bedouins. Goods from India and Africa reached Mecca by way of Aden and traveled along the shore of the Red Sea to Damascus and Constantinople. Yathrib, another major caravan post, prospered in its oasis about 250 miles north of Mecca. Jewish settlers—especially after the Emperor Hadrian had expelled their families from Palestine in A.D. 135—went about their affairs alongside their Arab neighbors. A merchant heading north from Mecca would meet some of these Jews at Yathrib as well as Christianized nomads as he approached Syria. In contact with traders, rabbis, and preachers, the Bedouins on the edge of the desert had made passing acquaintance with tales of both Moses and Christ.

A primitive approach to Arab monotheism had already been suggested by gods like Rahman the Merciful. But the moon god who brought the cool of night in the desert was no more easy to displace than was a god of flocks like Yahu—Yahweh or Jehovah—who lived in a holy tent and received Bedouin sacrifices. Since all of these various gods took second place to the sense of tribal loyalty, the Arab had no particular horror of Christian and Jewish beliefs. For most Arabs the revolutionary message of Christ had little appeal, and the more ancient message of Moses, his Covenant with Yahweh, and the Tablets of the Law had scarcely been credible to the wandering nomad.

During his lifetime in the thirteenth century before Christ, Moses himself had touched on Arab history. After killing an Egyptian in defense of his captive kinsmen, Moses fled to the Midianites, a tribe that had migrated from the Arabian Peninsula toward the Dead Sea. The account of his marriage to the daughter of a Midianite priest and of his adoption of Midianite worship seems to rest on accurate historical testimony. Zipporah, the daughter of Jethro, bore two sons to Moses, and a significant story is told of their departure from her tribe. Yahweh, the Midianite cult god, attacked Moses and threatened to kill him. Using a flint knife, Zipporah circumcised one of her sons and with this rite saved her husband's life. The episode preserves a primeval reminiscence of circumcision in connection with marriage and fits into known patterns of religious behavior. Yahweh's power was new to Moses, but at the same time Moses understood him to be the same god, the "God of the Fathers," as worshiped by his Semitic ancestors. After receiving Yahweh's revelation Moses returned to his people in Egypt and began the chain of events that reaches our own era.

Two thousand years after Moses, pilgrims and prophets

gathered in Mecca, listened to the poets, and noted the rise and ruin of distant empires. As Byzantines and Persians slaughtered each other, the Quraish, a high-ranking tribe of Mecca, maintained its traditional custody of the Ka'ba, where 350 idols had accumulated around the Black Stone. At the annual trade fairs Arabs indulged their customary enthusiasm for love, wine, gambling, and song. An occasional voice told of ruinous wars and heralded the apocalypse.

The Beginning of Islamic Conquest

A Thracian centurion named Phocas made himself master of Byzantium in A.D. 602 by beheading the emperor Maurice and his five sons. The empress and her daughters were also butchered. To press his campaign against the Persian armies of Khosrau II, who wished to avenge the death of Maurice, Phocas came to terms with the restless Arabs on his southern flank. In the eastern provinces he persecuted Jews and Monophysite Christians, and in his capital he grew increasingly savage. As Persian forces defeated his troops everywhere and carried the true cross off from Jerusalem, Phocas's rebellious subjects at last appealed to the Byzantine commander in Carthage to save the empire from its own tyrant. In A.D. 610 Heraclius arrived with a fleet from Carthage, killed Phocas, and displayed the mutilated carcass to the crowds. Hailed as the new emperor, Heraclius rallied Byzantine arms against Persia and administered a series of crushing defeats to Khosrau II, forcing him to surrender all he had gained against Phocas. A revolution followed in which Khosrau was deposed and slain by his own son. When the son died a few months later, the Persian empire was in anarchy.

Aging and diseased, Heraclius heard tidings in A.D. 634 of Syria overrun by "wild tribes" of Arabs. Seven years later, as the Arabs entered Egypt, Heraclius died. The civilized Byzantines and Persians had fought each other to the point of furious exhaustion. Instead of an apocalypse, a new voice never heard before had thundered over the peninsula. It had united the "wild" Arabs and summoned them to the stage of world history.

2.
Our God and Your God Are One

Mohammed, or Muhammad, is in its various spellings the most common masculine name in the world. It means "highly praised." The actual name given the boy born at Mecca around A.D. 570 was not recorded. The family name later bestowed on him was Abulqasim Mohammed ibn 'Abdullah ibn 'Abd al-Muttalib ibn Hashim. His father, a member of the prominent Quraish clan that guarded the Ka'ba, died before he was born; his mother died six years later. Our most important source for the life of Mohammed is the Koran as taken down from the Prophet's inspired words. Shortly after his death, devout Muslims started to write his biography (*sira*), often in idealistic tones. Lastly, there is the *hadith*, reporting the non-Koranic sayings of Mohammed on various occasions, handed down through authorities, and collected by subsequent keepers of the tradition.

An Uneventful Early Life

The orphan was taken care of at first by his grandfather, 'Abd al-Muttalib, and later by his paternal uncle, Abu Talib, both members of the Hashim division of the Quraish clan. When the fortunes of the Hashemites suffered serious reverses, Mohammed was given to a Bedouin nurse, Halima.

Mohammed must have spent his early years in poverty as a shepherd boy in the mountainous uplands near Mecca, becoming accustomed to the rigors of a nomadic existence. Later he accompanied some of the caravans, first probably those of his uncle, that Meccan tradesmen regularly sent north to Syria or south to Yemen. In his trading expeditions he proved successful and honest, so much so that a rich widow, Khadija, entrusted him with the management of her business affairs. At the age of twenty-five Mohammed married Khadija; and the match, which lasted until her death, was a particularly happy one. Many years older than her husband, Khadija was in every respect his truest confidant.

Until middle age Mohammed led a peaceful and prosperous life. In a town teeming with commercial speculators and in a masculine world where almost every Arab took part in armed combat, the early career of Mohammed appears comparatively uneventful. In a climate where men grow old ear-

The face of Mohammed (lower center) is veiled in this seventeenth-century Turkish miniature of the genealogy of the Prophet. Muslim teachings have generally opposed representation of the human figure in art.

ly, he was quickly past the age of adventure and ambition. Suddenly, when Mohammed was about forty years old, he had an overwhelming spiritual experience.

The Message

Mohammed had formed the habit of withdrawing periodically into the mountains near Mecca to meditate and pray. One night on Mount Hira, according to tradition, the word of God was revealed to him by the archangel Gabriel. As unlettered as any Bedouin tribesman, Mohammed was terrified by the message. As he related the experience, he heard an imperious voice. A luminous being grasped him by the throat and commanded him to repeat the sacred words. At first he tried to flee. Khadija later described his doubts, his self-questioning about the genuineness of the message, and his dread of resembling the visionary poets to be seen in the markets of Mecca who pretended to be possessed.Then came a period of inner emptiness when "the revelation was silent," and his distress was even greater. Finally, he was seized by the conviction that he had a message to convey. As he knew, the Jews and Christians had their revelations and their books while the Arabs, without a book of their own, were "ignorant." His hesitation ceased, and in about 613 Mohammed began to preach.

Mohammed's message took the form of a rhythmical recitative packed with exhortations and with vivid comparisons. It was a fervent and reiterated proclamation of the unlimited power of the one God, the creator of the universe, who would summon all creatures into his presence for judgment on the day of resurrection. But this God of justice was also a God of mercy who had filled the Earth with signs of his glory and grace. Every man was morally responsible to him for the conduct of his own life. Every man must respond to divine love and blessings by faith, prayer, and charity. Mohammed did not preach a new doctrine. He insisted that his teachings came as part of the prophetic tradition. His listeners were constantly reminded of earlier apostles of monotheism—Abraham, Moses, and Jesus. These prophets' "reminders" and "warnings," as the Koran calls them, were repeated in the Arabic tongue as part of the ultimate revelation made by Allah to Mohammed.

During the first few years Mohammed spoke only to a small, intimate group of his family and friends. Khadija was the first to believe in him and the first convert to the new faith. (A convert was known as a *muslim*, "one who surrenders" to the will of Allah. *Islam* means submission to God.) Mohammed gained a few other converts—his uncle Abu Talib, his cousin 'Ali, and his kinsman Abu Bakr. Most of the Quraish remained proudly aloof; but Omar, who at first rejected Mohammed, was later converted and, along with Abu Bakr, became a chief adviser. Those at the bottom of the system, slaves and members of the lower classes, were most inclined to believe in the new voice.

Exile in Medina

As Mohammed began preaching to wider circles in Mecca, a hostile reaction gradually arose. The hostility was probably due in great part to economic considerations. Mecca stood in a rocky valley without agriculture. Its profits came from trading and from pilgrimages that spawned fairs and markets. The council governing the mercantile republic included many of the richest traders. Mohammed's doctrine was a frontal attack on Mecca's economy, for the "idols" of the city brought pilgrims, trade, and money. His opponents first attacked him with mockery, sarcasm, and polemic. Then their persecution became more serious.

As Mohammed grew more influential he lost the protection that membership in the Hashemite clan had previously given him. In 615 he had to advise the most vulnerable of his followers to take refuge in Ethiopia, where the Christian monarch Negus ensured their safety and refused to return them to their Meccan oppressors. Because matrimonial and commercial relations between converts and the Hashemites were forbidden, more families joined the exodus. Personal grief was now added to Mohammed's trials. Both Khadija and Abu Talib died in 619, "the year of mourning." Mohammed began to look for assistance outside Mecca.

Yathrib was not a trading center like Mecca but a northern oasis where farmers lived by cultivating date palms. Two hostile tribes, the Aws and the Khazraj, were vying for precedence. The three Jewish tribes included the Kohanim, or "priests," who were evidently not the most learned of their calling. Tension between the Aws and the Khazraj had reached such a pitch that only an outside arbitrator could be effective. Mohammed, whose purpose was to transcend tribal divisions, seemed eminently qualified. Moreover, the presence of Jewish settlements may have given Mohammed hope that his monotheistic doctrine would find a happier reception if he emigrated to Yathrib. (In one of the Prophet's trances of this period he saw himself transported on a midnight journey to Jerusalem and thence to heaven. Muslim mystics later believed the Wailing Wall of the Jews to be the place where Mohammed's winged horse, with a woman's face and a peacock's tail, halted on the skyward flight. The power of this tradition was seen in the Palestine disturbances of 1929.)

The first secret negotiations with the oasis to the north inspired the pact of Aqaba in 622, in which Mohammed's disciples took an oath of fidelity. In small groups, Muslims began to settle at Yathrib. Alarmed at their departure, the Meccans decided to assassinate Mohammed, who was by then almost without protection. He managed to escape at night and, after hiding for a time on Mount Thaur, reached Yathrib on September 24, 622. These events marked the beginning of the Hegira (in Arabic *Hijra* or "emigration"). Muslims reckon their era from this year, starting with the day of the pre-Islamic lunar month that corresponds to July 16, 622. (The designation A.H., *anno Hegirae*, is used by Muslims just as A.D., *anno Domini*, is used in the West.) In 622 the faithful organized themselves as a community in Yathrib with Islam, "surrender to God's will," as its cornerstone.

Preacher and Politician

The year 622 marked another turning point in the career of Mohammed. The preacher became a politician and ruler and before long a military leader as well. One of his first measures was to integrate the refugees from Mecca with the original population of Yathrib (renamed after its hospitality to Mohammed as *Madinat an Nabi* or Medina, "the city of the Prophet"). A legal bond of brotherhood was instituted between each Muslim arrival and one of the Ansar ("assistants" or "helpers") as their hosts at Medina were called.

Mohammed also set out to win over the Jews, assuring them of freedom to practice their religion, including certain of their rites such as the custom of turning toward Jerusalem when praying. In return Jews were to accept the civil authority of the new arbitrator and were to contribute to military expenses. Such restrictions, however, appeared irksome to the Jews, who had enjoyed a hitherto favorable situation. Arguing against him from their own biblical writings, they refused to acknowledge Mohammed as a prophet, and relations became strained. Less than two years after the Hegira, Mecca, which was the sanctuary of the Black Stone, took the place of Jerusalem as the point toward which Muslims turned to pray.

If Mecca were to be the center of Islam, Medina could be only a place of temporary exile. Meanwhile, the Meccans, who controlled the trade of the peninsula, were bringing economic pressure to bear on the refugees and their Ansar hosts. The immigrant Muslims, who had lost their property, were beginning to feel the pinch of poverty. With a series of raids and skirmishes in the Bedouin manner, animosity between the Meccans and the Muslims at Medina grew into a war. Reprisals and counter reprisals were intensified. The losses were slight, but the prestige of victory and the disgrace of defeat had far-reaching psychological effects. In the spring of 624 the Muslims won their first considerable victory at Badr, where their bravery carried the day despite inferior numbers. Reflecting these events the revelations of the Prophet again took a different turn.

A Quraish prisoner who had been condemned to death asked who would take care of his little children. The Prophet's answer was uncompromising: "Hellfire." Practical decrees were issued dealing with booty and its distribution and with the problems of government. Islam had become a state as well as a religion. Becoming more militant, Muslims accused the Jews and Christians of having falsified their own revealed scripture so as to conceal the arrival of a new prophet. To show that he himself was the latest and last of the line, Mohammed took the title "the Seal of the Prophets."

War between Mecca and Medina

The Meccans were bent on revenging their dead at Badr. In 625 an army of three thousand advanced on Medina. The Muslims made an ill-disciplined sortie against the Meccans at Ohod; Mohammed himself was wounded, and his uncle Hamza was killed. But the Meccans could not follow up on their victory, and Mohammed was able to campaign more vigorously against his local opponents. Jews were accused of siding with the Meccans; six hundred men of their leading tribe were executed, and the rest were driven out. Muslims settled on the vacant date plantations. These Jews were the first tribe to hear the warning of Islam: "Convert, or die!"

By March 627 a number of Bedouin clans had taken up the cause of Mecca, and a strong new attack was mounted against Medina. This time Mohammed resorted to tactics unfamiliar to Arabs, accustomed as they were to the rapid movements of the *razzia*. He had a ditch dug around Medina, frustrating the Meccan horsemen and leaving them disconcerted and bored. Bad weather added to their discouragement, and the Bedouin coalition finally scattered homeward.

The people of Mecca began to tire of a conflict that was damaging their trade. They were somewhat appeased when, after one of his visions, Mohammed declared that he would not only make a pilgrimage to Mecca but also make the pilgrimage one of the basic duties of his religion. Having secured a truce for himself and his companions, he set out on a peaceful march to Mecca; but as he drew near the city, his way was barred by a hostile group. The Muslims halted and camped at Hudaibiya, where they received a Meccan delegation. Out of this conference came the pact of Hudaibiya. The Muslims agreed to return to Medina and not to visit Mecca until the following year, and then only for three days. Meccans who emigrated to Medina would be extradited on request and there would be a ten-year truce between the parties. Many of Mohammed's companions violently disapproved of these concessions to the "idolaters," but the pact forced the Meccans to recognize the despised fugitives and gave Mohammed another year to solidify his position at Medina.

Pilgrimage and Return to Mecca

As agreed upon, the pilgrimage took place in 629. The inhabitants of Mecca withdrew to the hills, leaving the town deserted, and the Muslims quietly arrived and departed. The time seemed ripe to settle all differences between Mohammed and the Quraish, his own people. The crucial opportunity was lost when Meccans broke the truce by taking sides in a tribal quarrel against allies of the Prophet. At the end of January 630, Mohammed and his Muslim forces advanced on Mecca. The city capitulated almost without a blow, and nearly all of the Meccans accepted Islam. Mohammed entered the sanctuary and ordered the idols to be smashed. The pagan shrine was made a Muslim holy place, its territory declared sacred and henceforth forbidden to unbelievers.

Mohammed displayed a generosity toward his former enemies that brought many tribal delegations from near and far to see the Prophet and to accept—if only for convenience perhaps—the new faith. Some may also have been persuaded by the apocalyptic mood of the previous years. As these converts confessed to Islam and submitted to the Prophet's tax, all Arabia appeared to be ready for unification. Jews and Christians were granted the protection of Islam in return for payment of the *jizyah*, a land and head tax for infidels. To these "people of the Scriptures" outside the fold, Muslims were told to say, "We have faith in that which has been revealed to us and in that which has been revealed unto you. Our God and your God are one, and unto him we are resigned."

Islamic Unity and Expansion

For pagan Arabs of the south some notion of unity had been foreshadowed by the Sabaean kingdom and by the common dialect of its poetry. Trade fairs had led to the keeping of holy months during which intertribal warfare was forbidden. For Jews, however, Mohammed's appeal to the Torah and to Moses was not effective. After the pact of Hudaibiya, Jews inclined toward the Meccans against Medina, and Mohammed captured the great Jewish oasis at Khaibar. Muslim relations with Christians were more satisfactory. A delegation from the Christians of Najran took part in a theological discussion with Muslims, and even though disagreement was total about the incarnation of Christ, Mohammed allowed Christians to continue their worship, setting aside part of the mosque for this purpose. (The ideal relationship between Islam and the older monotheisms was described in a celebrated saying attributed to Mohammed in the *hadith*: "You will follow the traditions of those who preceded you span by span and cubit by cubit—so closely that you will go after them even if they creep into the hole of a lizard.")

From the "year of the delegations" (630–631) onward the Muslim state began its expansion. Military expeditions were sent out, almsgiving was transformed into taxation, paganism —the worship of idols—was outlawed, and the bond of blood between clans and tribes was officially replaced by the bond of religion. The Muslim community, based on the tribal principle of equality, was governed entirely by Koranic laws as they were promulgated in various situations. Like Judaism, Islam became the religion and the state in one, and a mixture of old and new regulations guided the faithful.

Mohammed's Last Years

Mohammed took about a dozen wives, some for the sake of political connections, some for love. His favorite was 'A'isha, the daughter of Abu Bakr. His wife Mary, a Christian Copt, bore him a son named Ibrahim, but the infant did not survive. Of the children of Khadija, to whom Mohammed had been unswervingly faithful, only Fatima survived him. Fatima herself married 'Ali, Mohammed's first cousin and one of his earliest converts. (Hasan and Husain, the two sons of this union, might have succeeded the Prophet by right of birth if the Muslims had not abided by an elective system.)

In the days of growing glory and success, Mohammed continued to remain accessible to every suppliant, leading a simple life without luxury and living in houses built of mud and clay. As early as the pilgrimage of 631 he had designated Abu Bakr to preside over formal ceremonies. The following year Mohammed himself led the pilgrimage, even though he was suffering from the illness to which he eventually succumbed.

Mohammed's farewell pilgrimage was the occasion for a collective scrutiny of his lifework by himself and by the community. Tradition has preserved the moving terms of his last sermon. He urged his followers not to split up after his death, affirmed the unity of God and the brotherhood of the faithful, enjoined the community to watch over the rights of women, and proclaimed the abolition of blood feuds and usury. Mohammed returned to Medina and died in the pains of a severe headache on June 8, 632, while he was resting in the chamber of 'A'isha. Abu Bakr entered, kissed the Prophet's brow, and returned to the mosque. There the man who was to be elected caliph, or successor, spoke to the mourners. He reminded them that, although their messenger Mohammed was dead, their God was a living God.

After the death of the last messenger, "the Seal of the Prophets," tales of miracles were told about his life. But the Koran attributes no miracles to Mohammed. The book—correctly *Qur'an*, or "recitation"—is itself the "miracle," and Mohammed's one undoubted miracle was to have transmitted its divine eloquence.

The Koran

At first the revelations of Mohammed were recorded in memory, like the old Arabic poetry whose flavor they preserved. Because many of the memorizers soon perished in battle and since Mohammed himself had proclaimed that Judgment Day was near, it became imperative to write the message down. One of the Ansars or "helpers" of Medina was assigned the task of collecting the words of the Prophet from every possible source, and the authorized version, the first written book in Arabic, was organized about twenty years after Mohammed's death.

Unlike the holy books of Jews and Christians—some canonized, some apocryphal, some disputed—the text of the Koran was established once and for all time. Almost all Arabists agree that the beauty of its rhythmical and rhyming prose defies translation and is thus a witness for believers of its divine origin. Muslims make a pointed distinction between the beauty of traditional Arabic poetry and the supernatural splendor of the Koran. The Koran's language is the basis of written Arabic everywhere, and its content is the basis of Muslim education. In early Islam the Koran was the *only* education. Even today education in Muslim schools is indebted to the Koran. Its role in both religion and education probably make it the most widely read book in the world.

Less than the size of the New Testament, the Koran is composed of about eighty thousand words arranged in 114 *suras*, or chapters, of varying lengths, from scores of pages to about a dozen words. Except for "The Opening," which is brief, the *suras* at the beginning are the longest. Subsequent chapters are on the whole progressively shorter, somewhat like the Pauline epistles. In most copies of the Koran each *sura* bears, besides its title, the word *Madaniyah* or *Makkiyah*, "of Medina" or "of Mecca," indicating that according to tradition the revelation was received in one or the other city. Each *sura* starts with the formula "In the name of God, the Merciful and Compassionate." (The ninth *sura*, which contains strict warnings against idolaters and hypocrites, omits these conciliatory words.) The fiery and powerful Koranic style reverberates with a passionate demand for obedience to the will of a transcendent but watchful God.

Allah, the Arabic word for God used by Christian Arabs as well as by Muslims, was current in pre-Islamic times. The Koran constantly preaches Allah, his inaccessible mystery, his names, and his actions on behalf of his creatures. Allah is creator, judge, and rewarder. He is unique (*wahid*) and inherently one (*ahad*): "He begets not, nor is he begotten." He is omnipotent and all-merciful. Guided by him, human reason can find in transient creation testimony to the necessary and transcendental existence of the creator: "All must perish save his face." The formula that begins the *suras*—*bismillah al-Rahman al-Rahim*, often shortened in everyday speech to *bismillah* and meaning "In the name of God . . ."—is invoked by the devout Muslim before any obligatory or meritorious action. Another frequent formula of daily speech is *in sha' Allah*, "if God wills." The formula is not so much an expression of fatalism as it is a reminder of the nearness of God to the world and the actions of men.

The word of Allah as revealed in the Koran shows a familiar knowledge of Christian and Judaic scripture, not only of the Bible but also of the apocryphal lore of both faiths. Christ, Zacharias, John the Baptist, Mary, and other persons from the New Testament appear in *sura* 19 and elsewhere, but the Koran is above all related to the Old Testament and to the poetic lore of the Talmud. Although there are only five references to Mohammed, Moses is mentioned more than a hundred times by name. Only two of Mohammed's own contemporaries are named. There are many references to Jewish rabbis and learned men; indeed, the Koran shows a high respect for all true learning. Koranic tradition makes Arabs and Jews cousins, descended through Isaac and Ishmael, the sons of Abraham. The Koran also resembles the Talmud in its lack of conventional arrangement and as the cornerstone of education. (But it should be noted that the Koran is memorized without the debating relationship between master and pupil that characterizes Talmudic studies.) The Old Testament and the Koran can both be said to reflect the way of life of a male society of farmers, shepherds, nomads, and traders. Scholars have found in both traditions a "primitive democracy" in which, women aside, men are equal. Both traditions look forward to a Last Judgment. One small detail of the Koran reflects the cosmopolitan, Hellenized culture of the Near East at the time of Mohammed. Among the names given to the "fallen angel," the Koranic "tempter," is *Iblis*, a form of the Greek word *diabolos* that became *devil* in English.

Teachings of the Koran

The earlier chapters of the Koran are reminders of Mohammed's grim struggle against the Meccans and echo with warnings of the imminent judgment. The later *suras* of the Medina period are chiefly directed to the internal and external affairs of the Muslim community. The simplicity and concreteness of the Koran's ideas and ideals are a major part of the great appeal of Islam. The society envisioned in the Koran is authoritarian in its many laws of conduct but democratic in the absence of any human hierarchy to intervene between man and God.

In daily life the Koran places emphasis on charity and on kindness to orphans and slaves. Mohammed greatly improved the position of women with his teachings. His law entitles them, for example, to own and inherit property. (Daughters, however, are allowed only one-half the shares given to sons.) The husband's obligations are defined, and the maximum number of legal wives is reduced to four. The practice of killing infant girls is forbidden. (The inferior role given to women in some Muslim societies today rests mainly on later interpretations of the Koran.) As in the Old Testament, marriages within the clan are regulated according to kinship, and rules are prescribed about sexual activity, menstruation, divorce, and adultery.

As a general principle the Koran states that women's rights against men must be commensurate with men's rights over women, but "men are a degree higher." Husbands are adjured to be kind to their wives but may divorce them by proclamation. Intercourse with female slaves is permitted (verse 24 of *sura* 4 "of Medina," which is devoted entirely to women). A hundred lashes are ordained for the adulterer and his partner, although tradition restricts this punishment to unmarried persons. As in the book of Deuteronomy, death by stoning is the appropriate penalty for married sinners. (Some scholars have questioned whether the "Verse of Stoning" was in the original Koran, and some have remarked on the oriental severity of such punishments. Of course, other cultures provide equally horrendous deterrents.)

Koranic social law was intended to improve and reform the ordinary customs of Arabs. In matters involving money the basic principle is that wealth "should not be allowed to circulate among the rich only." The practice of tithing, which Pliny showed to be pre-Islamic, is imposed by the *zakat*, a tax on wealth. Helping the poor and needy and emancipating slaves are cardinal virtues. As in the Bible, usury is severely proscribed, but eventually both Muslims and Jews were to skirt the ordinance. Drinking alcohol and gambling are condemned.

With regard to diet, the Koran begins with the assumption that all "good" things must be allowed and then forbids four items: blood, meat from swine, meat from animals that have been found dead, meat from animals sacrificed or offered to idols. The third prohibition shows an obvious Jewish influence, and the last derives from an ironclad monotheism. But the Koran categorically allows food of "the people of the

In Jidda, Saudi Arabia, a bustling city with many Western influences, Muslims observe the traditional times for prayer during the activities of the day.

book"—Christians and Jews. The military traditions of the Arabs are not forgotten. According to the Koran, warfare is sometimes the will of Allah, even though it may be hateful.

In this system of law in which state and religion are one, the most fundamental factor is egalitarianism; all members of the faith without regard to race, color, or social or economic status are equals. There later arose a class of learned men, the *ulama* or religious leadership of Islam, but the Koran by itself remained the basic guide. Being simple and practical, it could be adapted to a tremendous diversity of cultures, and as such it hastened the spreading of Islam. The process was canonized in an alleged tradition of the Prophet: "Differences among my community are a mercy of God."

The Muslim creed contains five articles of faith that are the same for all Islam: belief in the one God; belief in angels; belief in the revealed books; belief in Mohammed and his forerunners; and belief in the Day of Judgment. As certain dogma was developed, belief in God's predetermination of good and evil was added to these.

The Five Pillars

The Muslim has five obligatory duties, the "five pillars" of Islam. They are the profession of faith, prayers, the payment of the *zakat* tax, fasting, and the pilgrimage to Mecca.

The profession of faith (*la ilah illa' Allah: Muhammad rasul Allah*, which translates "No god but Allah: Mohammed is the messenger of Allah") must be recited at least once in a lifetime. Made aloud with a full understanding and with assent from the heart, the declaration of itself makes the believer a Muslim.

The obligatory worship consists of five daily prayers at dawn, noon, midafternoon, sunset, and nightfall, said with the face turned toward Mecca. (Individual prayers, especially during the night, were later given much emphasis by the Sufi sect.) Ritual purity is required, as is the use of Arabic regardless of the worshiper's native tongue. Prayer at noon on Fridays is public and obligatory for adult males. In mosques the *imam*, a leader in worship and sometimes in war, can deliver a sermon, including prayers for the head of state. The men of the congregation stand upright in equality. Women have places set apart for them in certain mosques.

The third pillar is an obligatory tax called *zakat*, or "purification," that gives religious and legal sanction to property. The tax is payable each year, with the revenues intended

The Ka'ba containing the Black Stone is washed during a ceremony marking the Muslim feast of Bairam. The enormous embroidered black cloth that covers the building is changed annually.

primarily for the poor. Since the breakup of the Muslim community into various modern states, payment of these legal alms has been left to the individual and does not take the place of charity as stressed by the Koran and by tradition.

Fasting is required during Ramadan ("the scorcher"), the ninth month of the Muslim lunar year and a time sacred to pre-Islamic Arabs. Ramadan became a holy month for Islam because it was during that time that "the Koran was sent down as a guidance for the people." Being a period of atonement as well, Ramadan has a parallel in the Jewish Yom Kippur. Muslim regulations for Ramadan forbid food, drink, and sexual intercourse (in fact, any change in the body's composition) from the moment when "so much of the dawn appears that a white thread may be distinguished from a black" until darkness. The abstentions continue for twenty-nine days, with excuses for the very young, the very old, the sick, pregnant or nursing women, and travelers on extended journeys. In the final ten days of Ramadan additional prayers at night are considered especially meritorious.

The Pilgrimage

The pilgrimage to Mecca, the fifth pillar, is incumbent on every Muslim once in a lifetime, provided the person can afford it. The majority of pilgrims continue to be men. In the pilgrimage, or *hajj*, the worshiper upon reaching the holy border puts on two seamless garments, walks almost barefoot, and does not cut the beard, hair, or nails. The time of the holy season varies between October and December according to the last month of the lunar calendar. The chief activities of the holy season are visiting the sacred mosque, kissing the Black Stone, walking around the Ka'ba (three times running, four times slowly), visiting the sacred stone called Maqam Ibrahim (the "praying place of Abraham," who is believed by Muslims to have built the Ka'ba as a replica of the house of God), ascending and running between Mount Safa and Mount Marwa seven times, hearing a sermon at Mount 'Arafat, throwing stones at the three pillars at Mina (the "three devils" where Ishmael was tempted), and partaking of a sacrificial feast.

The Ka'ba, cube-shaped as its name indicates, is built of gray stone and marble and is oriented so that its corners roughly correspond to the points of the compass. The interior contains nothing but three pillars supporting the roof, from which a number of silver and gold lamps are suspended. At its eastern corner sits the Black Stone, now broken into pieces held together by a silver ring, awaiting the kisses and touches that bring forgiveness of sins to the believers. During most of the year the Ka'ba is covered with an enormous cloth of black brocade interwoven with gold inscriptions of the profession of faith and of Koranic verses. Changed every year, the brocade is made in Egypt and brought to Mecca with great ceremony by pilgrim caravan.

A Muslim may perform the pilgrimage by proxy, appointing a relative or friend, and there is a "little pilgrimage" of rites performed by any person entering Mecca at any season. The journey—with its solemn rituals, lights, and feasting—has gathered Muslims in a common bond over centuries, but it has also provided a forum for the spread of sectarian doctrines among faithful from various parts of the world. Since Mohammed led his first pilgrimage, scarcely more than fifteen European Christians have seen Mecca and Medina and lived to report their experiences.

Other Islamic Beliefs

After the five pillars, the most important religious practice of Islam is the *shari'a*, the total way of life as commanded by Allah. In its Bedouin origin *shari'a* meant "path to the watering place," but Muslim religious teachers extended its meaning to include belief in the doctrine and practice of Islamic law. The *shari'a*, therefore, embraces the Koran, the Sunna or Way of the Prophet, and the *ijma'*, or universal and democratic agreement of the community about doctrines present, past, and pre-Islamic. (Under *ijma'* many different practices were at first tolerated and then accepted.) A fourth principle embraced by *shari'a* is the reasoning process in theology that leads to progressive *ijma'*. The earliest theological controversy in Islam centered on the question of Allah's universal predestination as opposed to the exercise of human free will. Both sides of the controversy appear in the Koran. While learned men debated the issue, ordinary Muslims came to believe in the will of Allah as paramount in every circumstance, a form of "fatalism" that has been seen in the West as an impediment to progress and innovation among the masses of Arabs.

The Day of Judgment as described in the Koran and its depictions of Hell and Heaven depend on resurrection of the body. Generations of past infidels along with rebellious *jinn* roast in the fires of hell, suffering various degrees of torment.

They cry out for water from the inmates of paradise but are refused. In paradise, where rivers flow through gardens of eternal delight, the blessed enjoy banquets of fruit. Face to face upon couches, they are served delicious liquor that "shall not oppress the senses" and are embraced by wives of perfect purity.

Of all the sins of man, moral or ritual, the one without pardon is *shirk* (not related to the English word). *Shirk* involves denying the unity of God—through such doctrines as the Christian Trinity, for example or—associating other gods with Allah. For those who enter paradise the highest of pleasures is the vision of Allah and the chance to praise him forever. Muslim piety has collected in the Koran and in later tradition the ninety-nine "fairest names" of Allah, making up the ninety-nine beads of the Muslim rosary. To his followers Mohammed granted no religious day of prayer or rest, no Sunday or Sabbath.

Such, in brief, are the religious tenets that arose from the revelation of Allah to the Prophet. By the time of Mohammed's death, one-third of the Arabian Peninsula—Christians, Jews, and pagan tribes—had been converted to Islam. It would be hard to overstate the magnetism and power of his doctrine or the energy with which it was propagated.

The Caliphate

During the last decade of Mohammed's life, from 622 to 633, 'A'isha's father, Abu Bakr, had become a principal adviser. Most of the wealth he had accumulated as a small merchant he spent to free slaves and to advance Islam. He had accompanied the Prophet on his journey to Medina and had presided over public prayers in the days of Mohammed's final illness. Abu Bakr's position was clearly marked as second only to Mohammed, making him a natural choice for the Muslims of Medina to elect as *khalifat rasul-Allah*, the caliph or successor of the messenger of God. (Mohammed's son-in-law, 'Ali, only recognized the new caliph several months later.)

Despite the title, the caliphate did not become a religious office. The caliph might serve as the *imam* for a service of Friday prayer or give a sermon, but so could any qualified Muslim. Indeed, Mohammed could have no religious successor, inasmuch as the caliph was regarded as the protector, rather than the messenger, of the faith. The real nature of the office was military and political. The question of the caliphate, a living issue even today, was destined to bring Islam centuries of fraternal bloodshed on a scale far more vast than the Arabian Peninsula itself.

Abu Bakr was not elected without opposition. His supporters in Medina, called the Companions, believed in an electoral choice after the old tribal custom. Against them stood the supporters of 'Ali, the Legitimists, who argued that Allah and his Prophet could never have meant the succession to be decided in the heat of an election. As a paternal cousin, early convert, and son-in-law, 'Ali more than Abu Bakr was the legitimate deputy in their eyes. Both factions were opposed by the Omayyads, an aristocratic branch of the Quraish clan, who were late to accept the faith but whose great wealth and authority emboldened them to claim the caliphate. Political feuds appeared in the infancy of Islam.

No sooner than elected, Abu Bakr was confronted by the revolt of tribes in Hejaz and Nejd against the Medina government and its taxes. Rival prophets inflamed the tribes. Abu Bakr won over the Hejaz by persuasion, but the Nejd rebels were subdued only by military forces under Khalid ibn al-Walid. A desperate battle was fought in May 633, and the remainder of the restless peninsula was finally secured. Khalid raided the borderlands of Iraq, capturing the Christian community at Hira. In that same year Abu Bakr sent tribesmen into Palestine under Amr ibn al-As, the brilliant Quraish leader who had opposed Mohammed until his conversion in 629. Byzantine troops were met and defeated in southern Palestine, and before his death in 634 Abu Bakr had already taken steps toward the conquest of Syria. Islam was on the march. The anarchic tribes of the Age of Ignorance were becoming a military host, invincible in the desert.

The Ties of Faith

These were the Arabs the Koran distinguishes from the traders and townsmen of settled communities. With the rest of the faithful they formed the *ummah*, or congregation of Allah, in which the ties of fraternal blood were to be replaced by the ties of faith—insofar as a completely new religion could replace the ancestral memories and rivalries of the clans. The Bedouins were the least literate people of the peninsula, the least imbued with a national ideal. That they so speedily achieved a measure of discipline and social order under the banner of Islam is no less remarkable than the achievements of today's Saudi potentates, who themselves have reached world eminence in one generation with the modern weapon of oil.

Mohammed had not only named no successor but also had not created any kind of council along traditional tribal lines. In the waves of nomads riding out of the desert were the Companions of Abu Bakr, the Legitimist adherents of 'Ali, and the Omayyad aristocracy. Out of their rival factions future leaders of Islam would contend with as much cunning and fury as Byzantium and Persia had shown in their suicidal battles against each other. For the moment, however, Abu Bakr had managed to organize Arabia into ten provinces, each with a governor responsible directly to the caliph. The warlike spirit of the tribes was turned against the two ancient empires to their north. The Bedouins were responding to a single voice: "No god but Allah, Mohammed is the messenger of Allah." These are the first words a Muslim hears at birth and the last spoken over the grave. They were soon to herald the end of Sasanian Persia and to reach the ear of Heraclius on his throne in Constantinople.

3.
Century of Conquest

Scarcely any contemporary annals of the early Arab conquerors have survived. The chronicles of the Greeks and Persians leave much about the Arabs in obscurity, and Bedouin poets, like the primitive bards of Europe, wrote nothing down. The victorious followers of Mohammed who rode out of Arabia after his death are known today mainly through tribal sagas and heroic legends. The core of these preliterate traditions, however, has proven to be remarkably accurate and consistent.

Arabia became the heartland of heroes or, in more accurate terms, the starting point for the last great Semitic migrations. The impoverished nomads had nothing to keep them at home. Forbidden to indulge themselves in fratricidal raids, they had the sanction of the Koran to wage war against the infidel. The new victory cry was *Allahu akbar*—"God is most great!" When Omar succeeded to the caliphate in 634 at the death of Abu Bakr, his warriors by one estimate may have numbered no more than fifteen or twenty thousand troops mounted on camels and horses. With their scorn of death and hopes of paradise, however, they were almost irresistible. The desert had taught them endurance to hardship.

The Arabs' regular method of fighting was to charge in a long line, cast a shower of javelins, wheel back to their base, and repeat the tactic until the enemy showed signs of breaking. They also used arrows and slings until the time came to close with the enemy for hand-to-hand combat. What discipline there was sprang from tribal morale, each group of clansmen riding behind its own standard borne on a lance by one of its bravest. Being the aggressors, often against dispirited and divided opponents, gave the Arabs another immeasurable advantage in what came to be known as the Muslim "holy war."

Striving

Jihad, or "striving," the much misunderstood term for "holy war," is a religious duty imposed by Muslim law for the spread of Islam. It may be true that the Arab has on occasion offered either conversion or death as the only alternatives. The Koran (*sura* 9 "of Medina"), however, actually offers a third command—to make war on those to whom the biblical scriptures have been given, but who do not believe in Allah or the Last Day, until they pay tribute and are humbled. Tribute was thus added to the sword as a tool to achieve Islam's objective.

Islamic custom distinguishes different ways to fulfill *jihad*. With the heart the Muslim combats the devil and escapes his persuasion. With tongue and hand he supports the right and corrects the wrong. Modern Muslim spokesmen maintain that *jihad* does not necessarily mean an offensive war. In fact, the idea of the holy war is older than Islam, going back to southern Arabian inscriptions and to local Judaic kings. It was given the force of a pillar of Islamic faith, "the sixth pillar," by Kharijites, members of the earliest sect to arise in Islam. *Jihad* no doubt gave the caliphs a powerful impetus to expand the territories of the faithful. The idea may inspire an Arab terrorist today, but those who pursue *jihad* with heart, tongue, and diplomacy, those who stress peaceful goals, find much support in current Muslim thinking.

Early Military Successes

Differences between the Kharijites and other sectarians, although they went back to the dawn of Islam, could not deter the progress of the early caliphs. On his accession Omar took the title of *amir al-mu'minin*, "commander of the faithful," which was to be the formal title of all later caliphs. Against the Persians, Omar sent an obscure but devout general who led his Arabs across the Euphrates into a country of gardens and irrigation ditches defended by a fearsome cavalry of elephants. Dashing forward, the general was trampled to death by the lead elephant, a signal for the Arabian troops to tumble back toward a single bridge that offered safety on the other side of the river. Many Arabs were killed and many deserted in the panic of the Battle of the Bridge in 634, but a year later Omar's troops defeated a Persian onslaught at Buwaib. Khalid ibn al-Walid, who had subdued the false prophets of the peninsula, scored a decisive victory over Byzantine soldiers in the Yarmuk valley south of Damascus and took the city a few months afterward. Khalid's success against the army of Heraclius gave Omar freedom to organize a full-scale invasion of Persia.

The Conquest of Persia

In June 637, Arabs broke the main Persian army at Kadisiya,

and in July the Sasanian capital of Ctesiphon fell. At Kufa and Basra two garrison cities were founded for Arab troops—the policy being that Arabs were not to occupy subject land as owners or cultivators—and in these garrisons each tribe was allotted separate quarters.

The conquests made thus far by Arabs had been in the relatively flat and familiar area of the Fertile Crescent, or in barren areas where dust and sand were allies. Their possession of Iraq was to remain insecure as long as the Persians were at liberty to reorganize their forces in the Iranian plateau. Undeterred by difficulties of terrain, the Arabs adapted their tactics to mountain warfare. As they continued the systematic conquest of Persia, they found the Sasanian enemy not only weakened by prolonged conflict with Byzantium but also beset by Turkish attacks from the east. Yet the Sasanians managed to put up a fierce resistance in many provinces. Six years (638–644) were required for the Arabs to capture Khuzistan, while other Muslims were penetrating the highlands through the Hulwan gap. The western edges of the Persian plateau were conquered piecemeal. It was only on the final conquest of Fars in 650 that Arab troops were able to sweep across the plateau to occupy Kerman and Khurasan. The last Sasanian monarch, Yazdegerd III, fled before them and was murdered near Merv in 651 by one of his own subjects eager to escape with the crown jewels.

Western Expansion into Egypt

On their Syrian front, after the capture of Damascus the Arabs were able to occupy the northern cities and the coastal region of Palestine. (The territory of ancient Syria included the entire fertile strip between the eastern Mediterranean and the desert of northern Arabia.) Jerusalem held out against Muslims unskilled at siege tactics until 638. Caliph Omar received its surrender in person. Caesarea and Gaza fell in 640; Ascalon and Tripoli, the last Byzantine strongholds in that area, capitulated in 644 and 645. An Omayyad clansman, Mu'awiya ibn abi Sufyan, had meanwhile been appointed governor of all Syria.

The Byzantine armies responsible for the protection of Syria and neighboring areas were composed of Armenians, Arabs, and other troops who had little loyalty to the empire. The populations were often apathetic, and some of the Monophysite sectarian Christians had been harassed as heretics by the bishops of Constantinople. Local Semitic peoples, hostile to the emperor Heraclius, could actually welcome Semitic invaders. In Iraq, too, local subjects of Semitic stock had no reason to be loyal to their Persian oppressors or to the state religion of Zoroaster. Muslims could easily be seen as liberators rather than invaders. Muslim taxation was more equitable than the exactions of the emperors, and the warriors of *jihad* were far more flexible about religious differences than were the orthodox of other faiths.

On his own initiative Amr ibn al-As in 639 led four thousand Yemenite troops from Palestine down the ancient route along the coast into Egypt. Like Khalid, this Quraish general has been compared to Alexander, Hannibal, and Napoleon. Reinforced from Medina in 640, he concentrated his armies on the delta near Heliopolis. Advancing against him from the fortress of Egyptian Babylon, his Byzantine opponents were routed, and Amr negotiated the surrender of the Coptic Christian population. After taking the fortress itself in April 641 he marched on Alexandria, which surrendered after a truce of eleven months. Amr sent a report to Caliph Omar in Medina of the magnificent city that he had captured. Although in a state of long decline, the city of Cleopatra was still splendid enough to astonish a Bedouin general.

According to a thirteenth-century legend, the caliph ordered that the library at Alexandria be burned, saying its books were unnecessary if they contained the message of the Koran and unholy if they did not. The library had indeed suffered earlier destruction in a civil war under the Romans, but book-burning was, and is, contrary to Islamic tradition. ("The ink of the scholar," in words attributed to the Prophet, "is more sacred than the blood of the martyr." Mohammed said on another occasion, "Seek knowledge, even unto China.") The myth of the burning of the library was an invention of Christian propaganda to discredit the Saracens.

Arab Rule in Egypt

After the emperor Heraclius had succumbed to age and illness in 641, subsequent attempts by Byzantine naval expeditions to regain Alexandria failed. In this, the richest province of the empire, more than nine hundred years of contact with Ptolemaic, Roman, and Greek civilizations had failed to influence the mass of Egyptian people, who clung to their pharaonic culture even though their rulers had long been aliens. Two centuries of theological dispute had crippled the Christians of the city by the time they confronted the triumphant young faith of Islam. The attitude of the Copts toward their new Muslim masters, who spoke neither Greek nor Coptic, seems to have been negative. In return for paying tribute in money and kind, the Copts and other Christians were allowed to practice their religion and administer community affairs through their own chiefs.

Amr's choice of Al Fustat, the modern city of Misr al Qadimah, as the Arab capital in Egypt was dictated by military considerations. Like other Arab centers established in Syria and Iraq, it progressed from a temporary to a permanent camp, and later to a city. (But the Arabs, unlike the Byzantines, had no mind for town planning, and they let houses and huts spring up in confusion around their own mosques and administrative headquarters.) After sending expeditions to Nubia, to Cyrenaica, and westward to Tripoli, and after repelling the Byzantine navy in 645, Amr was master of Egypt.

In a great metropolis like Alexandria, as well as in the cultivated gardens of Iraq, the soldiers of Omar met their first taste of luxury. Unlettered Muslims, whose own Prince of the Faithful walked barefoot in the desert oasis of Medina, would sometimes give up unfamiliar gold in exchange for the silver that they could recognize. One soldier was scolded for selling a noble's daughter, his share of the booty, for only a thousand dirhams because he did not know that there was a higher number. Caliph Omar accused Amr of having become too rich in Egypt. In reproach to the proud and independent Amr, the caliph's messenger reminded the general that only his success in war had allowed him to escape a far simpler Arab life.

The Conquerors and the Conquered

Mohammed himself had made the rules for sharing the spoils of victory. After a battle all treasure, including captives, was brought together. One-fifth was sent off on caravans to Medina, and the rest was divided in equal shares on the spot among the soldiers. Because Omar had a puritan horror of luxury and dissipation, soldiers were given little opportunity to squander money in conquered lands. Together with whatever women and children they had brought with them, the first Arab victors were segregated into their encampments. Mixing with the natives, Omar believed, might diminish their fighting spirit. These initial policies, however, could not for long contain the seed that was to become the Arab world of many races.

Subject peoples were ruled in their traditional manner, with tolerance for the *dhimmis*, those who maintained their own religious practices as permitted by Islamic law. Owners kept their land; and local tax collectors shifted their revenues, out of which troops in the Arab garrison were maintained, to the new masters. The Arabs identified the Muslim religion entirely with their own race, receiving converts only as "clients," or *mawali*, just as clients had been received in deserts of the pagan past. Converts might be exempt from certain taxes paid by infidels, but they did not at first meet with more than contempt from the Arabs themselves. The goal of the early conquests was not missionary. Not always the most devout Muslims, Arab generals were out to win not souls but plunder. Although converts could gain a theoretical advantage, it was several centuries before the people of Syria and Persia embraced the religion of Islam in significant numbers.

Omar and Othman

As provinces wrested from Persia and Byzantium were added to the realm of the caliph, Omar closely supervised their administrators and punished delinquents—even going so far as to confiscate half of the booty taken by Amr. Profits from certain estates were taken directly by Omar for distribution at Mecca and Medina. Tall, physically strong, and of uncompromising piety, Omar is said to have condemned his own son to death for drinking. Many other anecdotes attest to his iron character, and Omar became the greatest name in early Islam after Mohammed. While Quraish nobles enriched their houses in Arabia, he wore a patched shirt and mantle and slept on a bed of palm leaves. One day shortly after sunrise as he led prayers in the mosque at Medina, Omar was rushed from behind by a Christian Persian slave who stabbed him six times with a poisoned dagger. The dying caliph was carried to his own house where he summoned a conclave of Quraish nobles to choose his successor. In his ten years of rule, from 634 to 644, Omar had become the master of an empire.

The zeal of the Quraish, Mohammed's own tribe, had largely created the early empire, and the same zeal in the form of clan rivalries was its greatest peril. After Omar's murder, the two chief contestants for the caliphate were 'Ali, the Prophet's cousin and husband of his daughter Fatima, and Othman, the husband of Mohammed's daughter Ruqayya. 'Ali was of the Hashim branch of the Quraish tribe. A member of the Omayyad branch, Othman had joined the emigrations to Ethiopia and to Medina. The conclave elected the already aged Othman over 'Ali.

Othman continued the policies of Omar. For six years or more Arab conquests proceeded steadily, and their Syrian armies began to probe further into Byzantine territory. Syrian and Egyptian fleets were organized, leading to the Arab occupation of Cyprus and to the first impressive naval victory over Greeks at the "Battle of the Masts" in 655. Tribesmen, however, began to resent the control exercised by the caliph and his governors, the exploitation of their victories by the commercial aristocracy of Mecca, and the favors shown to his Omayyad kinsmen by Othman. Preachers denounced the caliph's errors and innovations, especially his issue of an official text of the Koran with orders to destroy all others. Arab troops in Kufa on the Euphrates and at Al Fustat in Egypt broke into rebellion. Headed by the son of Abu Bakr, a party from Egypt marched to Medina in 656 and besieged Othman in his house. A mob of soldiers crashed through the doors and found Othman sitting on the floor reading the Koran. As they began to butcher him, his blood soaked into the manuscript. Othman met his violent end not at the hands of an infidel but from the ranks of the faithful. The Arab world was to suffer profound changes.

'Ali in Turmoil

During the caliphates of her father, Abu Bakr, and of Omar, 'A'isha had used her energies in family and social activities. The prophet's favorite wife, she had been made a childless widow at the age of 18 by the death of Mohammed. (Called "mothers of the believers," Mohammed's widows were not allowed to remarry.) As rebels and reformers arose against the weak and aged Othman, 'A'isha turned to intrigue, hoping to regain the caliphate for her family. When Othman was assassinated, 'A'isha held his rival 'Ali responsible and proposed to take vengeance. The mutineers and Medinians recognized 'Ali as caliph, but 'A'isha escaped to Iraq and won the support of a garrison at Basra. The soldiers of another garrison at Kufa, however, joined the faction supporting 'Ali. In October 656, 'Ali led his troops out of Medina—it was never again to be the Islamic capital—and combined them with his partisans at Kufa to march against his enemies at Basra. Mounted on a camel, 'A'isha became the center of a battle between the two armies ("The Battle of the Camel"), and 'Ali routed her forces. She herself was captured but was released upon her promise to abstain from politics.

'Ali's victory, however, was not complete. Mu'awiya, the governor of Syria, refused to recognize him as caliph and demanded requital for the butchery of his kinsman Othman. In May 657 Mu'awiya led the Syrians to meet 'Ali's forces at the Roman ruins of Siffin near the Euphrates. Faced with defeat during an indecisive battle, the Syrians are said to have waved Korans on the tips of their spears and to have shouted, "Let Allah decide!" (Accounts of these events have been colored by later propaganda.) 'Ali took their action as a ruse, but his more devout followers persuaded him to accept a truce. Representatives of both sides met and reached an agreement that the frustrated 'Ali apparently denounced. No further battle took place, but Mu'awiya gained control of Egypt and launched raids of increasing severity against Iraq. He could count on the obedience of loyal and disciplined troops, while 'Ali, having risen to power on a wave of revolution, was rendered powerless by insubordination. Some zealots held 'Ali guilty for agreeing to the arbitration at Siffin. Iraqi tribesmen refused to engage the Syrians again. Others were enraged because 'Ali had transferred the capital from Medina to Kufa. At the new capital a group of fanatical dissidents, the Kharijites or "outgoers," left the city and openly rebelled. 'Ali severely defeated the Kharijites in July 658, but similar uprisings flamed up in other areas.

The Rise of Sects

Already weakened by assassination, the religious and moral fabric of Islam was further weakened by sectarian disputes. The Kharijites, the first to become a sect, were opposed equally to Mu'awiya and to 'Ali. Engaging in campaigns of harassment and terror, they repudiated not only the two claimants to the caliphate but also all Muslims who did not accept their views, including *jihad* as the sixth pillar. Kharijites held that the judgment of God could be expressed only through free choice by the entire Muslim community. Anyone, they insisted, even a Negro slave, could be elected caliph if he possessed moral purity. Any Muslim, including the caliph, who committed a major sin was an apostate in their eyes and was subject to ostracism and even death. Luxury, tobacco, music, games, and concubinage without the wives' consent were to be forbidden. Intermarriage and association with less puritanical Muslims were strongly discouraged. The Koran was taken as truth letter by letter, and the Kharijites began to develop their own legal system and collections of *hadith* ("traditions") about the Prophet. (Today Kharijites survive mainly under the name of Ibadis in northern Africa, Oman, and Zanzibar. Their fundamentalist ideas, however, have had great influence on the Wahhabi ruling dynasty of Saudi Arabia.)

By 660 'Ali had lost control of the Hejaz, and in the following year he was assassinated outside the mosque at Kufa by a Kharijite rebel. His real personality has been hidden in the mass of reverent legend that gathered around him, but 'Ali seems to have been genuinely religious even if his statesmanship was a disaster. The legends were created by Muslims who sought a superhuman or charismatic leader and who found him in the husband of Fatima. These Muslims were the Shi'ah 'Ali ("the party of 'Ali") who believed that only 'Ali and his line could be true caliphs. (Their opponents, the vast majority of "orthodox" Muslims today, are Sunnis, people of the *sunna* or the "way" of Mohammed as revealed in traditions recorded during his lifetime.) Shi'ites believed that the caliph must be infallible, and on the fringes of Islam today there are sects who regard 'Ali as the incarnation of God. According to the Shi'ites, the charismatic leadership passed from Mohammed to 'Ali, from 'Ali to his sons Hasan and Husain (or to another son, Mohammed ibn al-Hanafiya), and thence to the descendants of Husain.

Expansion under Mu'awiya

Zealots had also attempted to assassinate 'Ali's rival, Mu'awiya. This son of the Omayyad clan, whose Quraish father was a rich and influential merchant of Mecca, proved an efficient governor of Syria. As 'Ali's power had slipped from his grasp, Mu'awiya had been proclaimed caliph at Jerusalem in July 660. At the death of 'Ali, Mu'awiya advanced into Iraq, where 'Ali's son Hasan abandoned his claim to the caliphate without a struggle. (In fact, this grandson of Mohammed was said to have been bribed into acquiescence, preferring to enjoy the embraces of his more than one hundred wives and to live up to his informal title as "the great divorcer.")

Once Mu'awiya had tightened his control over the provinces—although the Kharijites remained intractable—he decided to continue the policy of expansion. He founded new garrison cities at Merv and in Seistan, from which expeditions were sent into central Asia and northwestern India. Under Okba ibn Nafi', Egyptian armies began the invasion of northwestern Africa and founded another garrison city at Kairouan in Tunisia. As warlike as the Arabs, the Berbers of Africa had originally been fierce nomads. They spoke a tongue derived in part from the earlier Phoenician invaders who had founded Carthage. Their name is said to be an Arab variant of the word *barbari*, barbarians, contemptuously applied to them by Latin-speaking provincials. The Romans had never completely succeeded in Romanizing the Berbers, although many, like St. Augustine, became Christians. It took a hundred years for them to become reconciled to the Arabian empire. Nonetheless, Okba reached the shores of the Atlantic in a victorious march by 681, followed by a Berber and Byzantine uprising that drove the Arabs back to Cyrenaica.

The main Arab offensive under Mu'awiya was an attack against the Byzantine capital. With the support of the fleet, Constantinople was besieged in 669, but the following winter the Arab army was destroyed at Amorium. A fresh campaign was mounted in 673, and for four years Constantinople suffered an annual siege of several months. The invaders were repeatedly driven off by Greek fire—this weapon, whose secret was to disappear, was the same as the "Saracen fire" used against the Crusaders—and heavy losses compelled the Arabs to withdraw.

Caliph Mu'awiya was a typical Arab *sayyid*, a "gentleman." He governed not by force but by superior intelligence, self-control, mildness, and magnanimity. His was the virtue of *hilm*, which has been translated as "finesse." He succeeded for the first time in making the Islamic army a disciplined force. "I apply not my sword," he is reported to have declared, "where my lash suffices, nor my lash where my tongue is enough." He allied himself by marriage to the most powerful tribe in the army of Syria, and he took the bold step of removing his capital to Damascus—famous for its plums, figs, pistachios, and swords.

Founding of the Omayyad Caliphate

Well aware that the allegiance of the army was the sole guarantee of Islamic unity and that the old Arab method of election to the caliphate was no longer practical, Mu'awiya secured a general oath of allegiance to his son Yazid as his successor. This hereditary principle was an offense to Muslims such as the fanatic Kharijites, and it was especially disliked in Iraq, already restive over transference of the capital to Damascus and the predominance of Syrian elements in the army. Mu'awiya had the good fortune to find an excellent governor for Iraq in Ziyad, a former partisan of 'Ali. (Ziyad was reputed to be a bastard of Mu'awiya's father and was publicly acknowledged by the caliph as a brother.) Iraq remained quiet until Ziyad's death in 673. Old tensions then began to revive in the garrison cities, and tribal and political factions arose again. In many respects Mu'awiya ruled like the old-fashioned chief of a nomadic tribe, and history records him as the only caliph who never had a rebellion. By his introduction of the hereditary principle he became founder of the Omayyad dynasty.

Opposition in Kufa flared into fighting on Mu'awiya's death in 680. The Shi'ites, opposed to Yazid and favorable to the house of 'Ali, invited 'Ali's son Husain from Mecca to Kufa in order to claim the caliphate. Informed of this threat to his succession, Yazid sent Obaidallah, Ziyad's son, to restore order. Using the tactics that his father had used, Obaidallah summoned the tribal chiefs and made them responsible for the conduct of their men. Meanwhile, Husain had set out with his family, expecting to be received with enthusiasm at Kufa. Although warned on reaching Iraq of the change that had taken place, he journeyed onward and at Karbala was confronted with a Kufan force commanded by Omar ibn Sa'd.

Husain gave battle and, with most of his family and followers, was killed on October 10, 680. The tragic death of the Prophet's grandson and so many of his house caused a revulsion of feeling among Muslims everywhere, and the facts soon acquired a wholly poetic coloring. This event, rather than the murder of 'Ali, became the emotional focus of Shi'ism. Omar ibn Sa'd, Obaidallah, and Yazid himself came to be regarded as murderers, and their names were held accursed by all Shi'ites, who ever since have observed the date of the battle as one of public mourning. (The anniversary is also marked by a religious drama, with Husain as the hero, that is performed annually by the Shi'ites of Iran and India.) The Sunnis themselves saw in the horror of Husain's fate a cloud cast over the Omayyad house.

Yazid faced many enemies. After prolonged negotiations with his opponents, he sent a Syrian army against Medina. According to tradition, the city was conquered and plundered for three days. The Syrians then marched on a hostile Mecca in September 683 and found another rival caliph, 'Abdullah, ready to defend the city. The Syrian siege of Mecca lasted for sixty-four days, and the Ka'ba was damaged by bombardment. When the news came of Yazid's death on November 10, the army returned to Syria.

Yazid's young and sickly son succeeded him but died within a few months. 'Abdullah ibn al-Zubayr, the defender of Mecca, was recognized as caliph throughout Arabia, Iraq, and Egypt. Marwan ibn Hakam, of another branch of the Omayyads, was proclaimed caliph at Damascus, however, and in June 684 he defeated the local partisans of 'Abdullah. Marwan immediately reconquered Egypt for the Omayyads and installed his second son as governor. When Marwan died shortly after his return to Damascus in April 685, he left the disputed caliphate to his eldest son, 'Abd al-Malik.

The Mahdi

During this period of religious and political turmoil, popular Muslim belief gave rise to a new doctrine. Regardless of theologians, the Muslim masses had long believed in a messianic deliverer—the Mahdi, "the (divinely) guided one"—who would restore true religion and usher in a golden age of seven, eight, or nine years before the end of the world. (Orthodox Sunnis question this belief, but it is a necessary teaching of the Shi'ite faction of 'Ali.) Some accounts say that the Mahdi will slay al-Dajjal, "the Deceiver," or will assist Christ in slaying him. Some say that the Mahdi will be Jesus (the 'Isa of the Koran), who will descend to Earth, rule according to Islamic law, and confound both Jews and Christians. But others, among them the Shi'ites, say that he will be a descendant of the Prophet.

After the two sons of 'Ali and Fatima were dead, many partisans of 'Ali were disposed to follow his son by another wife, Mohammed ibn al-Hanafiya, although the son himself refused to lead them. When he died, it was taught that "his Mahdi" remained alive in his tomb on Mount Radwa and would reappear to vanquish his enemies. This idea seems borrowed from those who, like many Jews and Christians of the time, expected a second coming. Among Muslims this messianic hope appealed primarily to client converts, the *mawali* of the kind who revolted at Kufa in 685 as a rebellion against the "real Arabs." Because the Mahdi has been seen as the restorer of purity and justice, the title has often been claimed by social revolutionaries in Islamic society, especially in northern Africa. (In Shi'ite schools disagreement about who exactly the Mahdi will be has been a chief factor in separating sect from sect. The Isma'ilis, the Druze of Syria, the Bektashi dervishes of Turkey, and many other groups all have different interpretations of Mahdist doctrine.)

It must be noted that, even if fierce doctrinal issues arose in the formative century of Islam—differences that divide the Shi'ites from the Sunnis today—there have been no last-ditch religious wars since the early schism. Orthodox Islam has denounced heretics but seldom persecuted or burned them. There has been no Islamic inquisition. The nearest example is the persecution of Manichaeans that began at Baghdad under the 'Abbasid caliphs and a fanatical *ulama*. It should also be noted, however, that absence of prolonged theological bloodshed has not always made Sunni Muslims love their Shi'ite neighbors and has not always prevented combat between them.

The Empire of 'Abd al-Malik

When word of the Mahdi first went abroad in about 685, tribal factions in the east were openly hostile to one another. In Arabia the Kharijites pursued their reign of terror. The *mawali* revolt at Kufa, which included freed slaves, was aided by Yemenite Shi'ites who crushed their Arab opponents and eventually killed Obaidallah in Mesopotamia in 686. 'Abdullah, who was still a rival for the caliphate, was in nominal control of many provinces. His brother marched to reclaim Kufa from the Shi'ites and their *mawali* allies, and after a desperate resistance the Shi'ites were put down with great slaughter.

Meanwhile, 'Abd al-Malik, the actual caliph of Damascus, was wholly occupied with rebellious tribes in Syria. By 692 he had reunited these factions into a reformed army and had turned to reoccupy an Iraq exhausted by Kharijite ravages. In the same year an army of two thousand Syrians besieged 'Abdullah in Mecca for six months. In their final assault they killed 'Abdullah, who went down with sword in hand.

In Iraq and as far as the Oxus River and Afghanistan, governors appointed by 'Abd al-Malik were kept busy with battles and rebellions. The proud tribesmen of Iraq resented their plebeian overlords, the higher pay of Syrian troops, and the loss of their provincial revenues to Damascus. Cultivators, who had streamed into cities in the years of civil turmoil and had become Muslims, were embittered by their forced resettlement on the land and by imposition of the full tax despite their conversion. Reciters of the Koran were offended by the official text of Othman and the exclusion of their own manuscripts. On all these insurgent elements Syrian authority was once more brought to bear and it was maintained by the foundation of a new garrison city for Syrian troops. Forces from Iraq itself were never again called upon to campaign for Islam, and the chief Iraqi cities were given over to more peaceful pursuits. Caliph 'Abd al-Malik could resume war with the Byzantine empire on his northern frontiers and campaign in Africa.

He made no conquests in Asia Minor, but in Africa his troops, supported by a fleet, recaptured Kairouan—which had been lost in the Berber-Byzantine revolt—and after defeating a Greek navy expelled the Byzantines from Carthage. A new naval base was established in Tunis, and seaborne raids were extended to Sicily and Sardinia.

'Abd al-Malik also reorganized the empire in several ways. Damascus was linked to provincial capitals by a regular postal service with postmasters to keep the caliph informed about events and conditions in each area. The treasury, hitherto the domain of Greek and Persian officials, was reformed, and its business was conducted in Arabic. Greek and Sasanian coins were replaced in 693 with a new Islamic coinage. Al-Hajjaj, the masterful general who had pacified Iraq, made the text of the official Koran easier to read by adding vowel signs, which had never been required in ancient Semitic alphabets. When he died in Damascus in October 705, 'Abd al-Malik left his son al-Walid in charge of a much improved imperial system.

Next to that of Omar I the reign of al-Walid was the most brilliant in the history of the caliphate. The Syrian army ranged with impunity over Asia Minor and Armenia, while the Byzantines were torn by military revolutions. The African army swept to the far west in 708, and the Berber freedman Tarik was installed as governor of Tangier. Spectacular victories came in the east as Arab armies under al-Hajjaj conquered Bukhara, Samarkand, Khwarizm (modern Khiva), Fergana, and Tashkent and deposed Turkish and Sogdian princes. Another army invaded Makran and Sind, took the port of Daibul, defeated the Indian king Dahar, and after a lengthy siege captured Multan with enormous plunder. These Indian border provinces remain Islamized to this day.

Conquest of Spain

From his headquarters in Tangier, Tarik could look across the strait to a Spain shattered by dynastic feuds among the ruling Goths. The Arian Christian lords were hated by their Catholic subjects. While Roderic, the Gothic leader, was engaged in repressing the Basques, his enemies at home appealed to the Muslims of Africa for help. In 711 Tarik crossed to Spain with seven thousand men, mostly Berbers. He landed near the rock that bears his name, Jabal ("mount of") Tarik—Gibraltar. Roderic hastened to meet him, and Tarik called on Musa, the caliph's viceroy in Africa, for reinforcements. Tarik and Musa saw Spain as a rich field for booty rather than a land to possess. After Roderic was betrayed and killed near Medina Sidonia, Tarik swiftly occupied Toledo, the Gothic capital, while Roderic's rivals continued their negotiations with Musa and the Caliph al-Walid himself. The Jews of Spain, who had little reason to love either Goths or Christians, welcomed the arrival of Berbers and Arabs and helped to deliver Toledo to them. As religious passions flamed during the invasion, probably more Christians in Spain were killed by Christians than by Muslims.

Legend has it that at Córdoba a shepherd pointed out a breach in the wall to Tarik's cavalry. Malaga surrendered without a battle. By the end of the summer of 711, Tarik had gained half of Spain. In the following year Musa, not without envy of his junior's extraordinary success, landed in Spain with ten thousand Arab and Syrian warriors. He stormed the towns and fortresses Tarik had bypassed—Medina Sidonia, Carmona, and Seville. After a year's siege he took Merida in June 713. According to tradition, the victorious but still jealous Musa met Tarik near Toledo. Accusing the Berber freedman of various insubordinations, Musa put him in chains and flogged him. At the end of the summer after further conquests by Musa, Caliph al-Walid charged him with disobedience and summoned him to Damascus.

Arab historians paint a colorful picture of Musa's triumphant march back to Syria—his retinue of slaves, four hundred Gothic princes crowned and girdled with gold, and, perhaps an exaggerated figure, thirty thousand virgins captured from the Gothic nobility. (It is true, nonetheless, that slaves from many regions flooded the Muslim empire as a result of al-Walid's wars.) But the ultimate fate of Musa and

Tarik was to be one that had already happened to Arab generals before them. Both were accused of embezzlement, and both died in obscurity. Musa ended his life begging in the streets of a remote Hejaz village. His son, whom he had left behind to govern Spain, was murdered. Other governors for Spain were appointed by the caliph, and they were tempted to advance toward Gothic Gaul.

The Empire under al-Walid

Within a hundred years after the death of the Prophet the Islamic empire, from Gibraltar to India, had surpassed the earlier victories of Rome at its height. Under the reign of al-Walid agriculture, especially in Iraq, was intensely developed. Canals were constructed, marshes drained, and new lands plowed. Roads were cared for and wells dug for the convenience of pilgrims and travelers. The Arabs who had spearheaded military conquest had little culture of their own and little time at first to give to the study of their subject civilizations. Not settling down as owners of the land they conquered, they were continuously available for war and received an annual stipend from the caliph. Between campaigns they retired to their garrisons and encampments. By 700, however, their manpower was insufficient for the needs of the empire; non-Arabs like the Persians and Berbers became Muslims and *mawali*, clients who helped the armies continue their advance. In some provinces Arabs, like the small number who came to Spain, did begin to settle down. In urban centers a man who embraced Islam and spoke Arabic became, regardless of nationality, an "Arab." Intermarriage was beginning to dissolve racial barriers; and, as they settled outside Arabia, the Arabs themselves gradually felt the impact of different cultures.

Many characteristics associated by the West with Arabic Islam actually originated from this early cross-fertilization. A striking instance is the custom of the veil, or purdah, which both in Muslim and in non-Muslim minds is a practice of pure Islam. All the Koran enjoins, however, is a sense of modesty, in contrast to pre-Islamic sexual license. Women "should not make an exhibition of their beauty," although the Prophet's wives were held in a more strict seclusion. Outside Arabia, however, Arabs began to note the habits of their conquered subjects, especially the aristocrats, and to indulge somewhat in moral laxity. This gave rise to the large body of later tradition in which the Prophet allegedly warned against both male and female corruption on the eve of Judgment Day. In the milieus of these newly conquered lands much of the warp and woof of Muslim ethics was established. From these milieus, too, the idea of community was reinvigorated.

At the head of the social order everywhere were the ethnic Arabs who conquered and governed territories. They became the new aristocrats wherever their armies went. Next, in theory, came the converts, the *mawali* Muslims. In fact, however, these former infidels were often despised for reasons other than race. Their conversion meant that they paid lower taxes, which was a nuisance to the treasury, and the former Christians and Jews among them rankled against their Arab overlords and often tended to become the most sectarian and fanatic of the faithful. *Mawali* were also responsible for the spread of Mahdism among the poorer classes. Next to last on the social scale were the *dhimmis*, the "tolerated infidels," such as Christians, Jews, and Sabaeans. They could not bear arms, and they paid tribute in return for protection. At the bottom were the masses of slaves brought in by conquest.

The lot of Jews did not improve everywhere as it did in Spain. Spanish Jews welcomed the Berber invaders, but friction between Muslims and Jews continued in northern Arabia. Jews who were farmers and manual laborers at the time of the conquest tended to disappear; they reappeared centuries later as traders and merchants. In northern Africa, as Christian culture faded away, Judaism survived.

Under Islam slavery became a less harsh institution than it had been in many Roman or Byzantine lands. War captives, including women and children, supplied the slave markets; and although no Muslim could enslave another Muslim, nothing required him to free a captive who converted to Islam. Yellow slaves came from China; black, from central Africa. A Spanish slave brought almost double the price of a Turk. All children born to a female slave were slaves unless acknowledged by the master. A child fathered on a free woman by a male slave was free. (The last three Omayyad caliphs had slave mothers.) As moral standards relaxed and harems developed, eunuchs—as they had in the empires of Persia, Rome, and Byzantium—reached positions of political power. As conquered and conqueror mixed together, the "purity" of Arab blood was correspondingly weakened.

A Changing Culture

The sights, sounds, and smells of Omayyad Damascus were

Standing over the spot from which Mohammed is said to have ascended into heaven, the Dome of the Rock (top) in Jerusalem was originally built by the caliph 'Abd al-Malik in the seventh century A.D.; much of its present decoration was added in later periods.

much as in modern times. Vendors, tradesmen, metal workers, shopkeepers, and camels and donkeys crowded the noisy
streets. Still divided according to tribe, Arab aristocrats had
their own quarters and buildings. The Bedouin armies of
conquest had been accustomed to make their simple
mosques out of former churches or build them from local
materials. In 691, however, 'Abd al-Malik finished the oldest
existing Muslim monument, the Dome of the Rock at Jerusalem, which is a miracle of architecture and design. Using
marble and mosaic decoration, Caliph al-Walid converted the
Church of St. John the Baptist in Damascus, once a temple
of Jupiter, into the Great Mosque, a project begun by his
father. At the four corners of the sacred enclosure he turned
square towers into the first minarets of any mosque. (The
word *mosque* itself is from *masjid*, "a place of prostration.")
Persian, Indian, and Greek craftsmen made the beauty of the
Great Mosque a model for others in Syria, Africa, and Spain.
Al-Walid also enlarged and beautified the Aqsa Mosque in
Jerusalem and the Prophet's Mosque in Medina. The desert
conquerors were learning new ways.

During the first years of conquest desert poetry did not
change its traditional character. Under the Omayyads of
Damascus, however, invention and stylistic virtuosity flourished, and panegyrics were written to the caliphs. The *ghazal*
or love lyric was perfected by a Quraish poet of the Prophet's
clan and was influenced by a new style of professional music.
Over the protests of conservative Muslims the joys of love
and wine were once more celebrated.

Poring over the Koran, conservatives themselves developed
the arts of lexicography and philology. Arabic science, alchemy, and medicine began to flourish with the translation of
Greek texts. The Arabs' love of their language was enhanced
by these studies, while the need of converts to read the Koran
led to the development, especially in Persia, of formal Arabic
grammars.

A double process took place as the empire grew under the
caliphate of al-Walid. The Arabs infused new territories with
their faith and language, and they themselves were affected
by the cultures of the older civilizations of Persia, Greece,
and Rome. While others became "Arabized," the Arabs themselves never became "Hellenized" or "Persianized" in any
radical intellectual or psychological sense. They adapted to
their own requirements the best, the most practical, and the
most beautiful of other cultures.

An End to Expansion

After the death of al-Walid in 715 the rhythm of Arab conquest slackened somewhat. Al-Walid's self-indulgent brother Suleiman reigned for two years, during which Musa was exiled on his return from Spain. Another attempt was made on Constantinople, the last energetic assault Arabs were to mount against the Byzantine capital. The Emperor Leo III defended his city brilliantly, using "Greek fire" and stretching a massive chain across the Golden Horn to keep the Arab fleet out of the harbor. A severe winter compelled the caliph's land army to make a disastrous retreat through Anatolia in 717, while the fleet was destroyed by a storm. This shattering failure marked the climax and turning point of Islamic conquest. The destruction of the Syrian army removed the main prop of the Omayyad dynasty.

At this critical juncture Suleiman made the fortunate and unexpected move of nominating as successor his cousin Omar, a man of simple and universally respected piety. Islam gained a brief period of respite and relaxation of tension. Attempts to put all Muslims on an equal footing without respect to nationality encouraged further mass conversions, even though they threw the treasury into chaos. When his governors remonstrated, Omar II replied that "God sent Mohammed to call men to the Faith, not to collect taxes." Although he discouraged raiding in principle, border wars and the quest for booty went on. The riches of France, especially of churches and convents, had already begun to draw Arabs across the Pyrenees.

In 720 Omar II died, leaving a reputation for sanctity such as no other caliph achieved. He was followed by Yazid II, a son of 'Abd al-Malik, who was forced to take stopgap measures to bolster public finances and to meet dangerous outbreaks of violence. Political foes stirred up a general revolt in Iraq and southern Persia. These rebels fell in battle or were pursued to India and killed, but their faction survived to grow in intensity and finally to dethrone the Omayyads. Yazid II is chronicled, perhaps unjustly, as frivolous and pleasure loving amid his troubles. He was succeeded in 724 by the earnest and heavy-handed Hisham. The problem for Hisham was to stabilize an empire that had been organized solely for expansion. During the early years of his reign the Syrian army forayed in Asia Minor, and Spanish Arabs penetrated further into central France. In Asia Arab troops were kept on the defensive by the Turks. Hisham was meanwhile laying the foundations of a permanent Islamic bureaucracy for an "Arab" empire that had become, in effect, a Syrian empire maintained by Syrian troops dispersed all too thinly through many garrisons.

Defeat by the Franks

Having crossed the Pyrenees in 720, the Arab governor of Spain captured Narbonne but was repulsed at Toulouse, the seat of the Dukes of Aquitaine. Falling in battle against non-Muslims, the governor suffered not only martyrdom but also a defeat that signaled the failure of future Muslim adventures in France. The next governor, 'Abd al-Rahman, was attracted by the riches of Tours, where the body of St. Martin brought the offerings of many pilgrims. He met the Frankish forces of Charles Martel, dressed in wolf skins, between Tours and Poitiers. Charles, Mayor of the Palace at the Merovingian court, was a formidable warrior. After days of skirmishing, a battle took place in October 732, with 'Abd al-Rahman initiating the onslaught. The Franks never yielded an inch. By nightfall their swords had hacked down all of their attackers, including 'Abd al-Rahman. By the next day the Arabs had vanished from the field.

Western historians have seen the victory of Charles Martel in the centennial of Mohammed's death as a watershed in world history. The English historian Edward Gibbon, one of the first Westerners to recognize the importance of Islam, underestimated the fact that the Muslim empire under Caliph Hisham was dangerously threatened on other fronts when the Frankish swordsmen triumphed at Poitiers. The Arab withdrawal from France was hardly as decisive as the destruction eight years later of the main Omayyad forces in Asia Minor by Leo III of Constantinople. If Poitiers was less important, it was, however, a benchmark in the expansion of those "wild tribes" of Arabia. In the eyes of some, the Arabs had by this period elevated the Near East to an eminence it had not known even as "the cradle of civilization," long before Alexander or Caesar.

4.
Baghdad—Splendor and Decline

Defeated at Poitiers, France, by Charles Martel in 732 and defeated in Asia Minor in 740 by the Byzantines of Leo III, Caliph Hisham was forced to cut his losses and hold the empire together as well as he could with Syrian troops. On his eastern flank he drove back Khazars and Turks, but in Morocco a Berber revolt destroyed his army in 741. In the following year a large relief force of Syrians was cut to pieces on the Sebou River, and Hisham had to dispatch a third army to save Kairouan. Within its borders the caliphate was beset as ever by the fratricidal feuds Mohammed had hoped to suppress. Rebellious Shi'ites remained active, and Hisham could not control the ancient rivalry going back to pre-Islamic times between northern and southern Arabs. Even worse, Hisham rejected the nomination of his nephew, al-Walid, and made his own son heir to the caliphate. When the son was killed in a hunting accident, al-Walid—who had a passionate hatred for everything Hisham stood for—had his rights restored and claimed the throne in 743.

The Caliphate in Disorder

To pay for a new castle, al-Walid II sold a Yemenite rival, the leader of the southern tribes, into the hands of the governor of Iraq, a northerner. The Yemenite was cruelly murdered. The north-south antagonism was further inflamed when al-Walid proclaimed his two slave-born sons as heirs. The Yemenites rebelled and proclaimed a son of al-Walid I caliph in Damascus. A Yemenite force murdered al-Walid II in his desert castle after a reign of one year. His sons were also murdered, but the new caliph, Yazid III, lived less than six months after his succession.

After another battle between northern and southern tribes, Marwan II, a cousin of Hisham, was proclaimed caliph in 744. He was the last of the Omayyad dynasty. The authority of this house and of its kinsmen had been all but destroyed by ancestral Arab feuding and by political and religious factions. The problem of the succession—which continued to rock the caliphate as it had the thrones of Rome, Persia, and Byzantium—seemed to be solved only by bloodshed. Because of this disunity the northward advance of Arab soldiers was halted in the foothills of the Taurus range, which stand today as a linguistic boundary of the Arab tongue.

End of the Omayyad Dynasty

Between 744 and 747 Marwan II attempted to establish his rule over restive Syrians, Shi'ites, Kharijites, and rival governors of provincial garrisons. His troubles in Syria left Damascus in a shambles, and the main base of Omayyad power was defenseless. Marwan found his decisive and final challenge, however, in another quarter. During the Syrian uprisings the governor of Khurasan on the empire's eastern border had won the allegiance of the Arab chiefs. The southern Yemenites, generally hostile toward the governor and toward Marwan, rebelled against this arrangement. A stalemate resulted, and the door was open to intervention by a third party.

This third faction consisted essentially of Shi'ites, both Arab and converted *mawali*. They were united by their hatred of the Omayyads and by their hopes for the arrival of the Mahdi or savior from the house of the Prophet. Their secret missionary activities had begun in the time of 'Ali, Mohammed's son-in-law, and had been successful in winning over Yemenites in Khurasan as well as warlike Iranian converts. Under a black banner, which in popular belief announced the precursor of the Mahdi, these various foes of Marwan formed the 'Abbasid party. (The name came from Mohammed's uncle al-Abbas, whose great-grandson had been a Shi'ite revolutionary.) The general chaos of the times allows no simple lines to be drawn between the forces; but the conflict—consuming all of Islam—can be seen as northern Omayyads, formerly propped up by the loyalty of Syrian armies, against southern Yemenite 'Abbasids and their allies, dependent on the power of the Khurasan army.

Within the 'Abbasid group, an extreme Shi'ite sect called the Hashemites—Mohammed himself was a member of the Quraish house of Hashim—made the strongest appeal to those who believed that only descendants of the Prophet's family should lead Islam. On November 28, 749, the Hashemite Abu al-'Abbas declared himself to be al-Saffah ("the bloodshedder"), precursor of the Mahdi. He was proclaimed caliph. Up to this point the armies of Caliph Marwan had managed to maintain Omayyad supremacy. No power was greater than faith in the Mahdi, however, and volunteers from all sides flocked to join Abu al-'Abbas and his Khurasan forces. The moment of destiny came at the Great Zab River, which flows into the Tigris. There in 750 Marwan's army was given its final defeat by the Shi'ite 'Abbasids, made invincible by faith in their divine agency. Khurasan soldiers pursued Marwan to Damascus and from there to Egypt, where he was killed at Busir. Members of the Omayyad house were hunted down and put to death. Among those few who escaped, 'Abd al-Rahman, a grandson of Hisham, fled to Africa and then to Spain, where he was to establish a new Omayyad dynasty in Córdoba. Thus tribal feuds of the Age of Ignorance, despite the warnings of the Prophet, gave rise to hostile caliphates at each end of the Islamic empire. In the east the black flag of the 'Abbasids had triumphed, and Islam was opened to all the seductive influences of the Orient.

The First 'Abbasid Caliphs

The headquarters of the 'Abbasid caliphate were transferred to Iraq. The Khurasan army extinguished any rivalries that still flared among its predominantly Arab components, although tribal feuds continued in the armies of Syria and Mesopotamia. The fact, however, that 'Abbasid power rested upon the two provinces—Iraq and Khurasan—where the mingling of Arabs and Persians had gone furthest, favored the development of a common Muslim civilization in which the Arab no longer predominated. In language and religion Arabs remained supreme, but the 'Abbasid court and administration took on characteristics of the Persian empire.

The fall of the Omayyads of Damascus was not without sinister overtones. One 'Abbasid general invited eighty members of the cousin house to a feast, butchered them at his table, covered the dead and dying with leather skins, and went on with supper. The new caliph had, after all, proclaimed himself "the bloodshedder." The 'Abbasids were the first to lay down a leather executioner's carpet beside the throne of Islam. Even in their hour of triumph the 'Abbasids had to insist on the religious basis of their rule against determined Shi'ites, who set the party of 'Ali above the house of al-'Abbas. The enthusiasm of victory over the Omayyads was not enough to dissipate the risings and rebellions of rival factions.

After devoting much of his reign to the suppression of malcontents, Abu al-'Abbas was succeeded in 754 by his brother, who took the mahdist title al-Mansur, "the divinely aided." One of his first acts was to devise the murder of Abu Muslim, the leader of the Iranian converts who formed much of the Khurasan army. In his place al-Mansur put his own eldest son, happily named al-Mahdi. In Africa the caliph had to deal with further Berber and Kharijite revolts, and in Spain the dynasty of his cousins, the Omayyads, continued to defy him. All of al-Mansur's attempts to dislodge the Omayyads by supporting local rivals came to nothing.

At home two additional embarrassments developed. Contrary to orthodox practice, the fanatical Hashemites were paying divine honors to al-Mansur and had to be suppressed. The true Shi'ite faction, on the other hand, had transferred its loyalty to a claimant caliph of the Prophet's line. With the disciplined Khurasan army at his disposal, al-Mansur eventually overcame these opponents. In 766 he secured the establishment of the 'Abbasid house by founding a new capital at Baghdad, the old market town on the Tigris, linked by a canal to the nearby Euphrates.

Baghdad—The New Capital

If the history of the caliphate often evokes an old Arab proverb—"I against my brothers, I and my brothers against my cousins, I and my cousins against the world"—the story of Baghdad often evokes all of the civilized magnificence of Islam. Though built originally as a fortified garrison city, Baghdad expanded rapidly and grew into the great metropolis that, in spite of riot, flood, and siege, remained a center of Islam until the tottering end of the 'Abbasid caliphate. Although their power did not extend to northern Africa or Spain, 'Abbasid rulers gave Islam a "golden age" of five hundred years. Al-Mansur's triumph meant that Islam was to become a community of cultures no longer dominated by conquering Arabs. When Caliph al-Mahdi (775–785) created the new office of vizier, or provincial administrator, he filled the posts with freedmen of the 'Abbasid house who, being former slaves, were not of Arab blood.

Significantly, the name of the new capital was Persian—*Bag* ("God") *dad* ("has given"). The original Round City of Mansur called *Madinat al-Salaam* (the "City of Peace") stood on the west bank of the Tigris; but it has left no traces, and its exact site is unknown. The city was three thousand yards in diameter with three concentric walls, each pierced by four gates through which passed highways radiating from the palace to the four quarters of the empire.

The creators of this empire, the old tribal Arabs, were being diffused into the multicolored world of "the Arabian

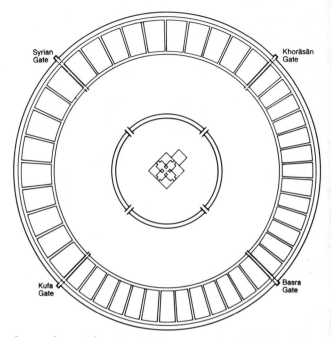

In accordance with ancient Persian custom, the original Round City of Mansur (Baghdad) was laid out in a circle to symbolize the sun.

nights." Once, they had eaten weasels, scorpions, and beetles as delicacies; now they could spread their tables with the chickens, nuts, and sweetmeats of Persia. It would be an exaggeration, however, to say that the desert Bedouin, with his sharp curiosity of mind, was overpowered by the superior culture of Persia. The Iranians, or "Aryans," of Persia may have regarded their Semitic masters as somewhat barbarian, and Persians may have served the 'Abbasids in many high ministries; but Arabic became the language of literature and learning, nevertheless, and subject people blended into an "Arabized" culture so thoroughly as to make the word *mawali* fall into disuse. Baghdad also had a flourishing Jewish community, one of the many hallmarks that distinguished 'Abbasid racial and religious tolerance, hardly equaled by any other ruling caste. On every level, however, an unofficial prejudice against blacks and those of mixed blood arose in the wake of conquest by white Arabs.

Harun al-Rashid

Religious tolerance did not diminish the zeal of al-Mansur and his successors for religious orthodoxy. Muslim sectarians continued to multiply and to be persecuted. The rising prosperity of the 'Abbasids and their improved administration, however, led to a brilliant civilization at a time when Charlemagne and his courtiers, as historians often note, could barely write their names. Charlemagne's great Arab contemporary was Harun al-Rashid, the fifth 'Abbasid caliph (786–809), whose world is reflected in the kaleidoscopic pages of *The Thousand and One Nights*. His reign marked a merging of Arab and non-Arab elements, a growth of industry and commerce, and a flowering of culture. Hindu science was translated into Arabic, and Baghdad rivaled Byzantium as a treasury of Greek thought, often in translations made by Jews. Harun's vast empire was helpful to Charlemagne against his Christian enemies at Byzantium, while the Holy Roman Emperor was useful in turn to Harun as an ally against the Omayyads of Córdoba.

Under Harun members of the Barmakid family, prominent Persians who had become Muslims under al-Mansur, obtained high posts. They built up the caliph's treasury and dealt with the unending military and social problems no administration could hope to alleviate among so many people across such a vast and diversified terrain. The power of the Barmecides—as they are known to Westerners and in the *Thousand and One Nights*—gave rise to rivalries and jealousies at court until, in 803, their enemies succeeded in winning Harun's favor. The Barmakid Ja'far, the caliph's boon companion, was beheaded, his family imprisoned, and their property confiscated. Their overthrow intensified internal strains. Harun himself died in 809, marching at the head of his 'Abbasid troops on the way to suppress another border rebellion. Two generations later, 'Abbasids ruled only at the pleasure of their Turkish troops. Of the thirteen 'Abbasid caliphs from 861 to 974, three were dethroned and blinded and five were murdered.

'Abbasid Culture

History, however, remembers the 'Abbasid caliphate not so much for its internal feuds or foreign wars as for its proliferation of culture and for an oriental luxury that, given the exaggerations of storytellers, was nevertheless truly astonishing. Al-Ma'mun (813–833) founded the famous House of Knowledge at Baghdad, where mathematics, astronomy, medicine, and philosophy were cultivated from many sources. Paper for books, an invention imported in about 750 from Samarkand, speeded the spread of learning. Arabic reached new heights as the language of poetry, of courtly society, religion, theology, philosophy, and science. In all of these arts the Arabs seized upon and embellished the concrete and particular, having occasional interest in alien and abstract philosophies but none in the epic poetry, drama, or history of ancient Greece.

Abu Nuwas, who died shortly after Harun al-Rashid, was the greatest Arab poet of his time, an exemplar of "Arab sensuality" and the subject of many apocryphal anecdotes. His father was a soldier of Damascus; his mother, a Persian. Genial, cynical, and immoral, Abu Nuwas and other 'Abbasid poets protested that they could not write in the tradition of deserts they had never seen. Drawing on all of the colorful life of his own time, Abu Nuwas developed the old Arab style with great freedom. Contrary to the command of the Koran, his genius found its best expression in the *Khamriyyat,* a collection of wine songs. Like the "obscenities" found earlier in Omayyad poetry, these songs marked a revolutionary spirit enhanced with artistry, elegance, and gaiety. Abu Nuwas has been called "the last of the Arabic troubadours."

The poetry of wine and love was to find a religious meaning centuries later in the literature of Sufi mystics. (*Sufi,* meaning "wearer of wool," had spiritual associations even in pre-Islamic times. In the 'Abbasid era Islamic mystics came to be called Sufis.) Known for their ascetic ways, Sufis emphasized the Muslim doctrine of God as the only absolute reality and strove for a personal union with him as the one true being. For the Sufi, prostration in prayer came to mean not an undefined humility but an extinction of the ego so that God alone remained. To repeat their litanies, Sufis began to use knotted cords and beaded rosaries with rhythmic movements of the body. (Such deviations as drug-taking, sorcery, jugglery, snake charming, fire-eating, and the spins of the whirling dervish, which Westerners associate with Sufism, affect only a small fraction of the whole community of Sufis.)

As Greek thought was translated into Arabic, Neoplatonisms entered the Sufi vocabulary, and their mystic theology was further elaborated. Although they tried to remain within the Sunni majority, the main body of Islamic sects, Sufis became probably the most aloof of all Muslims and the least accessible to Westerners. Turkey banned Sufis in 1925 for being too conservative, and Saudi Arabia banned them because their conservatism was not narrow enough. Approximately seventy different Sufi orders exist today, displaying a variety of mystical doctrines that, while thoroughly Islamic, owe something to the cultural diversity of the 'Abbasid caliphate.

Philosophy and Literature

The task of Arabic philosophers was to naturalize the Greek system of learning into the Islamic world. Almost everyone considered Aristotle the greatest philosopher. Plato's hypothetical *Republic* was neglected but not his Neoplatonist followers. Late Greek commentators were considered sufficient guides to classical texts of the Greek golden age a thousand years earlier. From the ninth century on a habit of philosophical reading spread throughout the entire Islamic world, from Bukhara to Spain and Morocco. At the 'Abbasid court al-Kindi declared that "we should not . . . be ashamed to recognize truth and assimilate it from whatever quarter it may reach us, even when it is brought to us by earlier generations and by foreign peoples." Both the Islamic world and the Latin Middle Ages were deeply influenced by ibn Sina (980–1037), born in Turkestan and known to the West as Avicenna. Logic, psychology, physics, meteorology, zoology, and especially medicine all attracted his encyclopedic mind. Writing both in his native Persian and in Arabic, ibn Sina had an impact on Islamic life that was prolonged and profound.

One of ibn Sina's most determined philosophical opponents was the Iranian al-Ghazzali, who was appointed professor at Baghdad in 1091. Sometimes called the greatest Muslim after Mohammed and "the Proof of Islam," al-Ghazzali spent ten years in mystical seclusion before combining theological orthodoxy with his private experience of meditation. Seeking to reestablish Muslim religion and prophetic inspiration by using Greek philosophy, he attacked other thinkers on their own grounds. His answer to the inner tensions of Islamic life proved more acceptable than the Hellenistic learning of ibn Sina, but it marked a decline in the force of Arabic philosophy.

The influence of abstract Greek philosophy was never as strong as that of Greek medicine and science. As scholars and students from Syria, Egypt, Arabia, and Persia mingled in

Baghdad, a new scientific literature was developed from many sources, reflecting interests that included history, geography, philology, grammar, music, mathematics, and the inevitable theology. Usually filtered through Syriac translation, Greek genius was felt only indirectly and had nothing like the immediate impact it made on the West during the Renaissance. In history and literature the Persian influence was stronger.

The golden period of Arabic prose showed an immense richness of vocabulary and idiom. Essayists, critics, theologians, and writers of fantasy flourished along with popular storytellers. The Arab love for didactic and humorous tales inspired many anthologies, which became a new type of literary genre, the *maqamat* or "assembly." The first anthology was made by al-Hamadhani (967–1007), who was known as "the wonder of his age." Making no pretense of being factual, the anthology consisted of picaresque stories in prose and verse woven around two imaginary characters. Veneration of the Prophet had already produced a body of legend and fable and to these were added legends about the wars of conquest and about the family of 'Ali. A romantic tradition sprang up together with a popular literature in which the various strands of empire could be seen. Sanskrit fables were Arabized; and the tales of *The Thousand and One Nights,* ranging over central Asia, India, and China, were to receive a fame and influence in the West second only to the Koran.

Astronomy and Geography

Although less proficient in theoretical speculation than in observing facts, Arab scientists were far in advance of the Christian world. The earliest followers of Mohammed had to determine the direction of Mecca by sights on the stars, and they built observatories for this purpose. The Greek writings of Ptolemy were translated into Arabic as the *Almagest,* and its calculations of planetary motions were perfected by Islamic astronomers. Muslim and Jewish scholars later introduced Arabic numerals, divisions of the circle, algebra, and the *Almagest* itself to European courts.

The geographical knowledge of the Greeks passed to the Arabs, whose trade with India, China, and the east coast and interior of Africa expanded the horizons of the world. Beyond their own horizons some geographers—like the tenth-century al-Mas'udi, a Baghdad native known as "the Herodotus of the Arabs"—justifiably assumed a sense of superiority.

Writing from his own travels and from hearsay, al-Mas'udi declared, "The peoples of the north are those for whom the sun is distant. Their bodies are large, their natures gross, their manners harsh, their understanding dull and their tongues heavy. . . . "

Mathematics and Alchemy

Mathematical studies at Baghdad combined the achievements of Greece, Rome, and India. The algebra of al-Khwarizmi in the ninth century continued Mesopotamian traditions, while his astronomy drew upon Greek and Indian components. By means of Latin translation, his genius brought Arabic numerals to the West at the same time that the Arab *sifr*—"cipher" or zero, a number not used in Greek and Roman systems—entered Western calculations. These numerals, properly called Hindu-Arabic, probably had been introduced to Islam by travelers and traders from India, where the decimal system also originated.

Alchemy, which began in Hellenistic times with attempts to convert base metals into gold, was closely allied with medicine and chemistry. In Syriac, Nestorian Christians brought their own Greek learning to the Baghdad court, and their books included alchemical manuscripts. A thriving school of Arab alchemists arose that, in practical fashion, took alchemy out of theoretical texts and into the laboratory. Among the most active alchemists were members of the Isma'ili sect, the mahdist branch of Shi'ites whose modern descendants follow the Aga Khan. Such famous physicians as ibn Sina and Rhazes were also alchemists. The best known of all Arab alchemists was the mysterious Jabir ibn Hayyan, who seems to have lived in the eighth century and written alchemical books and to whom mystical Isma'ili writings were attributed. Arab alchemists discovered important new chemicals such as caustic alkalies and improved technical processes like distillation. It took several centuries before Europe reached the point of understanding these Arabic accomplishments.

Medicine

Chemistry and its allied materia medica were the greatest Arabic contribution to medicine. As early as 765 Baghdad had a medical college. The physicians of Islam were not all Arabs by any means or even all Muslim. Coming from various parts of the great empire, some were Jews, and some were Christians. One of the earliest was Rhazes, a Persian born in about 864 near the modern city of Teheran. His most voluminous work was *Kitab al-Hawi,* the "Comprehensive Book," but his most famous work was a treatise on smallpox and measles that made a clear distinction between the two. The philosopher ibn Sina, often known as "the prince of physicians," was appointed doctor to the caliph's court. His chief medical work, *Al-Qanun fi'l-Tibb* ("The Canon of Medicine"), was used in France as late as 1650 and is said to be still consulted in the Far East.

Another court physician was Hunayn ibn Ishaq, whose indefatigable labors gave him the name "sheikh of the translators." The works of Galen and Hippocrates are counted among his Arabic versions. Hunayn's translations preserved the seven books of Galen's anatomy that vanished in the original Greek. Among his own writings is the earliest known work on eye diseases. Caliph al-Mutawakkil imprisoned Hunayn and threatened him with death for refusing to prepare poison for an enemy. "I have skill in what is beneficial," Hunayn told the 'Abbasid monarch, "and have studied nothing else." The caliph spared the life of the man European medical historians later ranked with the greatest doctors of the ninth century.

Law

As an integral part of Islamic theology, the study of law had begun as soon as scholars had leisure to analyze the Koran and the Hadith. Islamic law was elaborated under the 'Abbasids. The *shari'a,* "the path to God," even today includes everything that a Westerner would term law—public and private, national and international, as well as religious ritual and social ethics. (Much Islamic "law" is beyond the enforcement of any court and is left to the sanctions of eternity.) Schools of jurisprudence had been established in Iraq, Syria, and Hejaz. Like rival sects, rival theories of law were associated with the schools although there was much basic agreement on learned tradition.

Born at Baghdad of Arab stock in 780, ibn Hanbal founded one of the four surviving law schools of Sunni Islam—the Hanbali. A close student of the Koran and Hadith, ibn Hanbal rejected both orthodox and heretical reasoning and stood for acceptance of tradition alone. Imprisoned and scourged for his old-fashioned doctrines, he saw his views at last accepted by the caliphs, and he became a saintly figure with the people. His great work, still widely read, was an encyclopedia of thirty thousand traditions compiled by his son from his lectures. The dispute between ibn Hanbal and the 'Abbasid caliphs, between tradition and philosophy, involved politics as well as theology and pitted Omayyads against 'Abbasids. To an extent even greater than in European history, in Islam politics and religion and law and theology cannot be separated.

Architecture

Civil wars, Mongols, and natural disasters have obliterated the remains of Baghdad architecture in which Persian style made itself felt over the Hellenism of the Damascus caliphate. One 'Abbasid monument remains in Palestine, the Cistern of Er Ramle, dated by an inscription of Harun al-Rashid. It is the earliest example of a structure built entirely of freestanding arched arcades that support tunnel vaults. In 827 the 'Abbasid governor of Egypt doubled the size of the Mosque of 'Amr at al-Fustat by adding an area of equal size and shape to its west.

The most famous work of the 'Abbasid caliphs, however, was Samarra on the Tigris, a second capital about seventy miles north of Baghdad. Standing on the edge of a plateau, the palace was built of baked bricks with decorative dadoes of molded stucco and marble slabs in the throne room. The scale was immense.

The palace was followed by the Great Mosque of Samarra and the Great Mosque of Abu Dulaf, further to the north. The former was rebuilt in 852 and is the largest mosque in Islam; its famous spiral minaret, the Malwiya, towers on its immense northeast side. A miniature of the Malwiya adorns the slightly smaller Great Mosque at Abu Dulaf. The decorations used at Samarra went to Egypt when the governor, shortly after 864, decided to build a mosque with outer walls and windows of Egyptian design like the Mosque of 'Amr but with ornamentation in a newer style. Of its one hundred and twenty-eight grilled geometrical windows, only about four of those remaining today are original. (The Great Mosque of Kairouan, rebuilt in 836 and one of the glories of Tunisia, lay outside the 'Abbasid domain.)

Samarra, which had been founded in 836 by Caliph al-Mu'tasim after his unruly Turkish bodyguard forced him to quit Baghdad, became symbolic of the intrusion of foreign

The Great Mosque of Samarra in Iraq, built in the ninth century, is now in ruins. The nearby 176-foot spiral minaret may have been influenced by the ziggurats of ancient Mesopotamia.

politics and foreign art into Islam. Contrary to Muslim law, the walls of the palace displayed frescoes of huntsmen and nude females—which may have been the work of refugee Christian artists. (The Old Testament commandment forbidding the graven image had thrown the Byzantine empire into the great Iconoclastic controversies of the eighth and ninth centuries.) The Koran itself does not forbid image making; but the Hadith, the traditions of the Prophet dating from the ninth century, followed Jewish custom in denouncing makers of images as "the worst of men."

The Omayyads had not neglected the human form in their art, however, and under the 'Abbasids injunctions against human and animal forms were as idle as the prohibition of wine. One Baghdad caliph set the figure of a horseman on his palace dome, possibly as a weathervane, and sailed the Tigris with pleasure boats in the forms of eagles, dolphins, and lions. It took centuries for Islamic art to come into the service of Islamic religion.

Calligraphy, Pottery, and Music

Yet it must not be forgotten that the word of the Koran, Mohammed's only "miracle," was customarily held in such veneration by Islam that Arabic calligraphy became one of its most glorious arts. To copy the sacred text was to create not only beauty but also merit, and Islamic history remembers by name many more calligraphers than architects, painters, or craftsmen. The shape and line of Arabic letters were peculiarly suited to the reed pen of the Muslim calligrapher. Around the year 1000 as the 'Abbasids declined, ibn Muqla and ibn al-Bawwab, both of whom lived in Mesopotamia, helped develop the *naskhi* script for copying the Koran. Despite later styles invented in Persia and Turkey, it has remained perhaps the most popular script in the Arab world. The beauty of Arabic writing—as seen in inscriptions, on parchment and papyrus and paper, in faience tiles, and on the walls of religious buildings—is overwhelming testimony to the place this art has held in the Islamic heritage.

Among the other artisans of the caliphate, potters from Syria, Egypt, Mesopotamia, Persia, and Afghanistan had skills, often secret, to rival the finest work done in Europe or China. The first manufacturing centers were at Baghdad, al-Fustat, and Samarkand. Most of the pottery now in existence was excavated and survives only in fragments. Tombs are fruitless sources of pottery because Muslims did not bury pottery with their dead. The Omayyads left little ceramic remains of merit, but after Harun al-Rashid was presented with a number of T'ang porcelains, fine 'Abbasid pottery began to appear at Baghdad and elsewhere. Islamic potters aimed primarily for richness of color and decoration rather than for beautiful shapes and textures. Nearly all of their pottery was glazed and painted with elegant, rather stylized motifs. Again disregarding the Hadith ban on representation, they created spirited and rhythmical animal figures. Human figures tended to be stiff looking, resembling those found on contemporary miniatures.

Arabic script, including the *naskhi*, was a major ceramic ornament. Like their brothers in the laboratory, Islamic potters made important technical innovations including the rediscovery of tin enamel in the ninth century. First used by 'Abbasid potters to imitate T'ang wares, the technique went from Mesopotamia and Persia to Omayyad Spain and to Italy. Luster painting was probably invented and was certainly perfected by Islamic potters, perhaps as a response to the Hadith law forbidding gold and silver vessels.

Like so many proscriptions intended to defend Muslim simplicity against the luxuries and vices of subject peoples, the puritanism of the Hadith could not survive 'Abbasid prosperity. Behind the palace curtains of Baghdad singing girls defied the ban on music issued by the four orthodox law schools. Sufi mystics found erotic songs a way of representing divine love. Al-Kindi and ibn Sina philosophized about musical theory. Byzantine and Persian elements entered the native Arab musical tradition, and technical treatises—now mostly lost—were written. Of the nontechnical works on music, by far the most important was the monumental tenth-century *Kitab al-Aghani*, the "Book of Songs," which tells stories of poets and singers and reveals the role of music in court life. Virtuosi of the lute, fiddle, woodwind, and harp appeared; and as the art became more self-conscious, court music moved away from the old folk melodies of the common people. Along with changes in scale intervals and melodic modes, rhythmic structures grew increasingly sophisticated. Renowned for their wit and good fellowship, musicians commanded high fees. Harun freed his own favorite, the slave boy Mukhariq, and gave him a princely one hundred thousand dinars. When Mukhariq sang by the banks of the Tigris, he emptied the streets of Baghdad.

The Effects of 'Abbasid Wealth

Despite a powerful Persian influence, the framework of this "Arabian Nights" civilization was essentially Arabic. Many philosophers and scientists were Arabs, and most of the great poets could trace their descent through desert tribes. It is impossible to divide up the shares in Islamic culture between Arabs and non-Arabs, but Arab self-confidence and Arab values underlay much of early Islamic art. Through the great accumulation of wealth, begun by the Omayyads and continued by the 'Abbasids, the arts took on a new life. The rulers who commissioned great works were all Muslim caliphs, who often winked at artistic bans imposed by the Koran and the Hadith. Non-Arab craftsmen produced at Muslim pleasure. Yet over the expanse of the 'Abbasid empire the mingling of peoples in cosmopolitan settings like Baghdad was bound to have an irresistible effect, moral as well as cultural.

The caliphs shared their beds with wives and countless concubines of many races. In the early 'Abbasid period Arab women enjoyed a high status—sometimes, like 'A'isha, riding with the troops and sometimes, like the sharp-tongued women poets of tribal days, rivaling men in literature and courtly manners. By the year 1000 accounts told of women in Baghdad as lawyers, doctors, and professors. Soon after that, however, women were portrayed as the wily, seductive temptresses of *The Thousand and One Nights,* a change resulting from widespread concubinage and looser sexual morality. At the same time, the comparative tolerance of the Koran toward women was hardened into the seclusion of the harem and a rigorous separation of the sexes.

Official religious tolerance and the presence of dignified rabbis at Baghdad and of Christians in high office did not prevent the enactment of special laws requiring Jewish and Christian *dhimmis* to wear special dress and even to mark their houses with wooden "devils." The community of Muslim scholar-lawyers known as the *ulama* rose in prestige, and the aristocrats of desert tribes gave place to a new class of "priests," court officials, landowners, and merchants.

The vast wealth and enterprise of the merchants of Baghdad were echoed in the voyages of Sinbad the Sailor. Amid the records of luxury and splendor and of drinking parties and slave girls, the life of ordinary people under the 'Abbasids had few witnesses. Life on the small peasant farm—still despised by Arabs—and among the stalls and shops of the towns was probably much as it was in Arab countries until only recently. The literature of the time tended to preserve only the exciting and magnificent. Caliph al-Ma'mun's wedding was renowned for its jeweled splendor. The astonishing ceremony with which Caliph al-Muktadir received an embassy from Byzantium in 917 included seven thousand black and white eunuchs. (Luxury came to more modest homes in the form of the *diwan,* a three-sided sofa, and the *matrah,* a square mattress.) Archery, polo, and horse racing were among the daily diversions of the rich. Prey caught by falcons was duly slaughtered on the spot in accordance with Koranic law.

Like aristocrats in ancient Athens, Rome, or Persia, many Arab males were bisexual; they did not heed the words of the Koran (verses 165–66 of *sura* 26). Their songs were addressed to boys as well as girls, and Harun is said to have been shocked by the personal excesses of his favorite poet, Abu Nuwas—the poet derided in *The Thousand and One Nights* as "king of the Sodomites."

The Ebbing 'Abbasids

As 'Abbasid prosperity enhanced the arts and vices of civilization for the upper classes, it also provoked discontent among the humble, whose rebellious stirrings were aggravated as usual by sectarian disorder. (Under the religion of the Prophet, who set no day of rest for his followers, Baghdad evolved the five-day week; and as 'Abbasid wealth and power declined, free medical and educational programs were used to placate the poor.) Civil wars further weakened the authority of the caliphate.

Under al-Mu'tasim (833–842), the involuntary founder of Samarra, Turkish troops from frontier regions had been added to the old Khurasan guard, and Turkish officers rapidly attained prominent positions. Turkish generals were used to suppress Arab religious and political dissidents, and the caliph was more and more at the mercy of his Turkish guards. In 861 a Turkish commander murdered the caliph, and Turkish generals began to form ruling dynasties within their own families. In 935 the caliph appointed a Turk to be his *Amir al-Umara*, "commander of commanders."

As the Baghdad government was wracked by internal turmoil, its authority contracted. Along its Byzantine borders the enemy remained active, and orderly administration in the provinces vanished. An early symptom of such conditions could be seen in southern Iraq, where African slaves worked along the marshes in huge gangs. These Negroes had been converted to the Kharijite sect and had adopted its fanatical opposition to other Muslims. They made a successful revolt, and by 879 the black rebels and their allies had come within seventeen miles of the gates of Baghdad. After many reverses, they were eventually subdued by Caliph al-Mu'tamid in 883, and the head of their Persian leader was brought into the city on a pole. Henceforth the courage and ferocity of black soldiers were turned to the service of the caliphs.

The purpose of the Negroes' uprising was not to abolish slavery. The victorious Africans themselves took Muslim slaves. As allowed by the Koran, slavery existed on many different levels. Some slaves, like the Negroes in Iraq, performed manual and domestic labor. Others, however, enjoyed high military or administrative posts, and some were to have a decisive voice in the destiny of Islam. (It was only in recent times, after World War II, that the United Nations took effective action to abolish slavery in the Arabian Penin-

sula, Africa, South America, and other parts of the world.) In
Islam, as in the ancient world, slavery had no basis in race
or color. The concept of inferior slave races was the result
of the propaganda of later ages.

Chronic populist or sectarian uprisings within its borders
and chronic warfare along its borders against Byzantine or
barbaric raiders helped to disrupt the farming and home
industries that, with merchant trading, were the foundation
of 'Abbasid economic power. The caliphate might be recognized from Tunisia to Turkestan, but local chiefs and Turkish generals often held the real authority. From the ninth to
the eleventh centuries the Karmatians, an Isma'ili sect,
harassed the imperial armies with almost constant revolt.
Their military exploits carried them over Iraq, Syria, Yemen,
and Bahrain. They threatened Baghdad and in 929 raided
Mecca, taking the Black Stone to their own capital for twenty
years. During the same period two caliphs were deposed and
blinded by mutinous troops. Faction and treachery raged,
petty kingships rose and fell, and Baghdad sank to the level
of a provincial capital. In the general disorder the caliphs
were helpless.

Mahmud of Ghazni

On Islam's eastern border the great Turkish conqueror Mahmud of Ghazni (971–1030) established the Ghaznavid empire in Iran and Afghanistan after having conquered the
chief cities of Khurasan. Caliph al-Kadir conferred on Mahmud the title of "right hand of government and guardian of
the community." During the brief flowering of the Ghaznavid
empire a Turkish military elite, often of slave origin, held
power along with Persian tax collectors. As the caliphate in
Baghdad grew feeble, "Mahmud the Idol Breaker"—he had
plundered Hindu temples and persecuted the Karmatians—
attracted poets and scholars to his capital. Perso-Islamic letters revived, and in Islamic folklore Mahmud became an
archetype of the pious Muslim ruler. One of the famous
adornments of the Ghazni court was al-Biruni, a Persian
savant who excelled in the Arabic sciences, including history
and philosophy, and who exchanged letters with the great ibn
Sina. In geography al-Biruni advanced the daring notion that
the valley of the Indus had once been a sea basin.

The last years of Mahmud's reign were darkened by the
ambitious Seljuks, nomads converted to Islam whom he attempted to settle on the border region of Khurasan. In their

quest for an empire of their own, the Seljuk Turks were supported by Persian nobles in Mahmud's own court and by Islamic leaders anxious to suppress heretical Shi'ite sects. The Shi'ites, in turn, were supported by the new Fatimid dynasty of Egypt.

The Fatimids

The Fatimids took their name from Mohammed's daughter Fatima, claiming descent from her and her husband, 'Ali. As partisans of 'Ali, they were Shi'ites, and within the Shi'ite fold they became leaders of the Isma'ili movement that in the ninth century had begun to organize the overthrow of the 'Abbasid caliphate. From Syria to Kairouan, among Arab tribes and Berbers, the Isma'ilis were fractured by their own internal conflicts over theology and genealogy. By 911, however, their leader 'Ubaydullah, who called himself al-Mahdi, had been proclaimed the rightful caliph—or *imam* as the Shi'ites preferred—and he began to turn his attention to Egypt. After further sectarian battles Jawhar, a Fatimid general, conquered northern Africa as far as the Atlantic for the Isma'ilis and in 969 conquered Egypt.

The center of Fatimid power was transferred to al-Kahira, or Cairo ("the victorious"), a new capital founded by Jawhar just north of al-Fustat. The famous university mosque of al-Azhar was founded at Cairo by the invaders in the following year. From as far as China, Indonesia, Morocco, and Somalia, students and teachers still gather at al-Azhar in traditional robes and turbans to study the Koran and all branches of Arabic learning, and the university still exercises a vast influence throughout the Islamic world. But universal domain over Islam, the first and real goal of the early Fatimids, was to remain unfulfilled. Their rule lasted for two centuries but was confined to Egypt and its outlying provinces.

The Anarchy of Sects

A remarkable feature of the Fatimid caliphate was the rise of the Druze sect that survives today as a small community of fewer than two hundred thousand hill folk living in southern Lebanon, Syria, and Israel. Their political importance comes from a cohesion maintained throughout more than one thousand years of mid-East turbulence and from bans on intermarriage and on conversion away from or into their faith. In public the Druze may practice the creed of any majority group (by the principle of *taqiyah* or "dissimulation"), but their own religious system is kept secret not only from the outside world but also in part even from their own numbers. Only an elite of Druze initiates participates fully in their services and scripture. In 1017 this messianic sect, named after a leader called Darazi, united in worshiping the divinity of the ruling Fatimid, Caliph al-Hakim. The Druze apparently still believe that al-Hakim did not die but only vanished and will return in triumph one day to inaugurate a golden age. The Druze share this mahdist hope with many other Islamic sects. But their secret beliefs—which are said to include elements of gnosticism, Neoplatonism, and transmigration, all intellectual currents that had been active in the mid-East at the time of Mohammed—are peculiar to them.

By 1095 still another fanatic band of Shi'ite Isma'ilis had begun a reign of terror in northern Persia. The Assassins, as they came to be called, supported the Fatimid caliphs against Baghdad and the Seljuks. By the beginning of the twelfth century they had expanded their activities to Syria, where their chief was locally known as the "Old Man of the Mountain." (The sect still exists as a minor heresy whose Indian devotees are followers of the Aga Khan.) Stories of the terrorists' use of hashish (whence their name "Assassins") before setting out to commit murder and face martyrdom are doubtful, and there is no Isma'ili source to confirm tales of an artificial paradise into which drugged members were taken as a foretaste of eternal bliss. The sinister fame of the sect, however, has persisted in the mind of the West.

The Arabs in Spain and Sicily

While the Assassins and other Arab and non-Arab foes were accomplishing the internal downfall of the Baghdad caliphate, the Arabs of Spain, despite their own factional problems, were building the western branch of Islamic civilization. The 'Abbasids had attempted to establish their dynasty in Spain, but they never succeeded. 'Abd al-Rahman I, the surviving prince of the Omayyads whose relatives had been murdered, came to power in Córdoba in 756. Neither the intrigues of his 'Abbasid cousins, disputes within his own family, nor the pressure of Franks on his borders prevented him from reaching a brilliance that profoundly affected European life. Córdoba was filled with palaces and mosques, and its walls were extended. Al-Hakam II (961–976) gathered four hundred thousand volumes in his library, founded twenty-seven free schools, and lured scholars from the East.

The Great Mosque of Córdoba, begun by the Omayyads in the eighth century, today serves as a Christian cathedral.

A few decades later, after Córdoba had attained its military zenith, popular opposition to the Spanish caliphate degenerated into warfare between Córdobans, Berbers, and slave officials of the royal household. All sides used the caliphs as pawns and murdered most of them. In 1031 the last caliph, Hisham III, was imprisoned together with his family in a vault attached to the Great Mosque. He reacted to the news of his deposition by begging for a crust of bread. The leading families of Córdoba proclaimed a republic.

Although most of the original Islamic conquerors had been non-Arab Berbers, Spain under the Omayyads became more Arab than Arabia. Arab descent was so highly prized that non-Arabs invented Arab genealogies. Spanish Christians living under Muslim rule became so "Arabized" that a bishop complained that his students neglected their Latin for the charms of Arabic poetry. The earlier Christian culture was largely obliterated in Islamic Spain. In the ninth century in Seville the Bible was translated into Arabic for the use of Christian readers, and the Arab culture of Spain long outlived the Córdoban caliphate.

The same epoch saw Arabs move from northern Africa to Sicily, an island whose Byzantine protectors could no longer keep secure from the advance of Islam. In 909 Sicily passed into the control of the Fatimids. They continued the traditional Muslim policy of placing Christians in a position of legal inferiority, tolerating the practice of their religion, and imposing taxes that may have been less burdensome than those formerly paid to the Byzantines. A large Arab immigration from Africa took place during and after the Fatimid conquest.

Decline of the Arabs

From Morocco to Afghanistan the religion of Islam, which might have served as a bond for the empire, was permanently fragmented into sects. Arguments over religion, genealogy, and political advantage had split the caliphate into three houses—Omayyad, 'Abbasid, and Fatimid. The early 'Abbasids of Baghdad had placed the government in the hands of Persian viziers and then into the hands of Turkish sultans. (Later the Wahhabis of Arabia and the modern Muslim Brotherhood would date the decline of Islam from the time Turkish slaves became soldiers of the Baghdad caliph.) The caliphate of the year 1000 had become a throne to be manipulated by Persians, Turks, and sectarian factions within the Muslim community. Even the old north-south tribal rivalries had not been completely forgotten. Subject peoples adopted Arab lineages and took up the feuds of their ficti- tious ancestors, subverting the social structure as far away as Spain.

In Egypt the Fatimid al-Hakim was forced to execute sev- eral of his viziers. Born of a Christian mother, he demolished Christian churches. He did not spare the Church of the Holy Sepulchre in Jerusalem—an action in 1010 that helped to arouse the First Crusade. After declaring himself an incar- nation of God, as the Druze believe he was, al-Hakim died by violence. The Fatimid rulers of Egypt were unable to rely on the loyalty of their northern African and Sudanese troops. Just as the caliphs of Baghdad had been forced to do, they brought in slaves to fortify their armies. These white male Mamelukes (*mamluk* or "owned") were mainly Turks and Circassians from the territories of Rus, the Caucasus, and central Asia. Mobile and reliable soldiers, they progressively encroached on their masters until they became a military ruling caste, a "slave aristocracy."

In these chaotic conditions a general decline throughout Islam was inevitable. The surface of its world still had much brilliance. Arabic poets had many songs to sing and Arabic scholarship, especially in the western regions, much to ac- complish. But the military and political might of the ances- tral Arab conquerors had been dissolved into polyglot armies. Around calitic thrones Arabic itself was no longer the first language of the ruling class. Social upheavals speeded the decline of trade, a "feudal" economy began to take shape, and the dazzling and haunting visions of *The Thousand and One Nights* receded into legend as the Crusaders of Christian Europe appeared on the horizon.

5.
Christians, Turks, and Mongols

In January 946, Caliph al-Mustakfi had allowed an army of rebellious Shi'ites from western Persia to enter Baghdad. Ahmad, their leader, was one of three brothers of the house of Buya who had formed a powerful alliance of principalities from the Caspian Sea to the Persian Gulf. Al-Mustakfi sought to appease Ahmad by giving him a title, but the caliph was at once seized and blinded by the rebels. The Shi'ites considered abolishing the 'Abbasid dynasty altogether, but Ahmad was content to let the bankrupt line continue while he himself took over the administration. For a century the Buyids held effective rule in Baghdad, while the impotent caliphs lived on an allowance.

Eclipse of the 'Abbasids

Byzantine generals had been making spectacular advances into Mesopotamia and Armenia and later into Syria and Palestine. In 969 the emperor Nicephorus Phocas took Antioch. In the same year he was blinded and deposed by John I Tzimisces, his nephew, who then stormed Damascus, Tiberias, Nazareth, Acre, Sidon, and Beirut. The troops ravaged the countryside and departed, leading thousands of women and children off into slavery. Shortly afterward, the Seljuk Turks—the warlike nomads whom Mahmud of Ghazni had once hoped to settle peacefully on his borders—saw a chance to win a realm of their own. As Sunni Muslims they despised the Shi'ite Buyids as heretics and found support among Persian nobles in the caliph's shrinking bureaucracy. In 1040 near Merv the Seljuks inflicted a massive defeat on Mahmud's son Mas'ud; and in 1055 Togrul Beg, their chief, was invited to enter Baghdad and put an end to the anarchy of the Buyid regime. Togrul the Seljuk was given the formal title of sultan. The orthodox 'Abbasid caliphs saw a momentary restoration of their prestige, and for a century Seljuk sultans replaced Buyids as powers behind the throne.

Compared to their rivals in Egypt, North Africa, and Spain, the Baghdad caliphs had little more than memories of wealth and glory. For centuries they had been puppets—manipulated, blinded, deposed, and dominated by illiterate Turks. Often the victims as well of conspiracies or harem intrigues, they were by this time destroyed as Arab potentates. The rebellion of Negro slaves in Iraq had signaled the demise of trade coming from oriental ports to the Persian Gulf. Old Arab tribes like the Karmatians who sacked Mecca in 830 were seen as actual enemies of the Islamic caliph and his mercenary troops. As provinces fell away into misrule or defiance, the mercenaries themselves failed to provide even a semblance of stability.

Provincial Powers

In northern Syria the independent line of Arab Hamdanid princes held sway. Al-Mutanabbi, often regarded as the greatest Arab poet of Islam, arrived at their court in 948 and found a sovereign worthy of his admiration. The poet's hectic career, however, was typical of the uneasy times. Al-Mutanabbi, "the Would-Be Prophet," is said to have been leader of a heretical revolutionary movement among nomad tribes of the Syrian desert. After a term in prison he resumed his profession of extolling rich patrons in ornate, panegyric poetry. He had spent nine years with the Hamdanids when intrigues and jealousies forced him to depart for Egypt. There he attached himself to the Negro eunuch Kafur, who ruled effectively on the Nile before the Fatimid conquest. (Kafur was the only black to govern a country of "white" Muslims.) Unable to stomach Kafur's patronage, the poet found protection with another member of the Egyptian court and turned against the eunuch with scurrilous satire. When his new protector died in 961, al-Mutanabbi fled in secret to Iraq, wandered the desert for four years in search of another patron, and was killed by bandits.

The great dynasty of the Samanids was organized on feudal lines and occupied Persia, Khurasan, and Transoxiana, with its capital at Bukhara. The Samanids were natives of Persia and took their name from Saman Khudat, a noble converted to Islam after the Arab conquest. By the tenth century Samanid territories had attained a high degree of prosperity. Their coinage, found throughout northern Asia, attests to the success of their industry and commerce. But the Samanid rulers, too, were prey to internal rivalry and to rising Turkish power in central Asia. In about 960 a Turkish slave who was the commander of the palace guard at Bukhara fled to the mountains of Ghazni and established semi-independent rule. In the ensuing dynastic quarrels, Turks occupied the greater part of Transoxiana, and the Samanids came into conflict with the mighty Mahmud of Ghazni. Muntasir, the last Samanid prince and a warrior and poet, fought Mahmud and the Turks until he was assassinated in 1005. In the general collapse of the Samanid empire, the philosopher ibn Sina fled Bukhara to become a vizier in Iran.

Bukhara had produced its philosopher and its civilization at one end of Islam, and a galaxy of poets was about to appear at the other among the Muslims of Spain. As the tenth century drew to a close, however, Baghdad—the vital heart of this civilization—shone more in myth than in reality. After twenty years of travel throughout Muslim lands observing life and manners, the Arab geographer al-Maqdisi wrote that "Baghdad was a once magnificent city but is now fast falling into decay." And this sad reflection came seventy years before Baghdad opened its gates to the Seljuk Turks.

The Rule of Malik Shah

On the eve of the Crusades Malik Shah, the greatest of the Seljuk sultans, had consolidated the empire more through diplomacy and the quarrels of his enemies than through warfare. Acting for the caliph, he extended his control over upper Mesopotamia, Syria, Palestine, Mecca, Medina, Yemen, and the Persian Gulf. He was a patron of literature, science, and the arts; and he adorned his capital at Isfahan with splendid mosques. He employed the poet-astronomer Omar Khayyam, whose reform of the calendar made it the most accurate then known. The people enjoyed a reign of internal peace and religious tolerance. Assassins, however, murdered Malik Shah's vizier; his wives and sons intrigued over the succession; and his daughter was left in neglect by her husband, the caliph of Baghdad. Malik Shah ordered the caliph to leave the capital, but the sultan himself died in 1092.

After his death the empire, in a familiar pattern, disintegrated through internal quarrels. While it lasted, however, the brilliant ascendancy of this Turkish sultan emphasized the shadow into which the 'Abbasids and the Arabs themselves had fallen. As the language of learned men and diplomats, Arabic had also begun its decline. After the unbelievable rapine and slaughter that, in contrast to the Arab conquest, had characterized the arrival of the Turks, a Seljuk carried the torch of Islamic civilization.

Egypt and Spain

In Egypt the wealth and splendor of the Fatimids became

proverbial. The Fatimid caliphs were no strangers to violence and political disaster, and their claims to the caliphate were disputed by millions of Muslims, the majority of Islam. The Fatimids, however, saw Alexandria and Cairo, their new capital, flourish as centers of architectural magnificence as well as of the humbler arts of wood carving, metalwork, glasswork, and ceramics. The fanaticism of al-Hakim was not typical of Fatimid rulers, who sometimes had Christian wives or mothers. Like their rivals in Baghdad, however, the caliphs were inclined to rely on their viziers and surrender their power to subordinates. In the tenth century Arab tribes who were not fully Islamized were able to burst out of the peninsula and invade northern Africa, Sinai, and Syria. Along the coast of Africa to the west Berbers, who had been Kharijite Muslims for several centuries, remained utterly hostile to Fatimid authority. In 1091, just before the Crusades began, Roger of Normandy wrested Sicily away from the enfeebled Fatimid caliph and restored Catholic Christianity.

The Muslims of "al-Andalus" continued to foster a brilliant culture long after the Spanish caliphate of Córdoba was broken up. Like the 'Abbasids, the Spanish caliphs had employed foreign mercenaries ("slavs" or slaves) from France, Germany, and Italy who had been converted to Islam. Al-Mansur, the last great Arab ruler of Andalusia, replaced these mercenaries with Berbers and Christians, whom he led to victory after victory against Christian Spain. (His cruelties were not forgotten when Christians overthrew Muslims in the *reconquista* of Spain.) Although al-Mansur's death in 1002 was followed by political anarchy among his Muslim followers, Andalusia remained a literate beacon among the illiterate provinces of Europe.

Christians against Muslims

To the Christians of Europe, however, the Muslim world was seen neither as the matrix of a superior civilization nor as a vast empire fragmented by ethnic, religious, and political differences. For Christians, Islam was the monolithic enemy whose infidel forces had disrupted the travels of Christians to the Holy Land. The universal mission proclaimed by Mohammed as the Seal of the Prophets defied the universal authority of Pope Urban II as the vicar of Christ. After the battle at Manzikert in 1071 nomadic Turks overran the territories of Christian Byzantium, and soon Turkish emirs were fighting over nominally 'Abbasid provinces in Syria and

Palestine. Despite an official breach between the Greek and Roman branches of the Church, the emperor Alexius sent an appeal to the Pope in 1095 for recruits to use against these new and formidable oppressors.

Alexius, who simply wanted soldiers for his own armies, was forced to receive at Constantinople hordes of ill-disciplined fighters accompanied by pilgrims, clergy, and other noncombatants. They were led by ambitious Western princes whom Alexius could not keep under control. And so the Christians of Europe, divided by race and creed and political rivalry, began their Crusades against Muslims divided against each other in much the same way.

In a sense the confrontation of East and West could be seen as one of *dar al-Islam,* "the house of Islam," against *dar al-harb,* "the house of war"—the two divisions of the world as promulgated by Mohammed. (It could also be seen as a Western, Christian *jihad* against Islam just as many Arabs today are inclined to see Zionism when supported by its "Christian" allies.) Despite traditional Arab tolerance of Christians in Jerusalem and elsewhere, Western historians have often depicted the Crusaders as bannered warriors against an intolerant Islamic foe. In reality, of course, as the world of Islam declined, Muslims showed every degree of tolerance and intolerance. The Seljuk Turks of the Holy Lands were more engaged in civil warfare than in an anti-Christian *jihad.*

The Crusades

In turn Muslims lumped their Christian opponents together as "Franks," ignoring the political and religious antagonisms of Christendom. In fact, Franks and Byzantines had barely begun their journey across Asia Minor in 1097 when the Franks were enraged with their allies at not being allowed to loot Nicaea after its surrender. They had an instinctive hostility toward the Greeks, whose version of Christianity was different from their own and whose culture was far more advanced. At Antioch the progress of the First Crusade was delayed while Bohemund of the Norman duchy of Apulia quarreled with the rich and powerful Raymond, the count of Toulouse.

Nevertheless, the Crusaders advanced toward Jerusalem, held by the Fatimids, and took it by storm in 1099 with a barbaric massacre of Muslims and Jews. The Church of the Holy Sepulchre was recovered and the outrages of al-Hakim were revenged. Along the eastern shore of the Mediterranean the victors of this First Crusade established the Latin "kingdom of Jerusalem," together with other Christian states at Edessa and Antioch and later at Tripoli in Palestine.

The period of the Crusades lasted from 1095 until after 1270 when Louis IX of France died leading an eighth expedition against Tunisia even as his brother, Charles of Anjou, prepared war against the Greeks of Byzantium. In almost two centuries of hostilities, ostensibly against "Saracens," the Crusaders of Europe succeeded in destroying Christian civilization in Byzantium and witnessing the military triumph of Islam in the East.

The 'Abbasid caliphs and their Seljuk sultans never regarded the petty Crusader states as dangerous and never attempted to drive out the Franks. The caliphs of Cairo shared their attitude. Muslim rulers had long been accustomed to Christians among their subjects. In Syria itself the Turkish regimes at Damascus and Aleppo, out of mutual hostility, were sometimes ready to ally themselves with the Franks against each other. To the Turks the Franks were unlettered invaders who did not even use maps.

The real *jihad* against the Crusaders did not begin until Zangi, a Turkish Mameluke employed by the Seljuk sultan, seized the Mesopotamian city of Mosul in 1127, extended his authority in Iraq and Syria, and at last established a united Muslim front against the Christians. When Zangi recaptured Christian Edessa in 1144, it sent a wave of shock throughout Europe and caused Pope Eugenius III to proclaim the Second Crusade. Zangi's son Nureddin, a strict servant of Islam, continued to unify the Muslims. He annexed Damascus and brought Egypt under his control. Mosques, schools, hospitals, and caravansaries testify to Nureddin's devotion to the faith. His most important service, however, was to gather Muslims together under one banner and prepare future triumphs for Saladin, the officer who had helped him conquer Egypt.

These events held the attention of Europe, but for Islam they were as nothing compared to the catastrophe in their eastern provinces when Sanjar, the Seljuk prince of Khurasan, was defeated near Samarkand in 1141 by a confederacy of central Asian tribes. Transoxiana was lost, and Islam lay exposed to waves of barbarous invaders from the steppes. In Baghdad the 'Abbasids managed a brief renaissance of power when Caliph al-Muktafi defeated the army of the Seljuk sultan and extended his rule over most of Iraq to the borders of Mosul. This remarkable achievement, however, was not sufficient to save Baghdad from the Mongols who appeared a century later, a foe more savage than the Christians.

Saladin

For Westerners the bloody and useless fury of the Crusades has been ennobled by tales of chivalry between Muslim and Frank. These stories were also recorded by Arab historians. During the Third Crusade when Richard I, "the Lionhearted," arrived with his English troops in the Holy Land, he encountered Saladin of Egypt, the Muslim leader whose name still inspires romantic awe in the Christian world. Before Salah al-Din ("Honor of the Faith") arrived on the scene with Nureddin, the Fatimid throne had been beset with treachery, coups, and rebellions. For a short period Christian Franks were instrumental in saving Muslim Egyptians from Nureddin's Turks. In 1169 Saladin, a Kurdish officer, assassinated the Fatimid vizier and became commander of the Syrian troops in Egypt. Two years later he abolished the Isma'ili Fatimids entirely and proclaimed the return of Egypt to the orthodox Sunnis.

In complete independence, Saladin devoted himself to building up the economic and military might of Egypt. As soon as his armies were strong enough, he called for a *jihad* against the Franks. He won a decisive victory near Tiberias, overran Palestine, and, after offering generous terms to the Christian inhabitants, entered Jerusalem on October 2, 1187 — restoring the Holy City to Islam after eighty-eight years. The crown of the Frankish king of Jerusalem and the gold cross that the Crusaders had set on top of the Dome of the Rock were sent to the caliph in Baghdad. The Franks retaliated by laying siege to Acre until the city surrendered to Richard in 1191. The English king continued brilliant military exploits against the Muslims, but the armistice he concluded with Saladin in 1192 left Egypt in possession of everything but a coastal strip in Syria. The mutual courtesy between Richard and Saladin may have reflected in part the English king's upbringing in the south of France, where Arab manners and culture had left a lasting effect. As for Saladin, his actions on recovering Jerusalem offer a noble contrast to the behavior of its Christian captors eight decades earlier. It is true that he enslaved fourteen thousand Christians, many of them women and children. But Saladin did not, as the Franks had done, drive the Jews into their synagogue and burn them alive. The achievements of Saladin, who treated equally with the Christians of Europe and of Byzantium, profoundly affected the destiny of Islam. The personal dynasty he inaugurated in Egypt came to an end, however, with the death of his nephew in 1238.

Christian Expansion

After a Seljuk sultan had destroyed the Byzantine army in 1176 at Myriocephalon, the Crusaders had been forced to rely again and again on fresh troops from Europe. In 1203 the French and Venetians, having plundered a Christian city belonging to the king of Hungary, placed a pretender on the throne of Constantinople in the hope of bringing Greek Orthodox Christians over to the Pope. The people of Constantinople, however, detested the puppet ruler, removed him in a palace revolution, and defied the Crusaders. As a result, the French and Venetians assaulted the Christian capital, captured it on April 12, 1204, and committed indiscriminate pillage and massacre. Libraries of ancient classics were destroyed. Western Christians divided up the remains of the Byzantine empire and for sixty years systematically looted Constantinople of its treasures. Sacred relics were removed to the West, and bronze statues were melted down for coinage.

Having started as a small Christian order to protect pilgrims, the Knights Templar also showed interest in the wealth of the East. As their grand masters acquired their own territories and castles in the Holy Land and Sicily, they fomented confusion among Muslim and Christian alike. The Knights Templar were openly hostile to the Holy Roman Emperor Frederick II. As a result of his excommunication by the Pope, Frederick had to place the crown on his own head, without a priest to officiate, when he entered Jerusalem in 1229 and proclaimed himself king.

Led by Louis IX of France, in 1249 the Crusaders rallied for their last assault on Egypt. The seasonal rise of the Nile, fevers caught by troops floundering in flooded canals, and Muslim harassment made a disaster of the expedition. Louis and his knights were captured and then ransomed.

The Egyptian Mamelukes

When the sultan of Egypt died a year later, his son was summoned from Iraq to succeed him. The young man proved so offensive to the Mameluke guards that they killed him and

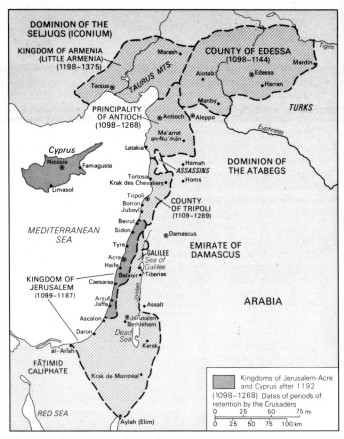

The Crusader states of the twelfth century occupied territory in what is now Israel, Lebanon, Syria, Turkey, and Cyprus.

recognized his mother as Sultana. She had herself styled *Malikat al-Muslimin,* "Queen of the Muslims." Her Egyptian amirs, however, appointed a commander in chief of their own choosing—Aybak, who married the Sultana. When Aybak himself antagonized the amirs by killing an officer, many Mamelukes fled to Syria to avoid the tyrant. He also aroused the passionate jealousy of his wife, who had him murdered in a palace intrigue in 1257. In revenge, the slave women of Aybak's first wife battered the Sultana to death with their slippers.

In Syria the refugee Mamelukes soon had to take the field against the Mongol chieftain Hulagu, a grandson of Genghis Khan, who had already descended on Baghdad and wiped out what remained of the 'Abbasid caliphate. The Mameluke forces won a crucial victory in Palestine in 1260, shattering the Mongol reputation for being invincible and saving Egypt from the bloodbath that always followed a Mongol success. Baybars, a Mameluke general, killed his own commander and took over the throne of Egypt. As sultan, he established a Mameluke dynasty that was to last almost three hundred years. His victory over the Mongols, a decisive battle in world history, saved Islam in the Middle East. The Crusaders had vainly hoped that the invading Mongols would adopt Christianity; instead, they chose the way of the Prophet.

Effects of the Crusades

Christian power waned in the Holy Land as one stronghold after another fell to Muslim assaults. The Crusades entered their last tragic period. The Knights Templar held out on the tiny island of Arwad (Ruad) until 1303. The Crusaders managed to sack Alexandria with great ferocity in 1365, but their energies were by this time directed homeward where the nation-states of Europe were emerging from the Middle Ages. The European Renaissance was due in no small part to the Arabic scholarship of Sicily and Spain. Although the Crusaders contributed little but bloodshed to the lands of Islam, they returned with more than plunder, more than the sugarcane they discovered in Syrian plantations, more than the techniques of Syrian glass that were to ornament the windows of their cathedrals. Their long adventures among the Arabs not only changed the handicrafts, commerce, and tastes of Europe but also left an indelible mark upon the Christian intellect and imagination.

Beyond the brutality of their invasions, Crusaders must also bear some blame for wearing away the tolerance that Islam had traditionally shown to unbelievers, to Christians and Jews, but which the sultans now became less ready to display. Together with Turks, Mamelukes, and the later Mongols, the Crusaders helped erode the old Arab aristocracies. From an enlightened and urbane culture once superior to the West, aristocratic Islam retreated to a narrow religious conservatism less favorable to secular learning.

Muslim Africa

The coming of the first Crusaders coincided not only with the general collapse of the Fatimids in Egypt but also with a similar decline and fragmentation in northern Africa. Descendants of the original Arabs of the conquest could be found here and there in the deserts, an uncivilized terror for settled communities. Local leaders tended to be Shi'ites; the Muslims of the coast were Sunnis, while the mountainous Berbers, who had been responsible for the conquest of Andalusia, were puritanical Kharijites. All three groups reflected different views about Islam and the Islamic state. Shi'ites believed in rule by a divinely appointed *imam* (Arabic "leader" in the sense of "an example to be followed") considered immune from sin. Sunnis believed that men might appoint the community *imam*, that he was liable to error, but that he should be obeyed as long as he maintained the laws of Islam. The Kharijites recognized no absolute need of an *imam*. (The three sects hold similar views today.) Bending to Kharijite public opinion, Berber chiefs abandoned their loyalty to the Fatimids, and in 1048 prayers were offered for the 'Abbasid instead of for the Fatimid caliph. In revenge, the Shi'ite rulers of Cairo unleashed on Tunisia three tribes of Bedouin Arabs from southern Egypt. The great city of Kairouan, a Sunni stronghold, was sacked in 1056 as Bedouins ravaged the countryside and uprooted the social structure.

During this time a confederation of Saharan Berbers, tribes belonging to the Veiled Sanhaja and closely akin to the modern Tuareg, were acquiring a new cohesion and strength. Returning from a pilgrimage to Mecca, one of their leaders brought back a Berber scholar to improve their rather sketchy knowledge of Islamic doctrine. The movement for religious reform began in a Senegalese hermitage, a *ribat*, and set in motion a broad military enterprise. Conquering Morocco and founding Marrakesh, the Veiled Sanhaja became known as Almoravids, from al-Murabitun, "people of the ribat." With strenuous effort they conquered all of Algeria before halting their eastward march. Yusuf ibn Tashfin, their general, assumed the title of "Amir of the Muslims" and paid homage to the 'Abbasid caliph in Baghdad.

The Almoravid Empire

At the same time the provincial rulers of Spain, who had divided up the old caliphate of Cordoba, were in retreat before their Christian foes. When Alfonso VI of Castile and Leon captured Toledo in 1085, the Spanish Muslims called on ibn Tashfin for help. A year later he halted the Castilian advance at the Battle of Sacralias and thereafter extended his rule over all of Muslim Spain except for the kingdom of Valencia.

Spain and northwestern Africa (the Maghreb) became parts of the same Almoravid empire, and the civilization of Andalusia crossed over to take root in African towns. The government administration was Spanish. Writers and artists also crossed the straits, and the great monuments raised by ibn Tashfin in the Maghreb were triumphs of pure Andalusian art with all of its richness and subtle beauty. The Almoravids, who used Christian soldiers against their enemies in the Maghreb and Berber troops against the Christians of Spain, brought the Berber clans to great political strength. As a foreign minority, however, they were ultimately powerless against the Christian reconquest of Spain. The capture of Toledo in 1085 by Alfonso VI had led to a powerful fusion of Christian, Arab, and Jewish cultures. The Almoravids were also doomed to failure against the sectarian fanaticism of their fellow Berbers, the Almohads.

The Almohad Empire

Like the Veiled Sanhaja, their predecessors, the Almohads of the High Atlas Mountains received their Islamic teaching from Mohammed ibn Tumart, a Berber who had studied in the East. A moral reformist, he insisted on the strictest concept of the unity of God. In addition, following Shi'ite doctrine, he proclaimed himself the Mahdi and sinless *imam,* a spiritual and temporal ruler. The Almoravid sultans forced ibn Tumart to flee from Morocco and to take refuge in the Atlas region. There he aroused the fervor of his fellow Masmuda tribesmen and formed a united confederation. On his death in 1130 he was succeeded by 'Abd al-Mu'min, who led the Almohads, or "Unitarians" as they came to be known, against the Almoravids of the Maghreb. Marrakesh fell in 1147 and under Almohad rule flourished even more.

'Abd al-Mu'min conquered the rest of northern Africa as far east as Tripolitania and as caliph brought Berber Islam to its zenith despite the hostility of Arab tribes. His son and the next caliph, Abu Ya'qub Yusuf (1163–84), conquered Spanish Islam. The Almohads imposed a Spanish form of central government on their own tribal hierarchy. They forgot their original puritanism, encouraged a revolutionary mystical movement in western Islam regions, protected philosophers like Averroes, and patronized artists no less than the Almoravids. 'Abd al-Mu'min built costly monuments with Andalusian craftsmen and ornamented his mosques with a classical elegance. His successors continued to serve the arts of Spanish-Moorish civilization.

After the fourth Almohad caliph suffered a shattering defeat in 1212 against a Christian coalition at Las Navas de Tolosa, the fortunes of the dynasty declined, and their Berber empire gradually broke up. Local leaders seized power at Tunis, Marrakesh, and other African centers. In Spain the Kingdom of Granada, the last Arab state, became in 1246 a vassal dominion of Ferdinand III of Castile. A flexible agreement allowed Muslims in Granada to enjoy two hundred and fifty ensuing years of high culture, developing the silk industry and guarding the straits, until their internal struggles made them too weak to resist the Catholic reconquest.

The Mongols

While the sun had yet to set on the western domain of Islamic civilization, the eastern area saw the arrival of the Mongols. Under the astonishing leadership of Genghis Khan (who died in 1227) these cattle breeders of the central Asian steppes, who reckoned time by the changing hues of grass, had become rulers of an enormous territory from the Caspian to the China seas. Superb horsemen and bowmen, they used the captives of one ferocious campaign to do the brutal and exhausting labor of the next. Before attacking, they offered terms of surrender. If these were refused, wholesale slaughter, death by hideous tortures, and enslavement—all carried out with unprecedented fury—could be expected by a defeated foe.

By 1250 the Mongol capital at Karakorum reflected the vast splendor of their empire. Christian churches, Muslim mosques, and Buddhist temples were observed by envoys who came to the khan's court from all parts of the known world. In 1255 Mangu Khan decided to send one of his brothers, Kublai, against the Chinese and another, Hulagu, against the Muslims of Iran.

Hulagu, the grandson of Genghis Khan, crossed the Oxus in January of 1256. He reduced Muslim fortresses in northern and eastern Iran with surprising ease, wiping out the Shi'ite Assassins who held these strongholds. As he advanced toward Iraq, rivalries between Muslim factions helped to clear his path. In January 1258, after routing the caliph's army, he reached Baghdad. The caliph refused Hulagu's summons to dismantle the city's defenses and to appear before him. Mongols and their captive troops surrounded the capital, forced its surrender, and put it to pillage. The 'Abbasid al-Musta'sim, the last caliph of Baghdad, was kicked to death. (In Cairo, a line of his cousins held nominal religious powers until the Ottoman Turks arrived.) Six centuries after the first Arab conquests, an Islamic era was thus brought to a close.

After his westward progress was halted by Egyptian Mamelukes in 1260, Hulagu settled in northwestern Iran and founded the Il-Khanid dynasty. Christians had welcomed him not only because Hulagu's Christian wife tempered his animosity but also because they saw him as a deliverance from the caliphate. Shi'ites welcomed the Mongols as allies against the Sunni 'Abbasids. When Hulagu died at Lake Urmia in 1265, he was buried with the last performance in Iran of a Mongol funeral rite—the slaughter of beautiful maidens.

Hulagu's nomadic conquerors maintained their primitive religious shamanism. Their fellow Mongols of the Golden Horde in southern Russia, however, adopted Islam and in 1261 made an alliance with the Mamelukes of Egypt. The pagan Mongols of Iran sought in vain for alliances with Byzantium, the Holy See, France, and England. In 1288 their khan appointed a Jewish vizier whose ruthless exploitation of Iran provoked anti-Jewish riots, while his attempts to provoke another Christian Crusade against Islam and the Holy Lands ended in failure. Iran lay in economic ruin until the reign of Ghazan (1295–1304), the khan whose conversion to Islam marked a turning point in Iranian and Mongol history. Although he repudiated the great Mongol khans of Peking, the influence of Chinese culture remained powerful in his realms.

The first Mongol ruler of Iran to bear a Muslim name was Abu Sa'id, who came to the throne in 1317 at the age of twelve. Two decades of internal struggle among the local amirs followed, and when Abu Sa'id died childless in 1335 the Il-Khan empire came to an end as a dynastic unit.

Tamerlane

Egypt grew richer as Mongol rule weakened in Iran. The

reign of the sultan Malik al-Nasir Mohammed (1310–1341), who has been called the Louis XIV of Egypt, saw a great flowering of the arts and extensive building of mosques and palaces. The sultan spoke Arabic instead of Turkish and enriched his Bedouin tribes with Arabian steeds. His extravagances and harsh taxation, however, resulted in his death. In 1382 the last of his line was dethroned, and Circassians, unrelated to the Turks, took over the Mameluke sultanate. Twenty-three of their able and fearless chiefs hacked their way to the throne, but they then split into factions led by separate amirs with separate bodyguards. Luckily for these slave-sultans, they managed to avoid destruction by Timur i Leng—"the lame Timur," commonly known as Tamerlane—the conqueror who, from his home in central Asia, had subjugated lands stretching from Moscow to India.

A Turk, Timur came from a family that had risen to power as ministers to the Mongol khans. By 1385 the warring amirs of Iran had fallen before his troops. In the next ten years he took over Iraq, Armenia, Mesopotamia, and Georgia, all the while waging war with the khans of the Golden Horde. The revolts that broke out across Persia during these campaigns were suppressed in a fashion typical of the Turks and Mongols. Whole cities were destroyed, populations were massacred, and towers were built of their skulls.

Around 1400 out of the spoils he took from a devastated India, Timur erected a mosque at Samarkand, a city he beautified with the labor of craftsmen from the many peoples he had conquered. He then set out to punish the Mameluke sultan of Egypt for supporting the Mongol ruler of Baghdad. Timur marched on Syria, stormed and sacked Aleppo, defeated a Mameluke army, and occupied Damascus, whose artisans were deported to Samarkand. In 1401 he also stormed Baghdad, massacred twenty thousand citizens, and destroyed all of its monuments. When the Mamelukes along with the Byzantines at last offered submission, Timur returned to Samarkand and began enormous preparations for an expedition against China. Not until his death in 1405 was Egypt safe from the threat of this "Asian scourge."

It should not be forgotten that, although barbarism often made havoc of civilized communities, commerce and religious life usually managed to survive even where destruction seemed complete. Muslim communities were entrenched as far away as China; Arab and Persian traders were active from Foochow to Java. Arabs dominated commerce in the

Malay Archipelago where twenty states had accepted Islam. In the multitude of racial strains that composed the world of Islam, the old Arab conquerors could be identified only by means of tradition and often embroidered genealogies. Their religion continued to triumph, even as their language and literature ceased to dominate. Paradoxically, Arab expansion had led to much loss of consciousness of Arab origins. Some groups still prided themselves on descent from the Prophet's own clan, but most of those whose language at the cradle was Arabic probably thought of themselves first as Muslims and only second as bearers of an Arab culture.

The Ottoman Turks

The Arabic name Othman, which has no ethnic significance, was a dynastic term derived from the prince Osman I, founder of what Europeans would later call the Ottoman state. Born in 1258, the same year in which Hulagu and his Mongols swept into Baghdad, Osman became leader of the Turkish nomads whose conquest of Byzantine territories had taken them to the western shores of Asia Minor. Converted to the Muslim faith, these Turkish border warriors and horsemen known as Ghazis based their mode of life on the *ghaza* or *razzia*—incessant raiding against Byzantine Christians not only for plunder but also as an obligatory *jihad* against the unbeliever. The conflict between Byzantine and Ottoman was slow and stubborn. Lacking the technical means of siege warfare, the Ottoman Turks sometimes had to blockade a large town for many years. Bursa surrendered in 1326, the year Osman died. In 1354 the Ottomans seized Gallipoli, their first permanent base in Europe. Conquest of the Balkans rapidly followed.

Timur defeated the Ottomans in 1402 at the Battle of Ankara but did not press his advantage against the Ghazis, whose *jihad* against the Christians he wished to continue. From 1413 to 1451 powerful Ottoman lords succeeded in patching together their feuds and added diplomacy, marriage alliances, negotiations, and lenient peace terms to the arsenal of tactics used against Christian and Muslim resistance. To help keep the central regime in control of restive provincial amirs, Ottoman sultans began the practice of exacting a tribute of Christian children to provide a loyal corps of palace officials, local administrators, and the famous soldiers called Janizaries. During this period Christian subjects far outnumbered their Ottoman masters. After generations of using captive women as concubines, the Ottomans themselves were a mixture of Asian and European races.

Unlike the Mamelukes who thought the use of firearms dishonorable, the Ottomans became masters of artillery. Sultan Mohammed II, "the Conqueror," having largely consolidated his rule in Ottoman lands, brought his cannon to the gates of Constantinople in April 1453. The year before he had blockaded the Bosporus; and, ignoring the chain that protected the Golden Horn, he had carried his fleet into the harbor by hauling ships overland. The final assault against Constantinople was made on May 29. The remaining inhabitants offered a desperate resistance; and Constantine XI, the last Byzantine emperor, was killed defending the walls. Last sacked by the Crusaders in 1204, the Christian capital fell to the Muslim sultan and for three days was subjected to pillage and massacre. After Mohammed II restored order, he began to rebuild, transferring his capital from Adrianople to the defeated city. The Faith ("conqueror") Mosque arose on the site of the Basilica of the Holy Apostles. Even before 1453 the new capital had acquired the Turkish name Istanbul from the Greek *eis tin polin*, "in the city." The final remnants of the Byzantine empire were obliterated.

The End of Islam in Spain

The Ottomans sealed their triumph in Asia Minor by converting Constantinople into Istanbul. At the same time Spain, the only country of Western Europe to have a diversity of religions and peoples comparable to Islamic lands, was being unified under Christian monarchs. In 1478 a bull from Pope Sixtus IV established the Spanish Inquisition to deal with the problem of Jews and converted Jews (*conversos*). In 1492 the first inquisitor general, Tomas de Torquemada, himself of a *converso* family, persuaded Ferdinand and Isabella as a pious duty to expel their Jewish subjects. When about one hundred and seventy thousand of these useful and rich citizens fled the country, Spain was left open to exploitation by German and Italian bankers. In the same year the Spanish were victorious in the kingdom of Granada, whose Moorish citizens were granted generous terms and religious freedom. But in 1502 the Moors also were given the choice of conversion or expulsion. Many chose conversion, but those Moriscos who remained in Spain were alien to the Catholics. Without Arabspeaking priests or money for education, their outward conversion could hardly become a religious reality.

The Court of the Lions is one of the most impressive areas of the Alhambra, a thirteenth- and fourteenth-century Islamic palace in Granada, Spain.

Muslim disunity, even more acerbic than the discords of their Christian foes, had helped bring about the downfall of Muslim Spain. Abu 'Abd Allah Mohammed XI, the last king of Granada, was an instrument of Spanish policy against his own father. His capital fell in January 1492. The following August, half an hour before sunrise, Christopher Columbus and his tiny fleet set sail toward the New World. Five years later Vasco da Gama sailed from Lisbon around the Cape of

Good Hope to Mozambique, where the inhabitants believed the Portuguese to be Muslims like themselves. In the port he found four Arab vessels loaded with gold, jewels, silver, and spices. The Conquistadores who followed Columbus to South and Central America took with them a culture partly Arabized, in which the Arab immigrant still finds a sense of identity today.

By opening up the sea route from Europe to the Indian Ocean, da Gama changed the face of the world. He shifted the balance of power from the nations of the Mediterranean, including many Muslim lands, to the Christian nations of Europe and the Atlantic. Instead of going by way of the Red Sea to Syrian and Egyptian ports, the commerce of the Orient with its immense profits could be conducted in Christian vessels going around the Cape of Good Hope. The religion of Islam had been diffused among Turks, Circassians, Mongols, and natives from the ports of Africa to Southeast Asia. The racial and intellectual force of the early Arabs was spent, but they had left a brilliant heritage—some of it as magnificently visible as the Alhambra's Court of the Lions, but much of it unrecognized by Western eyes until recent times.

6.
The Living Heritage

When Columbus set sail for the New World, he had on board Luis da Torres, "who had been a Jew and knew Hebrew and Chaldean and a little Arabic," in case they met the "grand khan." Like other Mediterranean navigators, Columbus also had the compass, an instrument first known for certain in China in about 1100 and mentioned in Arabian annals a century later. A Moor of Gujarat in India showed Vasco da Gama a coastal map of the entire subcontinent, more evidence of the early skill that Arabs had acquired in the arts of navigation.

Arab culture as such, which had helped create and then been absorbed into the wider world of Islam, was about to enter its long decline under the rule of the Ottoman Turks. To protect the Ottoman succession, the sultan Mohammed II, the conqueror of Constantinople, issued an edict requiring his descendants on taking the throne to slaughter any surviving brothers. Selim the Grim, his grandson, defeated the Mamelukes outsida Cairo in January 1517, entered the city, and added Egypt and Syria to his domains. From this date the Ottoman Empire—which was to include the Balkans, parts of Austria, Hungary, and southern Russia, Syria, Egypt, Iraq, and parts of Arabia and northern Africa as far west as Algeria—dominated the Islamic and Arab world for four hundred years.

Arab Influences

The Ottomans brought to an end what had begun with the Arab "imperial age." Many cultures flowered within a structure essentially created by Arabs, even though "pure Arabs" comprised perhaps only one percent of the population. Yet even in the magnificent black capital of Timbuktu Muslims heard Arabic in the mosques, and Arabic was the language of learning in its "university." Kankan Musa, the powerful Mandingo king, made his splendid journey as one of countless pilgrims to the Black Stone of Mecca, the Arabian heart of the vast Islamic world.

The Arabs were not only direct heirs to ancient Semitic and Persian cultures and the indirect custodians of Greek and Roman learning but also often the creators of a fresh "classical" tradition of their own. After the Seljuks captured Baghdad in 1055, Muslim culture no longer flowed from the East to Spain, but Andalusia itself became a fountain of the arts. Spanish fields and gardens displayed Arab agricultural gifts to the West—oranges, lemons, peaches, pomegranates, sugar, melons, apricots, shallots, scallions, rice, sesame, millet, ginger, and carob. Also Arabic in origin as well as name were candy, sherbet, and syrup—the latter, like *julep* and *soda* , a medicinal term from the Arabic pharmacopoeia and Arabic alembics. Columbus and his European followers were to use an Arabic vocabulary of navigation—*admiral, algebra, almanac, arsenal, average, azimuth, cable, shallop, zenith,* and *nadir*. Learned books were bound in cordovan or morocco if the owner could afford it, and thanks to Muslim contacts Christians learned to play chess.

Wood-block printing had made its way from China to Muslim Egypt centuries before movable type and cheap paper, which also originated in China, made possible the lore and learning of Islam. Books were often still written in beautiful calligraphy by scribes, and Jews used the flowing Arabic script for all but their religious writings. (Arabic itself often appeared in Hebrew characters.) Traditional Judaism can be said to have taken form during the zenith of the Islamic age. There was a long Jewish-Arab symbiosis as Muslim religious law developed along the lines of the Judaic law. Speaking many tongues, Jewish merchants linked the Christians of Europe to the lands of Islam. All through this extraordinary world different peoples and cultures blended even as they tried to exterminate one another.

Islamic Spain

Although the Holy Inquisition was installed in the New Alcazar of Córdoba after the Spanish reconquest, the city remained typically Moorish with narrow winding streets, orange groves in the hills, gardens beyond the western walls, and a Moorish bridge over the river to the suburbs. In Islamic times it had been celebrated for its huge paper mills, silversmiths, silk embroidery, leatherwork, Valencian pottery, and "damask" weapons. Under the caliphate, however, the same peoples who sustained this brilliant culture—Arabs, Berbers, Jews, European slaves, Spanish Muslims, and Arabized Christians—had been wracked by the mutual antagonisms that hastened Córdoba's decline even before Ferdinand III of Castile captured it in 1236.

Old Seville also remained typically Moorish, even today its doorways offering glimpses of beautiful arcaded patios. Here Muslims chafed under Almoravid masters, until the Almohad victory brought the city to greater prosperity and artistic accomplishment. Fragmented by rival Muslim leaders, the Almohads could not resist Ferdinand III, and another center of Arab civilization passed into Christendom. Toledo —famous since Islamic times for its steel, swords, and sweet marzipan—told the same story of cultural fusion. Christians, Arabs, and Jews were unable to resist religious and racial tension. In 1391 popular fanaticism led to great massacres of Jews under Christian protection in Toledo, Seville, and Córdoba. The expulsion of all Jews from Spain in 1492 was hastened by the abduction and martyrdom in Toledo of the Santo Niño de la Guardia.

Islamic Sicily

Sicily, another brilliant cultural gateway between Christianity and Islam, could boast three hundred mosques in Palermo alone before its conquest by Roger the Norman. In 1154 the Arab geographer, scientist, and poet al-Idrisi completed an encyclopedic work on the regions of the world for Roger II of Sicily. The entire work was translated into Latin, and its description of Sicily itself is of enormous historical interest. Even with a royal patron, however, it is unlikely that this great scholar remained in Sicily after the anti-Muslim riots of 1161, and it is not known when or where he died.

Although the Muslim population of Sicily was reduced by riot and conversion and Greeks along with Arabs became a minority, Sicilian civilization retained its composite character. Frederick II—the Holy Roman Emperor, self-crowned King of Jerusalem, and enemy of the Pope whose many territories came to include Sicily—maintained a semioriental court, including a harem, after his Crusade against Islam. He had translations made from Greek and Arabic and donated a huge repository of Arabic manuscripts to the University of Naples, which he founded in 1224. The university became a leading avenue for Islamic learning to reach other universities as far away as Oxford and Paris.

Reared in Palermo with a broad knowledge of Byzantine and Muslim cultures and an excommunicate and a skeptic by temperamant, Frederick nonetheless received absolution from a priest before he died. Muslim craftsmen and artists flourished under his rule; and the looms of Palermo, set up before the Christian conquest, continued for centuries to supply European courts with royal robes decorated with Arab inscriptions.

Islamic Education

Sicily and Spain were the principal centers where Western princes—few as literate as Frederick II—added Arabic manuscripts to their libraries and had translations mada into Latin. In Islam, too, education depended on the patronage of princes and rulers, beginning as early as 830 when the Caliph al-Ma'mun established his academy in Baghdad. Famous colleges had later sprung up in Nishapur, Damascus, Cairo, and many other centers throughout the Muslim world. The most celebrated of the early colleges was the Nizamiya, founded in Baghdad by a Seljuk vizier in 1067. With the great al-Ghazzali on the faculty, it taught law, theology, and tradition. More sumptuous and far wealthier in endowment, although it was founded in 1234 not long before the Mongols arrived, was the Mustansiriya of Baghdad. Its large staff served the four schools of Muslim law as well as other disciplines.

When Saladin destroyed the Fatimids in 1171, he replaced Shi'ite instruction at the Azhar with Sunni orthodoxy. In this respect the Cairo university resembled other Muslim places of learning—they were centers of sectarian indoctrination. Freedom of enquiry was not at the heart of Islamic education. The *madrasahs*, or Koranic schools that sprang up from India to Andalusia, emphasized theology, jurisprudence, and the linguistic study of the Koran. There were many distinguished Muslim scientists, but the ordinary student was not encouraged in scientific pursuits. Rather than remain at a single institution, students usually traveled throughout medieval Islam from one master to another, obtaining from each a certificate to teach either a book or a subject.

In this way the orthodox class of *ulama*, or learned men, became extremely powerful—but never powerful enough to prevent Sufi mysticism from sweeping throughout Islam. Although some Sufi leaders came to be worshiped as saints in defiance of traditional Islamic teaching, few Sufi heretics were brought before an "inquisition" of *imams*, and Muslim "witch-hunts" were sporadic. In Andalusia old maxims prohibiting women from learning to read and write were ignored. The women of Arab Spain were allowed to excel in poetry and literature; and the beautiful Walladah, a caliph's daughter who died in 1087, has been called "the Spanish Sappho."

Islamic Law

Public and private law maintained a primary role in Islamic education and life. A jurist qualified to go back to the original books and sources was said to possess the faculty of *ijtihad,* and he himself was termed a *mujtahid.* Inseparable from the Koranic tradition, the law also had orthodox and heterodox schools. Shi'ites tended to abide by the older practices of the *mujtahids,* and Sunni jurists were closer to the great body of opinions developed during the golden period of legal studies. (In practice, however, Shi'ite law has remained a little more elastic than the Sunni.)

Like Judaic law, Islamic law developed in the context of a revealed monotheistic religion and a holy book; and the scholars within the two systems, the rabbi and the mufti, had much in common. There were differences, however. Muslim law, unlike Judaic, did not recognize the right of the firstborn to a larger share of the inheritance. In addition, the Koranic ban on usury left most banking in the hands of Jews and Christians. So energetic was commercial activity on every level in medieval Islam, however, that this ban was variously interpreted and, as among Christians, frequently evaded. (When coffee was introduced to Muslim countries in the seventeenth century, conservative jurists agreed that like wine it should be prohibited. Again, practice prevailed over precept.)

By the time the Ottomans entered Constantinople, orthodox jurists had for centuries been attempting to administer law by interpreting ancient tradition through *ijtihad.* The Ottoman jurists in the early decades of their conquest announced that "The Gate of Interpretation has been closed." Today, in most Arab lands where the law derives from *sha-ri'a,* the ancient path of God, courts and statutes have been modified, and new codes have as much authority as medieval texts. Interpretation of tradition, however, remains officially embalmed.

Islamic Architecture

The first *madrasah* for theological students was built in Cairo after Saladin dethroned the Fatimids. Scholars forced to abjure Fatimid religious teachings could still be inspired by the glories of Fatimid architecture with its superb ornamentation, inscriptions, and arabesques. Islamic art expressed itself at its best in architecture. From the Taj Mahal to the Alhambra, its monuments reveal the grand centrality of Islam. The design of an arabesque itself, in its floral and geometric patterns, can be a reminder of the transcendence and unity of God. Yet it is somewhat misleading to speak of "Arab architecture." Like the early Arabs, later Islamic peoples used local skills and tradition to achieve their architectural aims. As artisans traveled throughout the regions of Islam, various traditions were blended and diffused.

In Egypt before the arrival of Selim the Grim, Mameluke architects had huge sums of money to lavish on structures that still delight tourists. The Mosque of Baybars introduced the large sanctuary dome, a feature that first appeared in the Isfahan Mosque built by Malik-Shah. The feature appeared again in the Mosque of al-Nasir Mohammed (1335) during a period that saw the final development and decline of stucco ornament, splendid dadoes of polychrome marble, and faience mosaics. Faience was a creation of Persian architects, whose skill in building vaults and domes, and in extensive polychrome decoration, was unrivaled in Islam.

Three Moorish Masterpieces

In Spain religious monuments of the Moorish period have vanished except for the Great Mosque of Córdoba, begun in about 787 by 'Abd al-Rahman I. Also known as La Mezquita, "the mosque," and now a Christian cathedral, it has undergone three enlargements. In the enlargement of 961, the Byzantine emperor is said to have sent craftsmen to work in gold and glass mosaic and to carve marble panels.

The greatest masterpiece of Muslim architecture in Spain is, of course, the Alhambra of Granada, one of the last and best expressions of Islamic genius. This palace and fortress of Moorish monarchs covers about thirty-five acres. It has been modified and rebuilt many times since the period (1238 to 1358) of its first construction. The Moorish portion included a palace, a castle, and a residential annex for officials. The Hall of the Abencerrages took its name from a legend according to which Boabdil, the last Muslim king of Granada, invited chiefs of the Abencerrage family to a banquet in the hall and massacred them. The original furniture of the palace is now represented by one splendid vase produced around 1320 from the "first period" of Moorish porcelain. In Seville the most magnificent survival of the Arab era is the Alcazar

Palace begun in 1181. Its splendid courts and state apartments are comparable only to those of the Alhambra.

The Islamic Aesthetic

As a visitor walks in wonder through the Alcazar, the Great Mosque of Córdoba, the Alhambra, or any other monument to Islamic genius, it becomes evident that all Arab-Islamic art serves a double purpose. Art is practical—a mosque for religious gatherings, a vase to contain liquids, or a tile to be part of a wall—and aesthetic—for delight and pleasure. In the Arab tradition there are no artistic objects—such as a free-standing piece of sculpture or a painted canvas hung simply for display—made simply for their own sake. The Arab-Islamic genius was used to ornament works that already had a specific utilitarian purpose.

In the decorative arts, especially in their use of calligraphy, Muslim artists almost never sought to represent nature as such. Their tradition officially forbade images of the invisible God or of the men and animals God alone could create. Instead of directly copying a leaf or flower, ornamental designs tended toward the intricacy and abstraction of the "arabesque." The geometrical form, true to its own symmetry rather than to nature, was repeated and varied according to the style of the designer. (In spite of this tradition of abstract forms, the modern Arab collector has shown little interest so far in the abstract schools of recent Western art. There is no reason to suppose any aesthetic bond between the Islamic artist of Persia or Andalusia and the easel painter of New York City.)

Nomadic art originated in the tent and on the loom, and the origins of Muslim art were apparent in the walls, carpets, and artifacts of the Islamic middle ages. A certain naturalism could be seen in the arts brought from Turkistan by the Seljuks. Statues and reliefs on the walls of Konya and Baghdad took the form of lions, eagles, dragons, and angels. Most representational art, however, was restricted to smaller works—glazed stoneware or highly stylized bronze figures of lions, elephants, and birds that were used as water vessels or as smoking utensils.

In their private rooms and on harem frescoes the Omayyads and ‘Abbasids used representations of hunters, musicians, dancing girls, and women bathers—all very much outside the Koranic tradition. Likewise, at the Alhambra the last Moors of Spain were shown as knights and troubadours

The Hall of the Ambassadors in the Alcazar of Seville was designed by Moorish architects in the fourteenth century for Pedro the Cruel.

in roof paintings of an almost Gothic style. Frescoes in the castles of Isfahan and Ashraf and in the harem apartments of the Mogul rulers of India were closer to East Asian and to Persian art. Like other representational art found within Islam, such figures showed non-Islamic influences—Christian at one end of the Muslim world and Buddhist at the other.

Islamic Ornament

Ornament remained the center of true Islamic art. Ornament used many techniques to enhance the walls of mosques and castles, the backgrounds of figure paintings, and the details of glasswork, pots and vases, bronze implements and carved furniture, arms and jewelry, and bookbindings and calligraphy. Later Arab dynasties took artistic motifs from the Turks and developed them into purely abstract styles of decoration such as the fillet, the arabesque, and the palm leaf. During the Mameluke period the fillet became a twined pattern of stars and rosettes, always mathematically accurate no matter how numerous or complex. After the Mongol period the motifs of the twining vine leaf, the palm leaf, and the tree of life of the ancient East were enriched in inextricable unity. These figures were even distorted into diabolical masks or Chinese cloud strata—so far did Islamic art venture from the old Arabic notion of abstract ornament.

The refinement of calligraphy can be seen in the stuccowork of the Alhambra, where new floral forms were used in which the tops of the letters blossomed into tendrils. The cursive *naskhi* script with its wealth of curves and twists never went out of fashion and often provided a delicate background to the heavier characters of earlier scripts.

After the Turks and Mongols, stucco walls and mosaics gave way to cheaper substitutes, most often tiles of faience. Walls were also overlaid with glazed bricks of varied shapes to make twined patterns with formalized words endlessly repeated. Rich ornament continued to be seen in many ways, notably in script friezes of glazed tile with dark blue characters on a ground of golden brown arabesques.

Islamic furniture in houses and places of worship was, and is, relatively sparse—a reminder that nomads, at least, used to sit on the floor or carpet. Chairs were a late luxury. Household objects, rugs and cushions, and lamps and candlesticks might be carved, inlaid, and ornamented according to the purse and taste of the owner. Early Islam had proscribed personal luxuries; the use of gold and silver, forbidden by the Koran, was rare. In the Seljuk and Mongol periods, however, faience painted with gold luster gave a magnificent style to ceramic art. Under the Mameluke domination of Syria, beautiful glasswork was produced at Aleppo. Lamps to hang in mosques were covered with bands of arabesque and script and with medallions in enamel colors and gold. In the later 'Abbasid, Fatimid, and Seljuk periods wealthy households could boast basins and braziers of bronze cast in the ancient Sasanian forms of peacocks, doves, sphinxes, and other creatures. In the fifteenth century Islamic techniques of decorating bronze, along with Muslim craftsmen, were imported from Syria to Venice to meet the enormous demand.

Islamic swords were famous for their wonderful blades of Damascus and Toledo steel, made by a laborious method of welding different types of iron. Until after the Ottoman conquest, the blades were straight; curved sabers and daggers did not become common until after 1500.

Beginning with the first Arab conquests, Islamic art and architecture fell deeply under Persian influence but later showed its nomadic character as Turkish leaders surrounded the caliphate. From the Seljuk period onward the influence of eastern Asia grew, but Islam typically continued to make a fusion of many cultures. The individual and abstract Islamic style reached its zenith between the tenth and sixteenth centuries. It extended through India to China and Java, from Russia in the north to the Sudan in the south, and westward along northern Africa to Spain. European culture in the Middle Ages and Renaissance was immeasurably indebted to it. When Islamic ornamental arts began to decay, the style was first veiled in extravagant outward splendor and then became more naturalistic under increasing European influence. By the middle of the nineteenth century, Islamic art was remote from its great age. The wealth of abstract ornament had been lost, and bouquets of "real" flowers were painted on vases for the Muslim market.

Islamic Poetry

It has been said that each verse or stanza of an Arabic poem, even each paragraph of a prose work, had its counterpart in the basic independent unit of the decorative arts. Repetition was another common point between literature and ornament. Many Islamic authors of the medieval period repeated in form or substance not only what others but also what they themselves had already said. Their major goal was not always originality. The form of Islamic music and poetry, however, was an irresistible novelty to the Christian troubadours of Spain and Provence.

In Spain, beginning with the first Omayyad caliphate, the Arabic passion for poetry cut across all classes. An Arab noble, who was confidential emissary of the Córdoban court, military commander, vizier, and lover of the lady poet Walladah, was equally famed for his own verse. National or regional poets, like the great Persians Firdausi (about 1000) and Jalal ud-Din Rumi (d. 1273), wrote in their own ancestral traditions and sometimes in their own languages. A supreme master of Sufi mystical poetry, Jalal ud-Din, founded the order of "whirling dervishes." His contemporary Omar Khayyam wrote a standard treatise on algebra in Arabic prose. His verse in the original Persian was at the time far less important than his astronomical reform of the calendar. The nineteenth-century English poet and translator Edward FitzGerald made innovative translations of Omar Khayyam's verses that popularized them in the West as the *Rubaiyat*. The work was a collection of quatrains that reveal not an Islamic mystic or Muslim philosopher but a charming agnostic.

Besides writers of ballads, love songs, and romances in Arabic, Islamic Spain also produced the great Hebrew poet Judah ben Samuel Halevi, who was born in Tudela in about the year 1085. Contrary to the usual custom, his philosophical dialogues were expounded in Arabic, while his verses in local courtly and liturgical styles were Hebrew celebrations of Zion, devoted to his plan to return to Palestine. Having complained that life in Spain was equally wretched under Christian or Muslim rule, he died in 1141 on his way to Jerusalem.

The Chazal and the Song

In this popular and cosmopolitan literary world, the classic Persian *ghazal* was never forgotten. The short lyric poem was brought to renewed perfection by another Sufi mystic known as Hafiz, "one who has learned the Koran by heart." Born at Shiraz in about 1325, Hafiz was destined to live in troubled times shadowed by the terrible approach of Tamerlane. In the *ghazal* he used a colloquial and unaffected Persian filled with homely images and proverbial expressions. He reflected the joyful and civilized life of medieval Shiraz, a love of humanity, and above all the mystic's search for the reality of God. Even today a Persian villager may sing a *ghazal* of Hafiz.

The history of the *ghazal* in Islamic literature had begun when it was adapted with supreme beauty by Omar ibn Abi Rabi'ah, an Arab of the Prophet's own clan, as the first Muslims were invading Spain. Long after the Moors had been expelled from Andalusia, Arab song remained in the cultural heritage of the West. Like the Moorish arch, tribal chivalry, and the myriad arts and crafts of daily life, Arab music also blended into the popular culture of southern Europe. Not the most obvious but perhaps the most lasting impression left by Muslims on the Andalusian character was a gift for crystallizing the fleeting emotion, aesthetic perception, or witty thought in an improvised bit of music or verse. An unknown poet engraved these lines on the tracery of the Alhambra:

This fountain is like a believer in ecstasy, rapt in prayer; and when the fountain shifts it is the worshiper, who stoops to genuflect and resumes his prayer.

It was but a step from these lines to the vision of the priest Luis de Gongora. The same sense of the evanescence of material beauty united the anonymous Arab poet with the poet Garcia-Lorca in the twentieth century.

Islamic Science and Medicine

While poetry continued to fascinate the Islamic mind, scientific progress had been slowed by the success of al-Ghazzali's orthodox religious doctrine. When he died in 1111, Arabic medicine, physics, and other natural sciences had already reached their zenith. The vast range of Islamic traders and the travels of pilgrims, however, continued to encourage the study of geography, history, and medicine. Yaqut (1179–1229) continued the encyclopedic tradition with his massive geographical "dictionary." A generation later ibn al-Nafis, a doctor of Damascus and Cairo, achieved some understanding of the circulation of the blood, three hundred years before the Italian surgeon Hieronymus Fabricius published his work. Cordoba had long since boasted a hospital equal to those of Baghdad and Cairo. Although Muslims considered surgery inferior to general medicine, a doctor of Cordoba, Abul Kasim, wrote the first illustrated book on surgery before the year 1013. Moorish Spain, in fact, was the center from which medical education in Europe largely came.

A thirteenth-century Arabic edition of Pedanius Dioscorides's *De Materia Medica* depicts the preparation of medicine from honey.

At the first organized medical school in Europe in Salerno, Italy, scholars such as Constantine the African (about 1020–87) continued to translate Greek medical classics from Arabic versions into Latin. The genius of Moorish pharmacists such as ibn al-Baytar of Spain led Europe to the creation of separate medical and pharmaceutical disciplines. When fourteenth-century Europe was decimated by the Black Death, ibn al-Khatib, a Moorish physician, defied the *ulama* of his own faith. Like Christian theologians the *ulama* insisted that the plague was a divine instrument, but the physician

argued that tradition had to be modified when it was con-
tradicted by evidence of the senses. His scientific vision and
courage were at the time as rare in Islam as they were in the
Christian world.

Ibn Battutah

By 1348 the Black Death had ravaged Syria and Egypt, where
it was observed by ibn Battutah, the most extraordinary Muslim traveler of the Middle Ages. A native of Tangier, he had
already made extensive and perilous voyages to the limits of
Islam in the East. Ibn Battutah began with the pilgrimage to
Mecca and went as far as the Mongol khan's court in Uzbek,
to Bulgar on the Volga, to Constantinople, Bukhara, and
Khurasan, and across the Hindu Kush to Afghanistan and the
Indus. Everything he saw in Muslim India—its peculiar customs and peoples and the mixture of cruelty and generosity
he found in the sultan of Delhi—made an indelible impres-
sion. In 1342 he began a journey to the Mongol emperor of
China but was wrecked on the Malabar coast. Later he visited
Sumatra, Canton, and other ports in the Far East.

From Cairo and the Black Death, ibn Battutah returned to
Morocco and reached Fez in 1349. He crossed the Strait of
Gibraltar to take part in the Muslim holy war against the
Christians of Castile but confined his visit to Granada. On his
last and most dangerous journey ibn Battutah set out across
the Sahara to the Muslim Negro states of the Niger Basin.
His narrative is the fullest account known of the Mandingo
kingdom of Mali and the Songhai capital at Gao. On orders
of the sultan of Morocco, he returned to Fez and ended at last
seventy-five thousand miles of travel. Ibn Battutah's books,
dictated at Fez to a royal secretary, are invaluable for geography, contemporary customs and manners, and curiosities of
every kind. He spent his final years as a *qadi* in Morocco,
hearing cases in the religious court.

Islamic Philosophy and Theology

To a student of humanity like ibn Battutah, the sacred texts
of Islam were an invaluable guide. To Arab philosophers,
beginning with al-Kindi in the ninth century, the problems of
reconciling prophetic revelation with rational inquiry resembled the problems of medieval Christian scholastics before
Thomas Aquinas. Out of the Arabic struggle—Greek thought
against the orthodoxy of the *ulama*—the Greek philosophical
heritage was transmitted to Christian thinkers. Much of it

came through translations into Arabic that Catholic scholars found in Spain.

One of the paramount figures of medieval Judaism, Sa'adia ben Joseph, devoted himself to the same problem. A subject of the Baghdad caliph, he produced in 933 the *Book of Beliefs and Convictions*, which like most of his works was written in Arabic. Showing a thorough knowledge of Aristotle and countering arguments of Christians, Muslims, and Brahmans, Sa'adia attempted to reconcile reason with Mosaic revelation. After the breakup of the schools of Babylonian Jewry in the eleventh century, his works were studied in Moorish Spain where Jewish learning flourished.

Even more influential, especially on Christian scholastics, was ibn Gabirol, a Jewish poet and philosopher born in about 1020 at Malaga in Spain. Writing in the tolerant atmosphere of Spanish Islam, he used Arabic meters for Hebrew poetry and the Arabic tongue for his chief philosophical work, known only in a Latin version as the *Fons Vitae*. (His poem "The Royal Crown" has been adopted into Jewish liturgy for the Day of Atonement.) A novel feature of ibn Gabirol's thought—his attribution of matter to angels and other spiritual beings—passed from Arabic into Latin to become one point of the famous conflict in Christianity between Franciscans and Dominicans.

Among Spanish Muslims the theologian ibn Hazm, born at Cordoba in 994, acknowledged only the literal sense of the Koran and the tradition. He rejected appeals to individual opinion or even to an *imam*. For his heresy he lost his position as a vizier, and he became one of the first students of comparative religion. In his chief work, the *Book of Sects*, he extended his critical methods even to biblical narratives. A century later ibn Tufail, court physician to the Almohads of Spain, wrote a philosophical "novel" about a man who spent fifty years alone on an uninhabited island. (Some critics have seen the work as a forerunner of *Robinson Crusoe*.) In the novel the hero found mystic contemplation superior to all philosophy and eventually reached a mystical union with God. The struggle between reason and revelation gave way to human intuition of the divine.

Averroes and Maimonides

Born in Cordoba in 1126, Mohammed ibn Rushd was a great defender of reason against revelation and was a champion of Aristotle against the mystical dogmas of al-Ghazzali. Known in the West as Averroes, he wrote on philosophy, medicine, astronomy, and Muslim canon law. He became a chief judge in Cordoba, was banished for a period because of his rationalist views, was restored to favor, and died in Marrakesh. Averroes left the works of his genius not so much as a legacy to Islam as to the Christian scholastics. Beginning in the first half of the thirteenth century, his commentaries on Aristotle were translated into Latin. They were a mine of ideas and information for Christian philosophers, to whom the Greek of Aristotle and Plato was a closed book.

According to Averroes, philosophy could lead to final truth, while sacred texts were at best simplified and childish accounts for people without learning. Although Christian theologians could hardly follow Averroes to this extreme, like the scholars of medieval Jewry they could hardly avoid consulting such a treasury of learning. Philosophy led theologians directly to the Greek tradition. Thomas Aquinas owed a particular debt to Averroes, but he could not approve the doctrines of the Arab master. In fact, there were no genuine Latin "Averroists" until the century following the saint's death.

Averroes also encouraged the return of Jewish philosophers to Aristotelianism, a trend that first developed among Jewish followers of al-Farabi and ibn Sina. Of these philosophers by far the greatest was Moses ben Maimon, known in the West as Maimonides. Also born in Cordoba and a contemporary of Averroes, he was a philosopher, physician, and master of rabbinic literature and of Islamic learning. Maimonides and other Jews fled Cordoba when the city fell to the Almohads in 1148. He eventually settled in Cairo, became court physician to Saladin, and declined the invitation of Richard I to come to England. (For Saladin's nephew he wrote a treatise on sex and impotency.)

Maimonides apparently never met or studied the works of Averroes but shared with him a profound influence on later Christians and Jews. The *Guide for the Perplexed*, the most celebrated work of Maimonides, was written in Arabic and attempted to interpret biblical and rabbinical theology in the light of Greek speculative thought. His work later became known to Aquinas, who also propounded the essential agreement of reason and theology although his methods differed. Another path entirely was followed by Maimonides' son Abraham, who led a Jewish pietistic movement and adopted practices of Muslim mystics.

Islamic Mysticism

Besides such Sufis as al-Farid and Jalal ud-Din Rumi, Arabic mysticism attracted other poet-theologians. The Spanish-born ibn 'Arabi acquired the title of "the greatest sheikh." He was educated in Seville and traveled in Egypt, Arabia, Baghdad, Mosul, and Asia Minor before settling in Damascus. Ibn 'Arabi claimed to have conversed with all prophets, past and future, and with God himself. Among the extensive works he completed before his death in 1240 were the dozen volumes of *Meccan Revelations,* a general encyclopedia of Sufistic doctrine. Guided by a lovely woman, ibn 'Arabi's spiritual voyages through heaven and hell have been linked in recent scholarship to *The Divine Comedy* of Dante, the fourteenth-century Italian poet.

The Sufi movement had become the bulwark of popular religion, while the theologians and *ulama* of Islam engaged in exalted debates. Among the many groups within Islam, even African animists and Asian shamanists, for example, could find support for their beliefs in Sufi teaching. Both could retain their ancient beliefs even as they became nominal Muslims. In India Muslims could follow the pre-Islamic practice of *sati,* by which widows burned themselves along with their dead husbands. In Indonesia, a region of comparatively late conversion, Sufism permitted many pagan traditions—even the matriarchal rule of certain tribes—to continue.

A Cultural Fusion

In numberless aspects of daily life there were many customs that were not specifically Arabic or even part of an extended Muslim tradition. Ancient practices as well as new refinements could be observed both in the world of Islam and in much of what only later came to be considered purely Islamic. The seclusion of women, for example, was hardly unknown in the classical Mediterranean, in Semitic culture before Mohammed, or in the ancient empire of Persia. The tribal blood feud so characteristic of nomadic life and the overriding obligations of kinship and masculine pride were not unique to the Arabs. The Moorish traveler who found elaborate baths with hot and cold water in each of Baghdad's thirteen quarters, as late as 1327 and long after its age of magnificence, was looking at the result of centuries of cultural fusion. The richly robed eunuch he saw in the streets might hold an office little different from that of Eutropius, the eunuch who became consul in the last days of the Roman Empire. In the mores of Islam —religion aside—it became, and remains, seldom possible to isolate a custom or institution as purely Muslim or as purely pagan.

In several institutions Muslim life reflected the sexist male aspect of Arabic erotic poetry. Despite the Koranic injunction against homosexuality, love songs were frequently addressed by men to other men, just as in Persian, Greek, and Latin literature. In remote villages on the banks of muddy rivers, the timeless rites of female circumcision and clitoridectomy were continued as a prop to male supremacy and superstition. Lesbianism, an inevitable result of harem isolation, was to become notorious in the huge seraglios of the Ottoman sultans. The ordinary woman could never really rise above her Koranic role as an inferior creature destined to remain in the home. In an essentially feminine household the male head of an urban family had the power of the master, but was sometimes more like a visitor into a woman's world.

In Cairo, Baghdad, Cordoba, and the other great capitals of Islam, the aromatized world of the woman in wealthy households was one of luxury, attended by eunuchs and boy slaves. (Because Islamic law forbade castration, eunuchs for Ottoman households were largely imported from Christian countries by Jewish merchants.) In the palaces the women's quarters could become the scene of jealousies and intrigues, which, as in the days of ancient Persia, could lead to the downfall of dynasties. Scholars who have noted these symptoms of decay, before the final ascendancy of the Ottomans, have often attributed them to the victory of subject peoples over their Arab conquerors, to the triumph of citified decadence over the warrior ways of the desert. There is no reason to assume, however, that the sexual customs and status of women in polygamous Islam during its imperial epoch were much inferior to what they have been in the great ages of comparable civilizations.

Slavery and Race

Neither Christian nor Muslim questioned the moral basis of slavery or had any religious reason to do so. The Koran enjoins the faithful to be color-blind, but Islamic attitudes toward African blacks on the one hand and barbarians from the forests of northern Europe on the other showed many variations, including outright racial stereotypes. While some exalted military commanders, Mamelukes, Janizaries, high viziers, and court officials were slaves in name only, the position of black slaves was, in practice, below that of nonblack slaves. Prejudice existed between nonblack and black races.

From the time of the first conquest and Arab diffusion, the child of an Arab father and African mother was visibly different. The huge trade in slaves from black Africa after the conquest meant that for many Muslims the only blacks they knew were slaves, usually domestic and manual laborers and often eunuchs. Commenting on the difference between white and black slaves, the historian ibn Khaldun wrote that the only people who accepted slavery were blacks. (The conservative *ulama* maintained their religious defense of slavery well into the nineteenth century.) Although the "pure Arab" Muslim felt superior to other races, believers and nonbelievers alike, the unity of the notions "black," "slave," and "inferior" never took complete hold in Muslim lands.

Ibn Khaldun

If there was decay in Islam when Columbus set sail from Christian Spain, it was perhaps more intellectual than moral. Muslim caliphs had tried on past occasions to stifle the path of inquiry by burning books or exiling the unorthodox. Such repression was symptomatic of the decline, and wreckage, of the spirit of free scientific inquiry. Philosophers and theologians turned to futile speculations and waged a battle of the books. Reverence for tradition became a chain binding Islam to its own past. It was a past so seductive as to compel the Inquisition to make bonfires of Arabic manuscripts in Granada. But the script used for Arabic, Persian, Turkish, and Urdu, and for Swahili today, could no more be destroyed than the message of the Prophet. And the age of intellectual decline produced Mohammed ibn Khaldun, the greatest historical philosopher of Islam.

Contrary to the Arab tendency to isolate events and places in history, ibn Khaldun was the discoverer, as he himself claimed, of a comprehensive social science. He was a pioneer in trying to find laws that determined the rise and fall of states and dynasties. Like Herodotus, he was one of the first historians to insist on the relevance of climate and geography —along with moral and spiritual forces—as factors in human development. He was born in 1332 at Tunis and spent a lifetime in political employment and intrigue, sometimes in high office at Fez or Granada and sometimes a prisoner or a refugee from rival factions. Ibn Khaldun became a chief judge in Cairo, attempted reforms, and was relegated to the academy. He made the pilgrimage to Mecca, had a series of conversations with Tamerlane at Damascus, and died in Cairo in 1406, having been restored to and dismissed from his judgeship four more times. Ibn Khaldun founded no school of historiography, Islamic or otherwise, and his great *Book of Examples* came just before the eclipse of Arabic historical prose and the arrival of the Ottomans.

The End of Classic Islam

Al-Maqqari, the last Arab historian of note, took Arab Spain as his subject. When he died in 1632, the Spanish novel *Don Quixote* had already been translated into English and was on its way to becoming, after the Bible, the most widely translated book in the world. Its author, Miguel de Cervantes, was an individual link between the two worlds of Islam and Christendom that blended even as they were bent on destroying each other. Sailing in 1571 as a common soldier in the fleet led by Don John of Austria against the Turks, Cervantes was maimed by gunshot in his left hand. In 1575, on another expedition, he was captured by Turkish galleys and sold as a slave in Algiers. In his five years of captivity under Hassan Pasha, the Spaniard could have seen little of the civilization that Muslims had built over the centuries. In the adventures of Don Quixote, however, the reader is often tempted to hear beneath the laughter an echo of the romance and chivalry left in Spain by its Arab conquerors. Classic Arabic literature —even before the death of al-Maqqari—had long since vanished when Cervantes wrote the first modern novel. By 1500, as Renaissance Europe made its rediscovery of Greek and Roman civilization, classic Islamic civilization had also vanished.

The Muslims had boasted no theaters, games, or political orators like the Greeks and no massive body of secular law like the Romans. Selim the Grim, the new master of the Arab world, had begun his reign in the manner decreed by his grandfather "the Conqueror"—he strangled his two brothers with a bowstring. After Selim had marched through Syria and beheaded the last Mameluke sultan in Cairo, he shipped their last 'Abbasid caliph, hardly more than the shadow of a puppet, to the new Islamic capital of Istanbul. During ages of cultural conflict and assimilation among the peoples of Islam, the very word *Arab* came to have little meaning except "nomad." In Ottoman Turkish, an "Arab" came to be equated with an Ethiopian or black. Without the long Arab heritage, however, there would have been no real empire for the Ottomans to conquer. Without Islàmic scholarship, there would have been a far more laborious Renaissance in Europe and no Arab awakening in modern times.

7.
A New World Faces the Old

After the capture of Cairo in 1517 Syria and Egypt became provinces of the Ottoman Empire. Selim the Grim also became the protector of the holy cities of Mecca and Medina. Two years earlier, this champion of religious orthodoxy had exterminated about forty thousand Shi'ite Muslims in Anatolia—an action sometimes compared to the massacre of French Protestants on St. Bartholomew's Day—that earned the sultan the title of "the Just." The year 1517 also marked the beginning of the greatest crisis in Western Christendom, when Martin Luther nailed to the church door in Wittenberg, Germany, his "95 theses" in defiance of the Pope. The intellectual Renaissance of Europe was in full ferment—the world had suddenly become round, printing had been invented, and gunpowder had revolutionized warfare. The Ottomans were about to bring the lands of Islam to the height of their material prosperity. Suleiman the Magnificent, Selim's only son, reigned from 1520 to 1566 as the greatest of all Ottoman sultans. The Arabs, however, languished deeper and deeper into decline, and their Turkish masters were followed by European colonists.

The Later Ottoman Empire

After Suleiman and his immediate successors the Ottoman royal house produced a long series of corrupt and degenerate rulers. Rich and absorbing as it is, their history touched for the most part only on the periphery of the Arab world. The focus of Ottoman influence was the Turkish capital of Istanbul, the heart of an Islamic empire that, in secular terms, eclipsed even the Golden Age of the Arabs. By 1529 Suleiman's troops were at the gates of Vienna. Although his siege was turned back, the sultan continued to devote his attention to other Ottoman territories in Europe. Between Istanbul and Gibraltar, Ottoman fleets were more than a match for the galleys of Spain and Venice. After defeat in the Battle of Lepanto (1571) in which the heroic Cervantes was wounded, the Ottomans built a new fleet and sailed to conquer Tunis in 1574.

At the same time the sultan had somehow to manage an often corrupt court and a complex system of monarchy based both on the Koran and on the ceremonial glories of Byzantium. This imperial edifice, whose every detail down to the color of the shoes worn by its subjects was regulated by order of the sultan or the chief mufti, was a New Byzantium on Islamic foundations. The rule of Ottoman sultans lasted until October 30, 1923. Defeated by the Allies in World War I, Turkey abolished the sultanate and elected Kemal Atatürk as president of a newly created republic. In the following year the caliphate was abolished, and the last members of the imperial house of Osman went into exile.

The Arab Dark Ages

Islamic scholars now recognize little real Arab history during the centuries of Ottoman splendor and decay, and Arab historians have called the period an "Arab Dark Ages." The deserts remained dry while the West began its industrial revolution. Turkish had long since replaced Arabic as the language of the ruling class. The Arabs produced few intellectual spirits of their own; as ibn Khaldun had already noted, Bedouins everywhere were dependent on adjacent civilizations. Some Arab historians see the Ottoman presence in Arabia and northern Africa not only as a cause of stagnation but also as an unwitting force that kept the Islamic heartlands intact until they could later confront European colonialists.

As the old world of Europe was transformed and the new world across the Atlantic rose to power, not only the Arabs but also the Jews of the Orient passed into the shadow of history. Until almost the present era Arabs and Jews shared a common birthright of suffering. Orthodox Sunni Muslims abandoned the tradition that the caliph would come from the Prophet's own clan. Under the Ottomans the words *sultanate, imamate,* and *caliphate* became interchangeable from one locality to another. Public prayer was always for the sultans, whose long rule over vast dominions eventually endowed the line with something of the prestige once enjoyed by the 'Abbasid caliphs of Baghdad. Turkish diplomats of the nineteenth century found it convenient in their dealings with Christian powers to make a false analogy between the caliph and the Pope. Ottoman sultans claimed spiritual domain over all Muslims—even those who, like desert nomads wandering over the Rub' al-Khali of Arabia, seldom heard the name of Istanbul.

Within Islam, Arabia and Egypt emerged as the two lands

that preserved a continuous Arab culture. They were never overwhelmed by the wars and invasions that continued to devastate other Muslim lands on the Mediterranean and in the East. Most of Islam, however, was an impoverished culture. Vasco da Gama's route to the Indian Ocean ruined the trade of Egypt. The shift from a commercial to a feudal economy, which had been in progress before the Ottomans, was completed with the reduction of Muslims in the Near East to a peasant class. Christians, Jews, and other infidels continued as merchants, a class so essential to the Ottomans that Suleiman gave the king of France the right to protect Catholics in Islamic territories. (In later centuries infidel merchants came to be despised.) Seaborne trade, which was in European hands, became more and more profitable. The Dutch were present in Java a century after the Portuguese.

Ottoman Rule

Ottoman fleets won several victories over Christian navies in the Mediterranean, the Red Sea, and the Persian Gulf. Their success contributed to a small revival of the trade from India through Muslim lands to Syrian ports. Ottoman sailors were determined that the coast of northern Africa remain Muslim and not fall under the dominion of Spain. On land from Hungary to Persia, the sultans were so occupied that Ottoman government was in a continual state of flux. Sultan Ahmed I (1603–17) relaxed the custom of killing his brothers at his succession and instead confined them to celibacy in walled gardens (*kafes* or "cages"). As a result, when later sultans were succeeded by a brother, the fledgling ruler was totally ignorant of his responsibilities.

Even the ablest sultans found it difficult to manage so huge and diffuse an empire. Their theoretically absolute power had to be distributed among the governors of thirty or forty provinces, some of them nearly autonomous. The sultan's "absolute" authority was also limited by the incessant cabals of his Janizaries and viziers. For all of its elaborate government, the New Byzantium was remote from many of its farming and tribal populations. Although the Ottomans proclaimed their allegiance to Islam and their holy warfare against infidel enemies, they never won the sympathies of their Arab subjects. Minor Turkish officials and tax collectors, however, could terrorize a Bedouin community at will, and for long centuries the Ottoman possessions were often ruled with more efficiency than many European countries.

The mainstay of the Ottoman armies was the Janizaries. These "new troops" consisted at first of captives taken as the empire expanded. In about 1450 Murad II organized the tribute of Christian children that became the principal means of recruitment. Converted to Islam and fortified by religious mystics, Janizaries were disciplined in every art of war. They were considered slaves of the sultan. The great cauldrons in which their food was cooked were as sacred as their military standards and were kept under special watch. Like the Praetorian Guard of the Roman empire, these naturally ferocious soldiers made and unmade sultans and extracted tribute as a price for their support. Always opposed to reforms, the Janizaries rebelled in 1826 against the enlistment of new westernized troops. Sultan Mahmud II unfurled the flag of the Prophet against them, assaulted their barracks with cannon, and executed the survivors. Once more than a hundred thousand men, the terror of Europe for four centuries, the corps came to an end. French and Prussian instructors, including Helmuth von Moltke, were then engaged to train the sultan's troops in the latest European methods of warfare.

Arab Lands under Ottoman Rule

Although war between Christians and Muslims was taken for granted at the beginning of the Ottoman era, neither side was willing to forgo the profits of trade. Following the agreement between Suleiman and the French king to safeguard Catholic merchants, French traders were not slow to establish posts in Egypt and Syria. Further Ottoman agreements, or "Capitulations," came with the Dutch, the English, and later with other European powers. Foreign colonies flourished in the ports of the eastern Mediterranean. At the western end of the sea Algeria, Tunisia, and Tripolitania fell under Ottoman protection. The Arabs of Morocco, which kept its independence from the Ottomans, remained an isolated medieval anachronism. Across the straits in Spain, King Philip III banished the entire remnant of Muslim population, making his realm the only land where an Arab culture had prospered and then—except for its memories—been destroyed.

Despite the fanatical hostility of Selim the Grim and the opposition of the majority of Sunni Muslims, the Shi'ite sect persisted in Persia. The ruling dynasty of Safavids had been founded in 1501 by the shah Isma'il I, the sixth in descent from a saintly Sufi sheikh who himself claimed descent from the Prophet. Shah Isma'il's own father had been killed in a battle against Sunni foes, and his troops were defeated by Selim. Before his death in 1524, however, Isma'il had mastered most of Persia and converted his Sunni subjects to Shi'ism, which became the state religion. The Safavids ruled Persia with a mixture of brilliance, intrigue, triumph, and decadence familiar to most dynasties. Isma'il II, a drunken tyrant, was poisoned after a few months of reign. Shah 'Abbas, whose troops were trained by the English adventurer Sir Robert Sherley, won a stunning victory over the Turks in 1603. With English aid 'Abbas also expelled the Portuguese from Persian ports.

Unfortunately, the shahs continued the familiar practice of locking the heir apparent in the harem until the moment of his succession. Although this measure—which began in the empire of Cyrus—may have protected the occupant of the throne, it also exposed the heir to the insistent influence of the harem eunuchs. As the dynasty declined after 'Abbas, cruelty, incompetence, and debauchery were not unknown. Under 'Abbas III, who was placed on the throne as an infant, the Turks were finally driven out of Persia by a masterful general. He then deposed the last Safavid in the spring of 1736 and took the title of Nadir Shah. At home, however, sectarian strife among the Muslims of Persia was by no means at an end.

Most Arabs, unless they served as soldiers or had contact with traders, would have heard dimly if at all of the upheavals and disorders in the Ottoman empire. Arabic was the sacred, not secular, language of the Ottomans, the language of law and doctrine. Turkish was used in the army, and Persian was often used for polite conversation and letters. The sharif of Mecca, who acknowledged Ottoman protection and control, would only have to journey a few days among the Bedouins of the surrounding deserts to find Arabs almost beyond the reach of Turkish protection or Turkish despotism. Yemen had expelled Ottoman forces in 1630. Along the coast of Lebanon a link between East and West was only tenuously maintained by Catholic Arabs of the Maronite faith. (The Maronite sect had been one of the heresies of early Christianity, but it had been brought into the fold of Rome in 1584 when Pope Gregory XIII established the Maronite College, which Jesuits administer to this day.) In the complex Ottoman fashion the religious administration of

Mecca and Medina was conducted at a distance by "the aga of girls," a black eunuch whose chief duty was guarding the women of the harem in Istanbul and controlling all communications with the sultan. The Turks did not impose their intricate layers of government in Arab regions, where older Muslim institutions were allowed to survive.

Ottoman Decline and Retrenchment

In Europe the Ottomans had continued to take on one Christian enemy after another. Sultan Mohammed IV (1648–87) succeeded his father at the age of six, but the Janizaries held supreme control, even monopolizing the sale of bread. Anarchy spread as a struggle for power was waged between the young sultan's mother and grandmother. Accused of trying to poison the boy, his grandmother was surprised in her apartments by his mother's partisans. She vainly attempted to use the oratorical skills with which she had once controlled rebellious Janizaries, but she was strangled with the cords of her bed curtains. Under Mohammed IV the Turks once again led a vast army against Vienna. The Holy Roman Emperor and his court fled from the capital in 1683. Only the timely arrival of King Jan Sobieski of Poland saved the Austrian cause. He led his cavalry against the besieging Turks and routed them. The failure of this last Turkish attack on Vienna marked the beginning of Ottoman decline.

The Ottoman defeat at Vienna was followed by the loss of Hungary to the Hapsburgs. In 1699 the Treaty of Karlowitz made Bosnia the northern limit of the Ottoman empire. In northern Africa, Ottoman generals and Janizaries fought against Spain, local dynasties, and each other. Ahmad Karamanli became the hereditary pasha of Tripolitania, which was under Ottoman suzerainty, by asking his Turkish and Circassian rivals to a feast that turned into a typical slaughter. After its golden age of piracy around 1600, Tunisia was nominally under the control of Ottoman garrisons until the first French arrived in 1830. Algeria had become an Ottoman vassal state in 1554, a base from which Barbary pirates also enjoyed a golden age. Turkish Algeria, however, was never really controlled by Istanbul. The local governor, or dey, had to contend with Janizaries, corsairs, and rebellious tribes. Twenty-eight deys were installed—the French brought a violent end to their rule in 1830—and of these, fourteen were assassinated. As Ottoman government weakened, the situation became worse everywhere for the Arab *fellahin*, or "peasants." Local pashas exacted heavier taxes, Bedouin tribes continued to raid, and farmers fled the countryside for the towns and cities. In Egypt, Sufi mystics charmed the public with occult exhibitions, and European travelers saw even their menservants consulted for medical advice.

After a century of Ottoman decline and misfortune abroad, Abdul-Hamid came to the throne in 1774. He had been secluded in *kafes* for forty-three years, and his weak mind showed the effects of the long isolation. Abuse and disorder in the army and palace were at their worst. Almost as soon as he took power the new sultan was forced by Russia to sign the most humiliating treaty ever forced upon the Turks. This document—the first diplomatic manifestation of Ottoman weakness, politely known as "the Eastern Question"—granted the sultan religious leadership of all Tatars between Poland and the Caspian Sea. In effect he was recognized for the first time outside his own territories as the caliph of Islam. The ironic honor came at a point when Ottoman losses could no longer be reversed. The same treaty more significantly allowed the tsar to protect all Orthodox Christians within the sultan's borders.

The Ottomans also suffered further defeats in Arabia. After the sharifs of Yemen and Hejaz expelled the Turks, Bedouin chiefs drove the Portuguese out of Muscat, drove the Ottomans out of al-Hasa, and came to dominate the grazing lands of Oman. The peninsula reverted to its time-honored pattern of tribal strife. A particular rivalry between two minor princes in Wadi Hanifah was destined to usher in a new era of Arab history—the Wahhabi empire.

The Wahhabi Movement and Empire

Othman ibn Mu-'ammar, the ruler of al-'Uyaynah, had welcomed into his territory a young reformist preacher, Mohammed ibn 'Abd al-Wahhab, who had returned from travels throughout the Middle East. In about 1750 Mohammed first began to proclaim puritan doctrines to Arab tribes whose idolatry and religious backsliding had become notorious. His aim was to restore primitive Islam to his countrymen. Although Othman accepted Mohammed's reformist teachings, the people were less receptive. In addition, the chief of al-Hasa demanded Mohammed's death, threatening to refuse his annual gift to Othman and even to invade the province.

In the face of such danger Othman, who was unwilling to kill the preacher, allowed him to find a place of refuge. Mohammed chose to walk under escort forty miles downstream in Wadi Hanifah to the seat of power of Mohammed ibn Sa'ud. The prophetic blessing that the preacher had sought to confer on Othman—". . . if you rise in support of the one and only God, God Almighty will advance you, and grant you the kingdom of Najd and its Arabs!"—became the reward of Othman's rival, ibn Sa'ud. Under ibn Sa'ud's protection men and women flocked around the new prophet. Old tribal wars were continued in the guise of a crusade against "the infidel," which came to mean anyone who refused to accept the Wahhabi interpretation of Islam.

The name *Wahhabi* is used only by Westerners. Adherents call themselves *Muwahhidun* ("unitarians") after their fundamental belief in the oneness of God. Other beliefs include a return to the literal base of the Koran, predestination, the inseparability of faith from good works, rejection of Sufism and other nonorthodox views, and rule of the Muslim state by Islamic law alone. Their admonishment is "to do good and avoid evil."

Among the earliest converts was ibn Sa'ud's wife, beginning a long alliance between the dynasty and the Wahhabi movement. In the guise of a new crusade against the non-Wahhabi, ibn Sa'ud swept his tribal enemies into oblivion one by one. His son, 'Abd al-'Aziz, inherited rule over all of central and eastern Arabia. By 1789 Wahhabi raids against pilgrim caravans invited Ottoman retaliation. In 1801 'Abd's son (later Sa'ud II) led his father's troops in sacking the holy Shi'ite city of Karbala', and he captured Mecca itself the following year. When his father was assassinated by a Shi'ite fanatic in a mosque in Dar'iya, Sa'ud II assumed leadership. (The preacher who had originally inspired the cause had died in 1792 after a ministry of fifty years.)

With the capture of Medina in 1804 the Wahhabi empire embraced virtually all of Arabia. As *imam* of the Muslim community, Sa'ud II presided over the pilgrimage year after year. The Ottoman sultan was forced to use Egyptian troops against rebellious Wahhabis and to give bribes to their subject clans. In 1818 the principal tribes that had never relished Sa'udi leadership joined with the Egyptians against Sa'ud II's son, 'Abdullah I. After desperate fighting among the palm groves of Dar'iya, 'Abdullah surrendered the Wahhabi capital. Dar'iya was razed to the ground, and 'Abdullah was sent to Istanbul and beheaded. Some members of his family escaped, and some were sent as captives to Egypt. The

Wahhabi empire had almost ceased to exist, but in defiance of the victors its puritan fire smoldered on in lonely desert spaces. Its religious doctrine was buried for a time and only later became a seed of the Arab awakening. Pitiless against fellow Arabs, Wahhabi fighters first raised their banner in the name of Islam, not of "Arabism."

Selim III against Napoleon

The sultan who ended the first Wahhabi empire had already begun the process of westernizing his lands. Selim III (1798–1807), although "caged" according to custom before his accession, had maintained a secret correspondence with the king of France. A passionate admirer of French culture— then in the midst of the Revolution—Selim wanted Turkey to be equal with the West in every kind of material progress, even in the structure of popular government at the local level. Selim reformed the army and attempted to disarm the jealousy of his Janizaries. Military schools were opened, the fleet was reorganized, and instructors were recruited from Europe.

But the country Selim admired so passionately also produced his greatest enemy. Trying to weaken England by opening a French route to India, Napoleon Bonaparte persuaded the French government to allow him to attack Egypt. His expedition captured Malta, took Alexandria by storm on July 1, 1798, and overran the delta region of the Nile. On August 1, however, the French fleet in Aboukir Bay was completely destroyed by the English admiral Horatio Nelson in the Battle of the Nile. Napoleon found himself a prisoner in Egypt, the land he had just conquered.

Selim, the nominal Ottoman master of Egypt, joined England and Russia in the war against Napoleon. To prevent a Turkish invasion of Egypt, Napoleon marched into Syria, was halted by the British at Acre, and began a disastrous retreat to the Nile. In August 1799 he returned to France, leaving his army in Egypt to face the contingents, mainly Albanian, that had been sent by Selim. The French forces were defeated by a combination of English and Ottoman attacks, finally accepted terms of surrender, and sailed from Egypt in the fall of 1801. On the departure of the French, Egypt lapsed into anarchy.

The European Impact on Egypt

Napoleon's brief adventure along the Nile had a profound

psychological effect on the Arab and Islamic worlds. The easy capture of Alexandria, the destruction of a Mameluke army at the Battle of the Pyramids, and the flight of the Mamelukes themselves removed the last vestiges of civil order and of whatever illusions Egyptians had of Islamic invincibility. Napoleon had proclaimed as his mission the restoration of Ottoman rule in Egypt, the ending of local Mameluke tyranny, and the preservation of Islam. He had brought with him one hundred sixty-five French scientists, artists, and men of letters. In Cairo these French savants set up Arabic and French printing presses and founded the Institut d'égypte. Its members studied the antiquities, languages, agriculture, and medicine of Egypt and surveyed a route for a future canal through the Suez. (The famous inscribed stone found at Rosetta, or Rashid, passed into British hands with the surrender of Egypt. During the following two decades it yielded the secrets of ancient hieroglyphic writing.) Learned Egyptians visited meetings of the institute, heard the conversation of Frenchmen from the land of the Revolution, watched chemical experiments, and inspected the Arabic press—the first in Egypt, stolen by Napoleon from the Vatican. The results of these labors were eventually published in the *Description de l'égypte* (1809–28), awakening the serious interest of Europe in the splendor of the pharaonic past, in Egyptology, and in Islam.

Officially "Ottoman" but actually part of the Arab world, Egypt began the process of westernization. Unlike Selim III —who selected what he wanted of Western culture but who could introduce printing only over objections from the Ottoman *ulama*—Egyptians felt the full, direct impact of French ideas as if by an intellectual invasion. Egalitarian notions were heard for the first time. Ideas of equality naturally remained no more than a murmur among people conditioned to accept harsh rule by centuries of oppression, whose *ulama* respected authority as a means to temper Arab feuds and rivalries. In cities and on farmlands it had long been observed that the mild, just ruler was despised and ineffective. Egypt, a country almost without roads, was not a prime seedbed for the politics of the French Revolution.

Even though the Arabs of the Middle East had languished in a "Middle Ages" until Napoleon arrived in Alexandria, the rediscovery of Egypt by Europe was a subtle continuation of the enrichment that early Arab conquerors had brought to their subject lands. For a hundred years after Napoleon, the story of Egypt and Europe was a paradigm for the relationship between Arabs and the West. After an initial shock, the arts and sciences brought by Europeans were welcomed. The *jinni* from Christian lands had much to give. But Europeans also presented an enormous bill—called "control," "protection," or "colonialism."

There was also a psychological price. The Egyptian Mamelukes who faced Selim the Grim had been defeated by firearms, a weapon they scorned as cowardly. The Mamelukes routed by Napoleon again raised the question of whether ancient Arab-Islamic virtues could endure the onslaught of Western technology. (The question remains alive today.) The *jinni* of the West was sending his steamships through the Mediterranean and to ports in the Red Sea, the Persian Gulf, and the Indian Ocean. Roads reappeared in Bedouin lands as overland trade became profitable once more. Railways were on the horizon.

Intervention by the United States

The United States appeared at the western border of the Arab world at the beginning of the nineteenth century. From the time of the Barbarossa brothers in the sixteenth century, the pirates of "Barbary" had raided the seas as far as Iceland. Based in Morocco, Tunis, and Algiers, the corsairs were a military subdivision of the Ottoman empire, paying ten percent of the value of their prizes to the local aga, dey, or bey. Many Europeans were in their service, and many were held as slaves. The United States, which had no navy, paid tribute to the Barbary states to protect its shipping. The agreements were fragile, however, and from 1801 to 1805 the pasha of Tripolitania, Yusuf Karamanli, was at war with the United States over the matter of shipping.

The pasha, who had aided Napoleon in Egypt, captured the frigate *Philadelphia* with captain and crew of three hundred. Seeking to depose Yusuf, the American adventurer William Eaton collected some local troops, including U.S. Marines, in Alexandria and started a march to "the shores of Tripoli." (Although Eaton had a low opinion of the "dog kennel" of Barbary, he once expounded to a group of sheikhs his theory that Muslims and Christians would enjoy separate regions of paradise and would be able to visit one other in the hereafter.) Eaton's expedition accomplished nothing. The United States did not arrive at a real settlement with the pirates until Commodore Stephen Decatur arrived in Algiers in 1815 with a squadron of the new U.S. navy. By that time the "Barbars" —properly Berbers—of Tripolitania had released their prisoners from the *Philadelphia*.

Ottoman Weakness and British Strength

Together with his futile wars against France and Russia, the Western reforms introduced into the Turkish army by Selim III provoked the Janizaries into one of their last successful revolts. In 1807 garrisons on the Black Sea rose in rebellion, and on July 28, 1808, Selim was murdered in Istanbul. His successor, Mustafa IV, reigned for only fourteen months and abolished all reforms in a period of continuous anarchy.

British policy during the nineteenth century was to keep Russia out of the eastern Mediterranean and out of the Middle East. The policy usually meant supporting the Ottomans against the Russian tsars. In the protection of Britain's strategic lines to Asia and Australia, Arab lands held a key position. In 1820, two years after an Egyptian expedition had virtually crushed the first Wahhabi movement, British alliances with sheikhs of the Persian Gulf signaled the beginning of British supremacy in the area. By 1836 the steamboats of Britain had begun moving along the inland waterways of Iraq. Lying near the southern entrance to the Red Sea along the route to India, Aden was taken over as a fueling station by the British in 1839 and soon was known as the "Coalhole of the East."

Mohammed 'Ali

The violence inaugurating the colonial era was not always European against native. In northern Nigeria Usman dan Fodio, the fanatical sheikh who was the leader of the Fulani tribes that settled among the Hausa, warred against Muslim and pagan Africans alike to create his own small empire in about 1810. Egyptians had crossed the Red Sea to battle Wahhabi tribesmen. The Egyptians were under the command of Mohammed 'Ali (1769–1849), the founder of the dynasty that ruled Egypt until 1952. He came to power in the turmoil following French withdrawal from Egypt. Albanian according to some but a Turk by his own family tradition, Mohammed 'Ali was defeated in the battles against Napoleon, but by 1801 he was one of two officers commanding Albanian forces along the Nile. He systematically rid himself of Mameluke and Ottoman rivals for power and won the support of the townsmen and *ulama* of Cairo. The Ottoman government tried to lure Mohammed 'Ali from Egypt by making him governor of Jidda but was forced in 1806 to acknowledge him as the viceroy of Egypt.

In 1807 Mohammed 'Ali showed his loyalty to Selim III by twice defeating British forces that were supporting a Mameluke faction at Alexandria. With their passionate temper and hatred of orderly government, however, the Mamelukes remained a potent threat. In March 1811, Mohammed 'Ali invited the leading Mamelukes to Cairo for the investiture of his son Tusun as commander of the expeditionary force about to depart for Arabia to fight the Wahhabis. No sooner had the guests arrived within the walls of the citadel than the gates were shut and a murderous fire opened on them. All but one were killed, and after a general slaughter of Mamelukes throughout Egypt a remnant escaped to Nubia. In the course of the campaign against the Wahhabis, in which the blundering Tusun died and Mohammed himself took the field, he earned the pilgrim's title of *al-hajj* on a visit to Mecca. In 1820 his armies began to penetrate the Sudan.

Having also built up a small Egyptian navy with the help of French captains, Mohammed 'Ali put his force at the service of the Ottomans in a doomed attempt to contain the rebellion of the sultan's Greek subjects. Twenty-eight Egyptian ships were lost in 1827 at the Battle of Navarino, where British, French, and Russian fleets supported the Greeks against the Ottomans. On land, Egyptian troops won some victories against the Greeks.

After his eventual withdrawal from Greece and the achievement of Greek independence in 1833, Mohammed 'Ali was disturbed by what he took to be the ingratitude of the sultan for Egyptian aid. Declaring war against Istanbul, Mohammed 'Ali sent his westernized troops to invade Syria in 1831, and he defeated the demoralized Ottoman soldiers. As it had been before Selim the Grim, the Egyptian boundary was again marked by the peaks of the Taurus Mountains and the banks of the Euphrates. Only when Europe came to the aid of the Ottoman sultan eight years later—and with a promise of hereditary rule in Egypt—did Mohammed 'Ali pull back his borders.

Although he was physically exhausted, Mohammed 'Ali remained mentally serene, having outwitted most of his enemies in his lengthy career. After a visit to Istanbul in 1846, however, he succumbed more and more to senility. By the time of his death in 1849 his eldest son, Ibrahim, had been in charge of the administration for two years. Mohammed 'Ali's supple mind had long been a match for European diplomacy—to the British a paragon of the antislavery movement and to the French a brilliant and voluntary pupil. Despite his wary opposition to the sultan, however, his reign can hardly be described as one of united Arabs struggling against Turkish oppressors.

Egyptian Reforms

In four decades Mohammed 'Ali had accomplished an enormous transformation of Egypt. With enthusiasm for French culture and education, Rifa'a al-Tahtawi was one of several Egyptian scholars who introduced a small but spontaneous revival of letters. Others devoted themselves to mathematics, astronomy, and theology.

A printing press set up in 1821 not only supplied the government with texts in Turkish and Arabic but also printed learned works in these languages and in Persian. French teachers came to Egypt, and young Egyptians destined for the professions were sent to study in Paris. Postal and telegraphic services became available. Mohammed 'Ali encouraged experiments that led to new crops and superior cotton. Waterwheels and irrigation canals improved farming, even if the Egyptian farmer never escaped his agelong poverty. In Alexandria a committee of foreign consuls advised the government and ran the board of sanitation. (Improved sanitation led, as such innovations still do, to an increase in population.)

In the westernized army, Egyptian peasants proved surprisingly effective, and the nucleus of a general staff was formed. The government was revolutionized. French steamships ran from Marseilles to Alexandria, and the British East India Company began a service between Suez and Bombay.

Mohammed 'Ali's very real reforms were accomplished at a period when the Ottomans, attempting to impose secular codes to replace Islamic law, achieved only superficial changes. As Mohammed 'Ali was driving the British from Alexandria in 1807, the cobblers of Istanbul were forbidden to make footwear with pointed toes. Whether hailed as a forerunner in a sense of Arab nationalism or damned as a ruthless exploiter of peasants and soldiers with little love for his Egyptian subjects, Mohammed 'Ali must be considered as the man who moved Egypt into modern times and gave it identity as a country.

A Cultural Awakening

Ibrahim Pasha ruled Egypt for only forty days after his father's death. An enlightened general and administrator on intimate terms with his French aides, Ibrahim had served the sultan against the Wahhabis in Arabia and against the Greeks in the Morea and had conquered Syria for his father. The incompetent nephew who succeeded him was mysteriously murdered in 1854. Arabs in Egypt and elsewhere were meanwhile not only discovering the ways of the West but also, thanks to printing and the spread of education, rediscovering their own classic heritage.

Rifa'a al-Tahtawi, who helped stimulate the revival, not only headed a school of languages in Cairo but also wrote poetry in traditional Arabic form and language. Among other poets of the literary renaissance, Khalil Mutran (1870–1949), who was born in Lebanon, translated several plays of Shakespeare. Arabic drama began in Lebanon and matured in Egypt. It came to include comedies, serious plays on heroic or historical Egyptian themes, and the "theatre of ideas" developed by Taufiq al-Hakim in the twentieth century. Egypt in the nineteenth century also produced novelists, essayists, critics, and polemicists. Daily papers often published current subject matter in archaic or poetical dialects.

The revival of Arabic letters in Syria and Lebanon owed much to Catholic publishing. Classical Arabic texts, dictionaries, and grammars came from the Imprimerie Catholique founded at Beirut in 1853. Arabic was further encouraged by the Protestant American University of Beirut, founded in 1866, and the Catholic Université Saint-Joseph, founded in 1874. The classic *maqama* style of narrative was revived by Nasif al-Yaziji (1800–71), who also wrote a manual of grammar and poetry in the classic style. The Bustani family was famous for scholarship—Butrus compiled an Arabic encyclopedia, and Sulayman translated the *Iliad* into Arabic verse. The first Arabic theatrical performance in Beirut was a musical adaptation of the French playwright Molière's *The Miser*, made by a Christian Arab said to have admired opera on a business trip to Italy. Playwriting spread to Damascus and Cairo, and school performances became popular.

In literary activity Egypt led the way until challenged much later by Syrian-Lebanese writers who had emigrated to America. These later Arabs, although writing in the United States, infused a new spirit into Arabic literature. Writers such as Khalil Jibran (or Gibran) became famous in their adopted country, but such modern Arab writers had come a great distance from the classical Arab spirit. Outside of Egypt, Syria, and Lebanon, other Arab countries did not join the cultural renaissance until the collapse of the Ottoman empire after World War I. The Sudan, Jordan, Saudi Arabia, Libya, Tunisia, Algeria, and Morocco had a flourishing literary revival only with the collapse of colonialism after World War II.

French Colonialism

The long Anglo-French rivalry in Arab lands had started when the British contested Egypt with Napoleon. In April of 1827 an argument arose between the dey of Algeria and the French consul over a trading concession. The consul became rude, and the exasperated dey flicked him with a fly whisk. This famous "insult" to French honor led to the dispatch of French naval and military forces that conquered Algeria in 1830. The French enterprise was represented as a mere protection against Algerian piracy, but the result was the seizure and eventual colonization of the whole country.

The French Foreign Legion, established by King Louis Philippe in 1831, had its headquarters at Sidi bel Abbes, and its polyglot, often pseudonymous volunteers were seldom idle. By 1846 forty thousand Europeans, largely ex-soldiers, had settled in Algeria. Between 1840 and 1847 Marshal T. R. Bugeaud de la Piconnerie devastated much of the fertile areas cultivated by natives. Abd-el-Kader, the great Algerian hero who had relentlessly opposed the French, went into exile. He later surrendered, was imprisoned for several years, and finally settled in Damascus, where in 1860 he saved 12,000 Christians from a crowd of fanatical Muslims. On a last visit to Paris, 1863–65, he tried in vain to influence France's Algerian policy.

Algerians were governed either by local French military authorities or by bureaucrats in Paris. Former Turkish provinces in the country were reorganized into French "departments." After a visit Napoleon III wrote, ". . . I am just as much emperor of the Arabs as I am of the French." A decree in 1865 declared the native Muslim to be a Frenchman—with all of the obligations of a subject, none of the privileges of a citizen, and harassment by special police regulations. Despite continued Algerian resistance and uprisings, the population was ultimately pacified by 1884 in what has been called the most extreme example of Christian-European intrusion into a Muslim-Arab country. A new Algerian people of European outlook was created—French, Spanish, Italian, Maltese, and native. One hundred and fifty thousand Algerian Jews became politically assimilated into Algerian society.

France had occupied several oases in Morocco, but in 1880 rival European powers agreed at Madrid to maintain Moroccan independence and an open trade policy. Italy and France both found excuses to intervene in Tunisia, which became a French protectorate in 1881 with a French resident general. The Maghreb—northwestern Africa—became the focus of French interest in the Arab world although trade, religion, and education as well as arms made the French presence also felt in the Sudan and along the Levant.

Wahhabi, Bab, and Sanusiya

In Arabia the Wahhabi tribes had been united again under the leadership of Faisal, a great-grandson of ibn Sa'ud. Bigoted, fanatical, uncompromising, surrounded by evil counselors, his sons with daggers drawn against each other, King Faisal had nonetheless managed to expand his realm after twice escaping from Egyptian captivity. (Hejaz remained in Turkish hands.) Sir Lewis Pelly, the British resident for the Persian Gulf area, made a state visit to the blind old king in 1865, the year of his death. Faisal's eldest son ruled until defeated by his brother Sa'ud III in 1871. In the next five years the throne changed hands seven times as members of the Sa'udi family fought for power. The Turks of Baghdad took advantage of the fratricide by occupying the province of al-Hasa for forty-two years.

Although rejected by the puritan Wahhabis, the mystical force of Sufism had never lost its appeal to other Muslims. In modern times Sufi influence has colored major reform movements in Islam from India to the Sudan and eastern Africa. In Iran, Mirza 'Ali Mohammed of Shiraz declared himself to be the Bab, or "gate," through whom the twelfth and last spiritual leader of the Shi'ite sect, who had disappeared around 874, would make revelations to his followers. Soon afterward, the Bab proclaimed that he was the actual leader himself, who had been expected to reappear. Among their complex and mystical doctrines, Babis came to believe that the Jewish Messiah prefigured the Bab and that prophecy, far from ending with Mohammed, would continue as long as the universe existed.

Most of the Bab's life after his "manifestation" in 1844 was spent in prison, and his followers were often persecuted. After his execution in 1850 they split into two movements, of which the Baha'is, led by Baha' u'llah, were to attain world prominence. After several deaths caused by sectarian quarrels, the Turks banished the Baha'is and their opponents separately to Palestine and Cyprus. Today the Baha'i world headquarters is in Haifa, Israel, with an archives building and a shrine of the Bab. Going beyond Islamic theology, Baha'is believe in the unity of mankind and of all religions. They have no priests or ritual.

In Libya most Bedouin Muslims today belong to the Sufi order of Sanusiya, founded near Mecca in 1837 by Sayyid Mohammed ibn 'Ali al-Sanusi (1791–1859), a conservative reformer known to his sectarians as the Grand Sanusi. A political as well as a religious leader, the Grand Sanusi was driven away by the authorities of Mecca, incurred the enmity of the Turks, and withdrew to the distant oasis of Jaghbub in Cyrenaica. There he founded a university and propagandized among the tribesmen of the Sahara and the Sudan. After organizing various sheikhs into a minor empire, the Sanusiya order ultimately lost its political functions during the harsh Italian occupation of Libya. In 1951 the Sanusiya amir of Libya became King Idris I.

Christian Influences

Religious tolerance allowed both Catholic and Protestant missions to prosper in Lebanon and Syria during the brief Egyptian rule under Ibrahim Pasha. In Lebanon many Maronite peasants had moved into areas owned by Druze landlords. Both Catholics and Muslims accepted the suzerainty of the powerful Shihab family, who once had been Sunni Muslims with Druze followers but who came to include Maronite members as Christian communities grew. After Mohammed 'Ali made his pact with the sultan and withdrew Egyptian soldiers from the territory, relations between the mysterious Druze and the Maronites worsened. The French were believed to support the Maronites; the British, the Druze. The Turks openly favored any policy that could lead to anarchy and Ottoman intervention. In 1860 hostilities between the Druze and Maronites culminated in a massacre of the Maronites, followed by a butchery of Christians in Damascus. Abd-el-Kader, the Algerian hero exiled in Damascus, received a medal from the French for saving several thousand Christian lives. Ottoman complaisance during the slaughter had permitted France, Britain, Russia, Prussia, and Austria to intervene.

In the following year Lebanon was granted autonomy under a Christian governor appointed by the Ottoman sultan and assisted by a council representing the various religious communities. The country lived at peace under this remarkable regime until the Ottomans seized total power during World War I. The arrangement that European powers had forced on the Ottoman sultan made Lebanon an important, though small, crossroads linking the world of Islam with the West.

The Beginnings of Nationalism

The notion of Arab nationalism was strong among Arab Christians, who were constantly exposed to the European concept of nation-states. European colonists helped unite Arabs in a common grievance against oppression. The fraternal battles that had always characterized Arab tribal life also kept alive a proud spirit of independence, deriving from the ancient "democracy" of nomadic councils. The learned men of the *ulama*, who once had cautioned the faithful against consulting infidel doctors, also helped give Arabs a sense of Islamic unity against a far more dangerous European invader.

The ways of the West, however, were not always to be denied. In 1857 under British, French, and Turkish influence, the bey of Tunisia issued the Fundamental Pact, a "declaration of the rights of man" similar to those that Europe had forced on the Ottoman sultan the year before. The pact was followed by a constitution. These measures, which unhappily involved higher taxes and concessions to Europeans, had to be abolished because of bad administration and popular discontent. The Berbers of Tunisia, however, had become the first Arabs to have a brief glimpse of republican rule. Bankruptcy and the political embarrassments of the Ottoman sultanate invited foreign intervention. Italy had a great many residents in Tunisia, but its claims over the country were quashed in 1878 when the British government quietly gave France a free hand in Tunisian affairs. In 1881 the bey yielded to a force of French troops outside Tunis and signed a treaty that led to a French occupation and protectorate.

As the West made incessant inroads into Arab life, some

Europeans dreamed of an Arab front against the Turks. They forgot, however, that Arabs had never been slaves and that the Ottomans, whatever their cruelties, were the nominal defenders of Islam. Although a feeling of Arab nationalism began to emerge after the middle of the nineteenth century, it took root only sporadically in an increasingly complex and westernized Arab world. Although native Arab crafts survived where they could, the Arabs whose ancestors had mastered the technologies of ships and steel could no longer compete with the manufactured goods of the West.

Increasing European Intervention

In 1851 George Stephenson of England was granted a contract for a railway between Cairo and Alexandria. In 1856 Ferdinand de Lesseps of France obtained a concession to build the Suez Canal. Under Isma'il Pasha (1863–79) Egypt began a period of economic development that benefited the country, ruined the pasha, and resulted finally in British occupation. Isma'il doubled the tribute he paid to the Ottoman sultan, receiving in return the Persian title of khedive and virtual autonomy within his borders. He imported Remington rifles and Krupp artillery. He put American veterans of the Civil War on his staff and used them to explore the Sudan. Isma'il clearly saw that the opening of the Suez Canal in 1869 had turned the Red Sea into a strategic waterway for the fleets of the West. (*Aida,* which the khedive had commissioned from the Italian composer Giuseppe Verdi to mark the inauguration of the canal, did not have its Cairo premiere until 1871.) Tourism under the auspices of the firm of Thomas Cook was becoming a source of revenue for Isma'il's administration. In the face of such Western activities the first stirrings of Egyptian nationalism arose.

The khedive's prodigality and mismanagement had so impoverished his country that he sold his Suez Canal shares to the British government. European creditors put Egyptian finances under the control of British and French officials. In 1878 an international commission took control of the khedive's personal estates. The army became restless at such intrusions, and the khedive responded by dismissing his European ministers. Britain and France appealed to the sultan. In 1879 a curt telegram from Istanbul notified the khedive that his son was appointed to be his successor. Isma'il sailed from Egypt, never to return.

Large audiences in Cairo had listened to Jamal al-Din al-

Afghani, a pan-Islamic advocate, call on Muslims to resist the West. (Pan-Islamic propaganda was not, however, endorsed by the regents of al-Azhar university.) Jamal al-Din was expelled from Egypt as Anglo-French control was reestablished. Resentment of foreigners continued to mount. Arabi Pasha, an Egyptian colonel of peasant stock, led a rebellion of junior officers against their Turkish-speaking army superiors, who were mostly Circassians. An officers' mutiny began in 1879 and spread. The embattled khedive appointed nationalist ministers and made Arabi Pasha his minister for war in 1882.

The dangers of a really serious uprising in Egypt brought the British and French fleets to Alexandria. In command of the "rebel" forces, Arabi was defeated by British expeditionary troops under Sir Garnet Wolseley at Tall al-Kabir in September 1882. After surrendering in Cairo, Arabi was tried for sedition. With other nationalist leaders, he was banished to Ceylon, but after an exile of nineteen years he was pardoned and returned to die in Cairo in 1911.

A week after Tall al-Kabir the Egyptian army was disbanded, and Sir Evelyn Baring took control of Egypt with upwards of fourteen thousand British troops at his disposal. Baring reorganized the government, finances, education, and the law. A triumphant revolt of tribesmen in the Sudan led by their newly proclaimed Mahdi was eventually put down by Lord Kitchener in 1898 after the battle of Omdurman—but not before Mahdists had seized a great deal of territory, captured Khartoum, and killed the famous British general Charles George Gordon.

Renewed Arab Nationalism

The Arab nationalist movement was revived by the turn of the century. In their newspapers young Egyptians read less about pan-Islamism and more about secular statehood. At Fashoda on the White Nile, Lord Kitchener in 1898 had forced a French column to retreat from Egyptian soil. By recognizing France's supremacy in Morocco in 1904, the British retained their supremacy in Egypt—ending a long period of tension between the rival governments. Egyptian nationalists were stimulated by a British occupation to develop pride in their own culture. Young Syrian immigrants were becoming active in publishing. Against opposition from conservative professors, reforms were introduced into al-Azhar. Intellectuals of the *salafiya* movement worked for a return to primitive Islam but also restated Islamic teaching in terms of modern science, which was held to be an ally of the faith. In 1900 a Cairo novelist caused a sensation by calling for the emancipation of women. A woman writer, Malak Hifni Nasif, discussed marriage, polygamy, and divorce.

Coming after the long torpor of "the decline," the ferment in the Arab world at the opening of the twentieth century was a real turning point. For many centuries large numbers of Muslims had interpreted the Koran as proclaiming the weakness of man and the futility of his will in the face of predestination. (In this view Islamic teachings were not different from many teachings of Greek, Christian, and Eastern origin.) Stagnation, as some taught, was pleasing to God. The fact of Arab "stagnation" under the Ottomans was once difficult for Arab historians to discuss. Today, however, they often refer to the whole period as one of essential Arab weakness, lacking in significant historical development.

Immense changes were to come. On the Arabian peninsula Kuwait had been coveted not only by the French and Germans but also by ibn Rashid, the great founder of the Rashidi dynasty who had conquered the Wahhabi regions in 1891. In 1902 'Abd al-'Aziz, a young Sa'udi warrior, reached the neighborhood of Riyadh with about two hundred men. On January 15, using only fifteen soldiers, he scaled the walls of the capital, defeated the Rashidi governor at the gate of the Mismak Fort, and ushered in the famous Arab era he dominated under his royal title of King ibn Sa'ud. The "blank pages" of Arab history were everywhere at an end.

8.
Awakening and Betrayal

Not since the Prophet had the Arabian Peninsula produced a leader comparable in stature to ibn Sa'ud. His victories, first over neighboring Arabs and later in his surprise attack on Riyadh and in battles against the Rashidis, raised the curtain on modern Arab history. At the time of ibn Sa'ud's birth in Riyadh in about 1880, the Arab world was barely awakening from its eclipse under the Ottomans. (The phrase "Arab awakening" was later popularized in a 1938 book by George Antonius, an Arab Christian of Palestine.) Almost all Arabs were ruled either by European Christians or by Turkish Muslims. Native Christians dominated Lebanon; the anti-Ottoman Arabs of Syria were mission-schooled Christians.

At about the same time two portentous events occurred. In 1882 Leo Pinsker, an Odessa physician, published an appeal to European Jews to escape persecution and settle in a homeland such as Palestine. In 1891 William Knox D'Arcy, a wealthy Englishman who had made his fortune in Australian gold mines, obtained a sixty-year petroleum concession in Persia, the first great oil production center of the Middle East.

As friends and foes appeared on the scene, ibn Sa'ud's first move in regaining his patrimony was to revive the ancient bond between his dynasty and the fundamentalist Wahhabis. He created a militant pantribal organization of "Brethren" that became a nationalistic Arab community. In 1912 the Brethren established the prototype for nearly one hundred future agriculture settlements. With arms and diplomacy, ibn Sa'ud was to bring his tribesmen into the mainstream of world history once again.

Abdul-Hamid II

Attempting to unite the Sunni and Shi'ite sects, the Turkish sultan Abdul-Hamid II became the patron of the infant pan-Islamic movement. Among his Arab subjects Abdul-Hamid II tried to use both force and generosity. After disbanding an 1877 conference—at which Arabs and other Ottoman representatives met in a short-lived constitutional parliament—the sultan was forced to preside over an ominous Islamic crisis as Western powers everywhere penetrated further into

Muslim lands.Even the journal *Pan-Islam*, founded in London in 1903, used Western concepts of humanism, liberalism, and socialism to contrast Islamic virtue with European vice. In such cultural conflict and fusion, it was surprising not that an Arab awakening was to fail in the tensions preceding World War I but that it could take seed at all. When Izzet Pasha, an Arab, became the second most powerful man in the Ottoman state, he was derisively dubbed "Arab Izzet" by his Turkish colleagues.

In 1908 a major oil strike was made in southwest Persia, and in 1909 the Anglo-Persian Oil Company was incorporated. For the Middle East, oil rigs signaled the beginning of the end of a "preindustrial" stage.

In 1898 the sultan had let Kaiser Wilhelm II have a concession to build railways in Turkey, with a line through to Baghdad. (Abdul-Hamid preferred Germans over the "liberal" French and English.) To further the ideal of pan-Islamism, between 1901 and 1908 the sultan constructed another railway from Damascus to the holy capital of Medina. Railways brought foreign workers and foreign ideas. Continuous intrusions of Western industrialism after 1900 had a more profound effect on the Islamic-Arab community than had all of the changes of the previous century.

After 1876 the ancient traffic in African slaves and eunuchs, which was centered between Zanzibar and the Arab sheikhdoms of the Persian Gulf, had declined to a clandestine operation. British gunboats enforced the sentiments of a European antislavery movement. The General Act of the Second Brussels Conference in 1890 played a major role in eventual abolition of the slave trade.

Nationalism and the "Caliph of Islam"

Yet Arab "stagnation" was hardly at an end. Mohammed 'Abduh (1849–1905), a Sufi disciple and pioneer of modern Islamic thought, had become the grand mufti of Egypt, which was under the "veiled protection" of Britain. He failed, however, to modernize his countrymen in the face of *taqlid*, the blind appeal to Muslim orthodox authority. (In the view of some historians, stagnation was not due so much to *taqlid* as to the incessant activities of colonists and their Christian missionaries.) Despite the early efforts of certain Arab leaders to express the voice of Arab nationalism, the notion ran counter to the view of all Islam as one "nation of believers." No independent state had Arabic as an official language before World War I. Hatred of the West and of Europe was in fact a stronger force for unity than any particular Arab movement. Although his superb skill as a reciter of anti-Western verses made Mohammed Hafiz Ibrahim "the poet of the Nile" and director of literature in the Cairo library, he died in 1932 after an essentially unproductive career. The British had more to fear from an old-fashioned Mahdi than from a nationalist poet.

Arab nationalism remained an untested novelty. Indeed, as "caliph of Islam" whose Muslim missionaries were competing with Christians in Asia and black Africa, Abdul-Hamid made a strong claim on the loyalty of his Arab subjects. But at home his oppressive censorship and his network of spies had inflamed the opposition of the Young Turks. Coupled with revolts in the officer corps, their secret activities led to the restoration of the constitution in 1908. (The sultan was forced to dismiss about thirty thousand spies throughout his lands; one of the exultant captains was Mustafa Kemal — later Kemal Atatürk — the future "father" of modern Turkey.)

Besides innumerable racial and religious minorities, the sultan's empire included seven and a half million Turks and ten and a half million Arabs. Many Arabs welcomed the new Ottoman constitution, especially those who had been exposed to "liberal" ideas through missionaries and educators. The sense of Arab nationalism aroused by French Jesuits, American Protestants and other Westerners began to take on new vigor. (Some have seen the seeds of the Arab awakening as springing directly from the success of the Young Turks.) Reactionaries and rebels, however, soon attacked the new constitutional regime. In southern Arabia the people of Yemen, long a foe of Turkey, rose in revolt until Izzet Pasha arrived to pacify them in 1911.

Abdul-Hamid's attempted reforms were too little and too late for most of his subjects; their various ideals were too deeply rooted to be swept aside by momentary enthusiasm or to be united in a constitutional framework. Fanatical opposition arose in Istanbul itself. After an army of Young Turks from Salonika suppressed a military revolt in the capital, Abdul-Hamid was deposed in 1909, and his brother Mohammed V took his place. Confined to a palace on the Bosporus, Abdul-Hamid died in 1918. Like a sultan in the old days of Ottoman fratricide, he had so mistrusted his court that he had prepared his own medicines and extracted his own teeth.

The Zionist Movement

In the developing tide of national feeling sweeping over subject peoples—whether ruled by Turks, Habsburgs, or Russian tsars—the infant Zionist movement had become a small but worldwide phenomenon. The first Zionist congress was assembled in Basel, Switzerland, by Theodor Herzl in 1897. A foreign correspondent and literary editor of the leading Viennese newspaper, Herzl had not at first conceived of Palestine as a Jewish national home or Hebrew as a national language. The anti-Semitism he experienced in France— notably in the passions aroused by the Dreyfus trial—and as a daily part of life in the Habsburg capital, however, led Herzl to publish in 1896 his famous pamphlet *The Jewish State*. Under Herzl's leadership the Basel congress drew up a program proclaiming that ". . . Zionism strives to create for the Jewish people a home in Palestine secured by public law." Meanwhile, a small group of oppressed Russian Jews—inspired by Pinsker and financed by Baron Edmond de Rothschild of Paris—had begun to settle in Palestine as farmers and artisans.

Named after the Philistines of the Old Testament, Palestine did not have an "official" boundary in modern times until after World War I. Traditionally known as the Holy Land, it came to include, without precise definition, a region from Dan to Beersheba, bordered by the Mediterranean on the west and the Arabian Desert on the east. Its location and roads were of timeless strategic value. Herzl visited Palestine in 1898, possibly to seek help from Kaiser Wilhelm II—who was on a spectacular journey through Syria, Damascus, and the Holy Land—but partly to see the foreign settlements. Although Zionist congresses continued, Herzl failed to win a charter for Palestinian autonomy from the Turks. He did find money and sympathy in England, where the government caused a temporary split in Zionist ranks by offering Jews land in Uganda. In 1905 the seventh Zionist congress rejected any territory outside Palestine and its adjacent lands. Herzl, only forty-four years old, died in 1904 while Zionism was still divided on the issue.

Although Zionism had gained a world impetus, only a small minority of Jews were Zionists at the time of Herzl's death. Many preferred to live in the countries of their residence, especially where Jews were a distinct group with their own traditional culture. Many of these Jews believed that a return to Palestine could be accomplished only by divine guidance. Zionism, however, had stimulated orators and pamphleteers, established its own newspapers in many languages, and inaugurated a "Jewish renaissance" in arts and letters. Pogroms in Russia and anti-Semitism elsewhere inevitably aided its cause. "Practical" Zionists went directly to Palestine, while "political" Zionists insisted on a charter as a prerequisite for colonization. Russian Jews emigrated to Palestine as pioneers, used Hebrew as their spoken language, and discouraged the employment of Arab labor. By 1914 there were about ninety thousand Jews among the largely Arab majority of Palestine. There were thirteen thousand settlers, many supported by Baron Rothschild, scattered among forty-three Jewish agricultural homesteads.

Such was the spearhead that came from the romantic longing for a Jewish return to the Middle East. (A classic novel of nineteenth-century Hebrew literature—Mordecai Ze'eb Feierberg's *Whither*—expressed this sentiment.) Palestine lay in Ottoman hands, however, and the Young Turks with nationalist ideals of their own had little use for Jewish national aspirations. Nevertheless, Japan's defeat of Russia in 1905 led many Eastern peoples, including Muslims, to take a somewhat sanguine attitude toward incursions from the West.

The Pan-Arabic Movement

The Anglo-French agreement of 1904 gave France a free hand in Morocco and established British power in Egypt. The agreement made Mustafa Kamil, a young Egyptian nationalist, realize that his countrymen could not rely on French support to oust the British but must redouble their own efforts. In June 1906 a clash between the Nile villagers of Dinshaway and British officers on a pigeon shoot resulted in severe penalties, including floggings, for the natives. Liberals in England were outraged; in Egypt the incident united the peasants and middle class against the British presence. Mustafa Kamil was as much a pan-Islamist and champion of the Ottoman sultan, who made him a pasha, as he was a foe of the British. By the time of his death in 1908, however, separate national movements in Muslim lands were making havoc of the pan-Islamic ideal. The clash of local interests against an idealized unity became a hazard of the movement.

Arabs could not be enthusiastic pan-Islamists after the Young Turks turned their energies from Ottoman reform to the defense of Turkey against European enemies and to un-concealed Turkish nationalism. Syrian patriots formed political parties to propagandize against the Ottomans. Their goal was Arab autonomy within the sultanate. The Young Turks responded by tightening their hold on Arab countries. In Paris anti-Turkish students formed al-Fatat, or the Young Arabs, a secret society whose purpose was total independence from the Ottomans. In 1914 Arab officers in the Turkish army formed their own secret association.

In 1912 the sultan had to agree to an arrangement between France, Spain, Germany, and England that parceled out divisions of colonial Africa. The agreement also gave the French a protectorate in Morocco to be shared with the Spanish. In the same turbulent year Italy took Tripolitania and Cyrenaica from the sultan, who was desperately engaged in the Balkan Wars. In the years of crisis before World War I, Europe was engaged in endless secret dealings, often involving colonial populations, while at the same time secret political parties were agitating for freedom on European soil.

In June 1913 al-Fatat called an Arab national congress in Paris; most of the delegates came from Syria. The Young Turks promised Arab leaders to make Arabic the official tongue in all Arab provinces and to increase the number of Arabs in high government posts. Like the colonial programs often advocated by European powers, these Turkish concessions were mere promises. World War I was about to engulf Europeans and Ottomans and to provide a real chance for an Arab rebellion against the Turks.

World War I

The Serbian army had fought well in the Balkan Wars against Ottoman Turkey. The "Black Hand," a secret society of Serbian nationalists, was ready to move against the hated House of Habsburg that ruled Serbia from Vienna. (In typical fashion, the head of the clandestine society was officially employed by the Austrian emperor as the head of Serbia's military intelligence.) On June 28, 1914, a Serbian conspirator named Gavrilo Princip shot and killed Francis Ferdinand, the Austrian archduke, and his wife as they drove through Sarajevo, in neighboring Bosnia-Hercegovina.

Europe awoke from its illusions of peace and prosperity and stumbled toward a state of war. Russia supported the Serbs against Austria, but the Kaiser supported Austria. After all of the secret treaties and open alliances had been sorted out and ultimatums issued by various powers, in September 1914 Serbia, Russia, France, Belgium, and England became Allies against the Central Powers of Germany and the Austro-Hungarian Empire. Turkey joined the side of the Central Powers against Russia, its traditional enemy. Italy joined the Allies the following year. The outbreak of war was greeted with jubilation by the masses on both sides, each side believing in the victory of right against might, and many people believing that the war would be over in a few weeks.

Acting as caliph, the sultan on November 14 called all Muslims to a *jihad* against Russia and the Allies of Christian Europe who had so often invaded Muslim lands in Africa and forced him to sign so many humiliating Capitulations. The Turks had at least professed Muslim equality with the Arabs, while Europeans like the British at Dinshaway had often shown an intolerable arrogance. The world of Islam, however, was divided. In India seventy million Muslims were subject to the British crown, and Arabs were serving in the French army.

When Turkey joined the Central Powers, Egypt became an open protectorate of Britain and entered the war against Turkey. The Egyptian people accepted their new obligations. Despite the presence of numerous persuasive Turks in harems kept by Egyptian aristocrats, Egypt never joined the sultan's *jihad*. Britain safeguarded Egypt from Ottoman vengeance. Like a host of other Muslims, if the Egyptian people wished the Turks success, they did so without active support.

Before returning from Egypt to England to run the war, Lord Kitchener had established a friendly relationship with Husain ibn 'Ali, the sharif and amir of Mecca. Husain, who had opposed the Turkish railway from Hejaz to the holy city, negotiated with the British at the onset of the war. Consequently, the "authorized" call to *jihad* never came from Mecca. As the war progressed, Arab optimism and nationalism were further aroused. With Turkish and German support, the Sanusi brotherhood of Cyrenaica attacked British posts in Egypt. Most of the Muslims of northern Africa, however, posed no threat and gave no active support to the Allies. Arabs by the thousands served under the French flag in Europe. In June 1916 Husain raised the Arabs of the Hejaz in a revolt against the Turks. By autumn, however, this revolt was threatened by a Turkish expedition.

Adding to the strategic importance of the Suez area and the Arab Middle East, the British Admiralty had signed a contract in May 1914 with the Anglo-Persian Oil Company to supply fuel to its navy. The change from coal to oil had begun in 1904, and the war speeded every technological advance. Submarines had diesel engines; military planes and automobiles required gasoline.

Husain, Faisal, and "Lawrence of Arabia"

Three pashas—Enver, Talat, and Jemal—dominated the Turkish war machine. Having sworn to capture Cairo, Jemal was made commander of the Ottoman forces in Syria, where he carried out atrocities against Armenians and Arabs. The barbaric control he maintained over Syria left the work of resisting the Turks to Husain and his tribesmen. Following Kitchener's proposals, Husain corresponded in 1915 and 1916 with Sir Henry McMahon, the British high commissioner in Egypt. In these florid and complicated letters the British held out some promise of Arab independence, but the question of Palestine was left in confusion. Arabs still accuse the British of double-dealing, while British defenders have asserted that the pressures of war dictated the terms of their diplomacy.

Husain proclaimed the independence of the Hejaz in June 1916 and accepted the surrender of the Turkish garrison at Mecca. In October he was proclaimed as king of the Arabs, and he summoned all Arab tribes to battle against the Turks. In December the British recognized Husain's kingship of the Hejaz. Husain had established the modern Hashemite dynasty that was based on an ancestral line that could be traced through Fatima and her husband 'Ali to the house of Hashim, a subdivision of the Prophet's own tribe, the Quraish.

In command of the Arab revolt was Husain's son Faisal, once a member of the Turkish parliament, who had later been horrified by the atrocities that he had seen in Syria. The Allied high command was under General Edmund Allenby, as the Turks in the autumn of 1916 received reinforcements and threatened to recapture Mecca. Faisal was joined by T. E. Lawrence, a young British archaeologist attached to the military intelligence staff in Cairo. An unconventional, often irritating personality, Lawrence remains a subject of controversy to this day. His brilliance and magnetism, however, succeeded in firing the spirit of Arab independence across one thousand miles of desert.

Lawrence guided or inspired raids that pinned down Turkish resources as they strove to protect their lifeline, the

Damascus–Medina railway. Prospects of the British campaign, which had received several disastrous blows from the Turks, were galvanized into new hope when Lawrence, with some Arab chiefs and a few hundred men from the Syrian desert, attacked Aqaba, a port on the northern end of the Red Sea. They entered the town on July 6, 1917, killing or capturing twelve hundred Turks with a loss of only two of their own men. There were further Arab attacks against the nearly thirty thousand Turkish troops that would otherwise have been used against the British in Palestine. Faisal led the Arab army, but Lawrence—a man with deep sympathy for Arab culture and aspirations—was its flamboyant, eccentric, and often heroic spirit.

Betrayal

Between 1915 and 1916 France and Britain were in secret negotiations to divide up the territories they hoped to control after defeating the Ottoman empire. Sir Mark Sykes, the chief British representative, was an active champion of Arab freedom. The resulting Sykes-Picot agreement signed in May 1916 ratified an arrangement under which a British sphere of influence was established in Mesopotamia and in the ports of Haifa and Acre. The French sphere included Syria and southern Kurdistan, and Russia was to receive Armenia and other territories. Specifically, the Sykes-Picot document divided Arabia into foreign spheres of influence, even though the area was organized into Arab states. (The major part of Palestine was to be subject to international control.)

These secret agreements came to light in November 1917 as a result of the Russian Revolution. Having opened the tsar's files, the victorious Russian Communists, who were anxious to expose "imperialist" intrigues, showed the Turks certain Sykes-Picot documents. The Turks used the documents to demonstrate how the Christian powers of Europe planned to betray the Arabs and other Muslims. Still dependent on British arms, Husain and Faisal could do little more than demand explanations from France and Britain and mourn especially the loss of their trust in England. The feeling of betrayal that then took root has never been forgotten.

Also in November 1917 Arab suspicion of the Allies was further aroused by the famous letter from Arthur James Balfour, the British foreign secretary, to his countryman Lord Rothschild. Balfour declared his government in favor of "the establishment in Palestine of a national home for the

Jewish people" without violating the rights of "existing non-Jewish communities." The declaration had been inspired by Chaim Weizmann and Nahum Sokolow, leaders of the Zionist movement headquartered in London at the time. The British ministers hoped that by supporting Zionism they would rally Jewish opinion in the United States—which had declared war against Germany in April—and that a future Jewish population in Palestine indebted to British friendship would add to the protection of the Suez area. Although vague in certain points of wording—"a" instead of "the" national home and no mention of a national "state"—the declaration was welcomed by Zionists. (The only Jew in the British cabinet, Edwin Samuel Montagu, was a staunch foe of Zionism.)

The principal Allies endorsed the Balfour proposal. Assured that no actual Jewish state was contemplated, Husain saw some possible advantages in having Jews immigrate into Arab countries. The Jews of the United States, many of whose families had suffered the horrors of Russian anti-Semitism, now had evidence of the Allies' good intentions. Christians, too, could see in the Balfour declaration a hope that Jews could return to their biblical "promised land."

The End of the War

The British took Baghdad from the Turks in September 1917, and General Allenby captured Jerusalem in December. Maneuvers by Lawrence and Allenby culminated at the Battle of Megiddo on September 19, where defeated Turkish forces trying to escape were bombed into chaos. Soon after, British soldiers of the Desert Mounted Corps met their Arab allies for the first time. Until then the tribes had been an almost invisible host. In October the Arab Legion entered Damascus and representatives of the Ottoman government signed an armistice aboard a British cruiser off the island of Lemnos. Turkish rule in Arab lands was finished. Gertrude Bell, one of the few Englishwomen to have traveled in the Arabian Peninsula, served the new administration in Baghdad. A brilliant Oxford graduate and an expert in the labyrinth of Middle East politics, she was a firm proponent of Husain and the Hashemite dynasty.

Despite all promises the English and European hands continued to be heavy in Arab affairs after World War I. The Arabs themselves may have experienced a real awakening, but their disappointment—their "betrayal"—was an inevitable result of the Paris Peace Conference of 1919 and the

League of Nations created by it. With the exception of U.S. President Woodrow Wilson, the statesmen who imposed terms on Germany and broke up the defeated Ottoman empire were men like British secretary of war Winston Churchill. Raised on imperialist notions, they had no trouble distinguishing people who naturally ruled from people who were naturally subjects. At the end of the war Arabia, the most "underdeveloped" Arab area, gained a measure of freedom, while Arabs whose cultures had evolved under Western domination remained subject to the West. In Tunisia, Algeria, and Morocco, Arab intellectuals continued to write in French. The "original Arabs," however, were renewing their own culture on the peninsula.

Europeans like Balfour could agree that, in secret negotiations like the Sykes-Picot agreement, the West had indeed betrayed the Arabs. It was done, they argued, in the interest of a higher cause—victory. The Treaty of Versailles specifically called for an end to such secret diplomacy, but Arabs had to live with the results.

The Postwar Arab Lands

Divested of its subject territories and transformed into a republic, with the sultanate abolished, Ottoman Turkey began a long program of westernization under Kemal Atatürk. The capital was moved from Constantinople (later officially named Istanbul) to Ankara. The Latin alphabet replaced Arabic script, and an official drive was launched against Arabic-Persian customs and even vocabulary. Iran, a nominally neutral territory, continued its concessions to the Anglo-Persian Oil Company. Husain, the sharif of Mecca, saw his son Faisal crowned as king of Iraq, which remained under British mandate until 1932 when it joined the League of Nations as an independent country. Faisal's brother, Abdullah, was recognized by Britain as the amir of Transjordan, which he ruled from 1921 to 1946. Guided by British advisers, he maintained his country's independence from Palestine.

After waves of nationalist activity immediately following the war, the British protectorate over Egypt was abolished in 1922, and the sultan Fu'ad was proclaimed king. A constitutional government was formed around the Wafd Party, the spearhead of Egyptian nationalism. The Sudan remained under British administration. Across the Red Sea, the sheikhdoms of southern Arabia and the Persian Gulf remained quasi-protectorates of Britain, while the greater part of the peninsula was united into the Kingdom of Saudi Arabia under ibn Sa'ud.

French military operations against Abd el-Krim, a resistance leader, were resumed in the Rif Mountains of Morocco after the war. The Muslims of Algeria were allowed a token share in local governments as a reward for wartime loyalty. Heeding President Wilson's call for self-determination, the Young Tunisians vainly attempted to win freedom from France. Libya was annexed by Italy and later colonized by Italian settlers.

Under the Versailles Treaty, France maintained its historic presence in Syria and Lebanon by the terms of a "mandate." The system of mandated territories was an experiment set up by Article 22 of the League of Nations, an organization the United States refused to join. The mandate was a compromise through which the Allies could grant a measure of independence to former colonies of the kaiser and the sultan, while retaining interest in and control of their activities. (The United States subsequently made treaties to protect its own interests in mandated countries.) In 1920 a Syrian Congress elected Faisal king of a united Syria, but the French exiled him from Damascus. Thereafter a French high commissioner had to deal with the persistent demands of Syrian nationalists and take charge of Lebanon, where aspirations for independence also were ablaze.

Unrest over Palestine

In this pattern of continued colonialism, rule by mandate, and limited independence, many Arabs felt their sharpest sense of betrayal over Palestine. The territory had been ravaged not only by the war atrocities of Jemal Pasha but also by locusts and epidemics. A British military government had been established after the capture of Jerusalem, and it continued under the League of Nations. In 1919 a Syrian general congress rejected the Balfour declaration. A commission sent by President Wilson reported that the Arabs formerly under Ottoman rule rejected Zionism and that Zionists themselves contemplated the dispossession of Arabs in Palestine. The commission recommended modification of "the extreme Zionist program."

In April 1920, five Jews were killed and two hundred wounded by anti-Zionist rioters in Palestine—Arabs who felt cheated in their hopes of independence and who were fearful of subjection to Jewish settlers. The military government was dissolved, and Britain sent Sir Herbert Samuel to be high commissioner of a civilian administration. Zionists were not pleased when Sir Herbert, a practical and skillful politician, temporarily suspended Jewish immigration in 1921 and issued a pardon to Haj Amin al-Husaini, a leader of the riots who was to become a spokesman for the Palestinian Arabs. Organized into Christian-Muslim associations, Arabs continued to oppose Jewish immigration, while the British sought quotas based on the economic capacity of the country.

In July 1922, a mandate for Palestine was approved by the League of Nations, incorporating the Balfour declaration and stressing the historic Jewish link with Palestine. Article 6 required the British administration to permit Jewish immigration "while ensuring that the rights and position of other sections of the population are not prejudiced." Transjordan, once included in the original British mandate for Palestine, was excluded under Zionist protest when the league terms became official in 1923. As British colonial secretary, Churchill had endorsed the development of "the existing Jewish community," but he announced that his government did not intend to allow "the disappearance or the subordination of the Arabic population, language, or culture in Palestine."

Nationalism versus Colonialism

It was only natural that the thrust of Palestine into the Arab world would give impetus to a sense of Arab unity. Movement toward unity was difficult, however, against roadblocks created by victorious Allies as they divided the Arabs up into artificial states and territories. While Wahhabi puritanism flourished under an independent ibn Sa'ud, Ferhat Abbas was urging Algerian intellectuals to become, in effect, cultural Frenchmen. Both Jews and Arabs could feel that the victory of their "friends" in World War I had brought little more than arbitrary accommodations here and there. Faisal, who had met Chaim Weizmann in Palestine in 1918, was encouraged by Lawrence and the British to accept an agreement with the Zionist leader in London the following year. In his own hand Faisal added a proviso that all agreements depended on the Arabs obtaining their independence. The proviso was put into a rough English translation by Lawrence, who showed it to Weizmann. (The translation may have been too loose a paraphrase.)

Faisal had as much reason to fear the French, who had

expelled him from Damascus, as he had to fear the Jews. After Syria and Iraq failed to become truly free, he aroused a new sense of Arab identity and unity. "We are Arabs," he declared, "before we are Muslims." In June 1919 Faisal stated that "there is neither minority nor majority among us, nothing to divide us. We are one body." Churchill had deplored the presence of African troops in Syria to enforce French rule but had sided with the French against Faisal, the friend of Britain. At the same time, Faisal had received the unstinting support of Gertrude Bell in Iraq. She invoked British power against his tribal rivals for the kingship and even had one of them deported to Ceylon.

In another high-handed accommodation, the boundary between Saudi Arabia and the amirate of Transjordan was drafted after lunch in Jerusalem by Churchill. A wavy kink in the frontier is known as "Winston's hiccough." Between Churchill, Lawrence, and the British government—as many Arabs read events—their cause had been at best trifled with and at worst betrayed.

Ibn Sa'ud and Saudi Arabia

Immediately after the war, ibn Sa'ud with British help had conquered remaining Rashidi territory and had assumed the title of the sultan of Najd. Through possession of strategic trade routes and oases in the southern Syrian desert, he came into contact with the mandated territories of Iraq and Transjordan. His headstrong Wahhabi Brethren charged across these borders in sporadic raids that caused crisis after crisis. Relations with Faisal and Abdullah, the Hashemite rulers, worsened rapidly.

During the war Husain, their father, had become the king of the Hejaz. In 1924 he proclaimed himself caliph. The cost of uniting this region under ibn Sa'ud was a Wahhabi massacre of the townsmen of Ta'if in the Hejaz and a protracted siege of Jidda. Husain abdicated, his son 'Ali surrendered, and on January 8, 1926, ibn Sa'ud was hailed as king of the Hejaz in the Great Mosque of Mecca. A year later he became the king of Najd, and in 1932 he united all of his kingdoms under the name of Saudi Arabia.

To assuage the sectarian conflict provoked by these conquests, King Sa'ud convened an Islamic congress at Mecca in 1926. He gave guarantees for the welfare of the holy cities and the honest treatment of pilgrims. The major Western powers, including the U.S.S.R. and finally the United States, began to give him diplomatic recognition. In 1934, after a brief war, King Sa'ud concluded a long hostility with the *imam* of Yemen by granting generous peace terms. His statesmanship reconciled Iraq and Transjordan—although ruled by sons of his enemy Husain—along with Kuwait and Bahrain. The famous Saudi-Iraqi "treaty of Arab brotherhood and alliance" of 1936 was later signed by Yemen. During this period of peaceful negotiation King Sa'ud took the momentous step, at the advice of an American expert, of granting a sixty-year concession in 1933 to the American oil company now called Aramco. Oil royalties began to fill the Saudi treasury.

The Development of Oil

The American interest in Middle East oil had begun after World War I. The U.S. government protested the division of former Turkish oil interests in Iraq among the Anglo-Persian and Anglo-Saxon (Shell) companies, the Compagnie Francaise des Petroles, and Calouste Gulbenkian, a former adviser to the sultan. In return for royalties, Anglo-Persian gave up half its shares to a group of U.S. companies, including Standard Oil of New York, Standard Oil of New Jersey, Atlantic, and Gulf. Pipelines to the Mediterranean began to be built in 1931. By 1937 the Anglo-Iranian company—Reza Shah Pahlavi renamed Persia as Iran in 1935—was producing more than ten million tons a year, a figure exceeded only by the United States, the Soviet Union, and Venezuela.

In 1925 the sheikh of Bahrain had granted exploration rights to a London company, whose options were soon taken over by Gulf. Various English, American, and Dutch companies came into Arab lands after Bahrain began exporting oil in 1934. The Kuwait Oil Company was formed the same year, and in 1938 a field with huge potential was discovered in the Burgan area. That year the total production of Middle East oil amounted to only fifteen million out of a quarter billion tons worldwide. (This balance was to shift radically after World War II.) The international western companies known as "the Seven Sisters" had divided up the world petroleum market, and the royalties they paid saved King Sa'ud and his fellow rulers from the Great Depression that overtook the West after 1930.

The four new Arab countries that emerged from Ottoman territories after World War I entered the era of Stalin, Hitler,

In Dubai, one of the United Arab Emirates, a passing oil truck is reminded of the need to watch out for camels crossing the highway.

and the depression little better equipped to deal with their problems than they had been before. In any event, Arab destinies still lay outside Arab control.

Syria and Lebanon

France was responsible for developing Syria and advancing its self-government. French politicians, however, hesitated to make concessions to Syrian Arabs that might have repercussions in their northern African colonies. The French also wanted to protect Christian interests. As roads were built, state schools established, towns improved, and the University of Damascus founded, many local minorities wanted the French to remain and continue their help. The majority of educated classes and urban residents, however, wanted an enlarged independent Syria, to include the Druze districts, Lebanon, Transjordan, and Palestine if possible. A rebellion organized in 1925 under the People's Party sent bands into Damascus in the same year and also seized much of the countryside. With French conciliation the revolt subsided by 1927, and elections were held in 1928 with a victory for the nationalists. The French high commissioner was not satisfied with the new constitution, and the nationalist assembly was dissolved in 1930.

Six years later the government of France—following the British actions in Iraq and Egypt—agreed to Syrian independence. The Syrian nationalists elected a parliament and chose Hashim al-'Atasi as president. By the end of 1938, however, the Syrians were again due for disappointment. The French were not ready to ratify their agreement, the Syrian government resigned, and World War II put an end to independent political activity. For its own strategic reasons France had ceded to Turkey the district of Alexandretta with its large Turkish population—a territorial "betrayal" not recognized on Syrian maps to this day.

The population of Lebanon was about evenly divided between Maronite Christians and Muslims. During their twenty-five years of mandated rule, the French openly favored the Maronites, and relations between the two communities were often tense. The constitution of 1926—curiously resembling the old Ottoman arrangement—provided for a Maronite president, a Sunni Muslim prime minister, and a Shi'ite Muslim speaker for the chamber. As they were in Syria, the French in Lebanon were reasonably efficient. Higher education was left almost entirely to religious bodies.

Although agriculture was weakened by the decline of the silk industry, Beirut prospered as a trade center. A 1936 Franco-Lebanese treaty of friendship was never ratified by the French government. After the fall of France to Hitler's troops in 1940, Lebanon was occupied first by forces of the Vichy regime and in 1941 by British and Free French soldiers. Independence remained only a hope.

Iraq, Transjordan, and Iran

The British administration of Iraq has been termed the most successful of the mandates. Despite the efforts of some colonialists to make Iraq into another India for the crown, advisers such as Gertrude Bell supported Arab and Hashemite interests. Rebellious Kurds and lawless Bedouins were brought under control, as were restive Shi'ite teachers in their holy cities. The League of Nations decided a boundary question with Turkey in Iraq's favor and recommended continued British control. (The land Iraq won from Turkey proved rich in oil.) Under British sponsorship, Iraq joined the league in 1932. King Faisal was established as the independent monarch of this free but still troubled state.

Just before Faisal's death in September 1933, an Iraqi army unit massacred more than three hundred Christian Assyrians, and the surviving Assyrians fled to Syria. Under his son King Ghazi tribal and political factions led to a coup by the ferocious general Bakr Sidqi in 1936, but he was murdered the following year. Anti-British feeling mounted and Nazi-style youth groups appeared in Baghdad. An ominous precedent for the new Arab world had been set by the military coup and the murders that it provoked. When King Ghazi was killed in an accident in his sports car in 1939, suspicion of the British led to riots in Mosul. The throne was passed to the infant Faisal II, a child of three. German war victories and the fall of France increased the power of anti-British generals. Amid bitter political strife, the regent for the young king fled the country, and a revolutionary regime was formed by pro-Hitler officers.

Although part of the Palestine mandate, Transjordan was excluded from agreements on a Jewish state. King Abdullah had attempted to rouse the tribes of Jordan in support of his brother Faisal in Syria before the French exiled Faisal. In 1921 the British persuaded Abdullah to pull back and take over the territory to be called Transjordan, and in 1927 Transjordan was recognized as an independent state under

British tutelage. In 1939 an elected cabinet replaced the executive council. Abdullah's new kingdom was open to border raids from the Wahhabi warriors of Saudi Arabia, and to help put them down his own Arab troops were joined by John Bagot Glubb, a young officer and another of the remarkable Britons who took up the Arab cause. Glubb transformed Abdullah's fierce but anarchic Bedouins into elite modern soldiers. As Glubb saw it, the Arab future lay in alliance with the West, and King Abdullah steered a pro-British course. In 1939 Glubb became the commander of the Transjordanian Arab Legion.

With its minority of Arab tribes in Khuzistan and in the area along the Persian Gulf, Iran touched the Arab world with close Islamic, geographic, and economic ties. Under Reza Shah Pahlavi (1925–41) the Trans-Iranian railway was completed and central government introduced, at times with harsh measures. Although he built the railway without foreign loans, the shah's desire to improve industry resulted in the presence of two thousand German technicians in Iran on the eve of World War II. In 1941 British and Soviet troops deposed him in favor of his eldest son Mohammed Reza. The refineries and pipelines of the Anglo-Iranian Oil Company were saved from sabotage, and in 1943 Iran declared war on Nazi Germany.

Egypt and Northern Africa

During the decade before World War II many pan-Arabist writers, whatever their local loyalties, did not include Egypt as a leader in the Arab world. Beginning in 1923, Egypt had a parliamentary government under King Fu'ad I. Under martial law, however, British troops protected British interests under a high commissioner. After the assassination in Cairo of Sir Lee Stack, the governor of the Sudan, an Anglo-Egyptian crisis developed. The Egyptian parliament was dissolved at the end of 1924 but was restored in 1926 with an overwhelming majority for the nationalist Wafd Party. Control of the Sudan remained a problem even after 1936, when Britain signed a treaty for an end to occupation and for friendship with King Farouk, then only seventeen years old. (The Wafd Party was meanwhile threatened by the rise of a fundamentalist fanatic group that called itself the Muslim Brotherhood.)

When the Egyptian officer corps was opened to candidates on a merit basis in 1937, both Gamal Abdel Nasser and Anwar el-Sadat were among the cadets. One leading pan-Arabist took the bold view that, although dominated by Britain, Egypt was endowed with qualities that obliged it to take leadership in the awakening of Arab nationalism. Most Egyptians, however, put their own independence above pan-Arabism. A struggle raged between the Wafd Party and Farouk, who had a personal hatred for the Wafd leader and the British. A new party, the Sa'dists, was formed in 1939 to cooperate with the government. When Italy joined Hitler's side in 1940, Italian armies in Ethiopia and Libya clashed directly with British troops in the Sudan and in an unstable Egypt.

Italian rule in Libya was repressive. Some roads, schools, and hospitals were built. Settlers reached the plateaus, and Muslims were granted limited citizenship in 1939. Arabs, however, were not allowed to enter Tripoli or Benghazi after dark.

By the treaty of Fès in 1912, the sultan of Morocco had divided his country into French and Spanish zones. Abd el-Krim, the Berber hero, routed a Spanish army in the Rif Mountains in 1921. After the Spanish withdrew, the French advanced against him. Not until an army of one hundred and sixty thousand attacked Abd el-Krim in 1926 at his capital of Ajdir was he defeated. (Spanish Morocco, under General Francisco Franco, successfully revolted against the republican government in Madrid beginning in 1936.) After Abd el-Krim went into exile, the French attempted to put the Berbers under tribal law instead of Muslim jurisdiction—an action that urban Moroccans saw as a threat to Islamic unity. Acting in the name of the sultan of Morocco, the French and Spanish did their best to transform a medieval empire into a modern kingdom. Roads, ports, railways, schools, and hospitals were built. Tangier was made an international zone. Rabat, Tetuán, and Casablanca flourished as new capitals. As early as 1926, however, young Moroccans were forming political societies and agitating for reforms. As Mussolini and Hitler became formidable, France increasingly relied on the resources of Morocco. When France fell in World War II, Morocco remained loyal to the puppet Vichy government until Allied troops landed in 1942.

In 1936 the French settlers of Algiers defeated a plan to give twenty-one thousand Muslims an equal vote. The immigrant Christian minority enjoyed a European standard of living, but the Muslim majority—undernourished and often without jobs—could find places in primary schools for only one in eight of their two and a half million children. The tragic attitude of many French colonists toward the natives could be seen in a sign posted outside an estate near Algiers: "No Arabs, Jews, or dogs allowed!" Resentment was fired by a general Arab awakening among the natives and led to two political groups. One was dominated by Ferhat Abbas, born in 1899 as the son of a local Muslim administrator. Educated entirely by the French, he never spoke fluent Arabic. "Algeria is French soil," he wrote in 1931, "and we are French Muslims." Although his love of French culture was bitterly tested in 1936 when his countrymen were denied the vote, he was not unmindful of his political future and served as a volunteer with the French forces of World War II. Another Algerian party, under the working-class leader Messali Hadj, had a completely nationalist platform.

Tunisia had been modernized by France in typical colonial fashion, and a phosphate industry had developed. The Destour ("constitution") Party of Tunisia demanded complete independence after 1920. Under the leadership of Abd al-Aziz al-Thaalibi, a distinguished Arab of the old tradition, propaganda was circulated among the working classes. After disorders and repressions, in 1934 the younger nationalists founded the Neo-Destour Party, led by Habib Bourguiba, a thirty-year-old lawyer.

Born in 1903, Bourguiba had studied in Paris, and he started a nationalist newspaper in French on his return to Tunis. At the outbreak of World War II he was on trial in Paris for his political activities. The Germans freed Bourguiba but could not enlist his support. Although Bourguiba was allowed to return to Tunisia, the Free French forces ignored his proposals for gradual independence, and he escaped in disguise to Egypt. Tunisia had meanwhile become a battleground between the Allied and Axis armies.

The Muslims of northern Africa living west of Egypt under Spanish, French, or Italian authority were somewhat affected by the Arab awakening after World War I. They had, however, no share, even indirectly, in the Arab revolt of that war and no immediate contact with the bitter problems produced by mandated divisions in the Middle East.

Palestine and Zionism

In Palestine the years from 1923 to 1929 were relatively quiet. Jewish immigration had dropped to a trickle. But in

1929, as Zionists expanded their activities, Arabs in Jerusalem became fearful of Jewish domination. Religious riots took place at the Wailing Wall, a monument sacred to the Jews, and elsewhere throughout the country. The following decade was marked by further riots as the British, attempting to reconcile Jewish and Arab interests, made enemies of both. A general strike begun by Arabs in 1936 almost flared into an open rebellion. Another of many royal commissions of inquiry reported in 1937 that the mandate was unworkable and that Britain's obligations to Jews and Arabs were impossible to honor. The commission recommended partition of the territory, the first official mention of a Jewish state.

Meanwhile, immigration had picked up as more and more Jews were put to flight by the scourge of Hitler. The Arabs had long been convinced—especially by an explanatory letter in 1931 from the British prime minister to Weizmann—that Zionists in London could shape policy to their will. The general Arab revolt continued well into 1939 while the British prepared a proposal calling for seventy-five thousand Jews to be admitted to Palestine over the following five years. Thereafter quotas of Jews would be subject to Arab "acquiescence."

Zionists were shocked by the proposal, and Arabs, although in agreement, felt that they could not trust it. Its publication marked the end of any understanding between Britain and the Zionist movement. By this time Jewish landholdings in Palestine had increased to nearly four hundred thousand acres, and nearly four hundred and fifty thousand Jews formed thirty percent of the total population. Zionist underground organizations included the Haganah ("defense") of David ben-Gurion that was openly active against Arab opponents and its extreme wing, the Irgun Zvai Leumi ("national military organization"). Volunteers from Syria and Iraq were supporting the Arab cause.

World War II

When World War II broke out, Zionists were in the paradoxical position of opposing both Hitler and Britain. In 1942 a Zionist conference in New York called for establishment of a Jewish state in the whole of Palestine and for unlimited immigration. Tension mounted in Palestine as Hitler's extermination of European Jews continued. Jewish terrorism was ignited in 1943 as the Irgun Zvai Leumi joined the Sternists, a splinter group, in widespread anti-British attacks. These attacks culminated with the murder of Lord Moyne, Britain's minister of state, in Cairo in November 1944.

In the wake of early Axis victories the Free French supported by the British had proclaimed the freedom of Lebanon and Syria. Elections were held in Lebanon in 1943, but the new government was too independent for the Free French, and almost all of its members were arrested. Arabs could see no end to European hypocrisy. Europeans had caused the turmoil in which Jews were fleeing Hitler; yet Hitler's foes, including the United States, did little to admit refugee Jews. Official Zionist policy itself demanded that Jews go to Palestine, not to Canada, Australia, or other areas of the world.

Most Arabs were not militantly involved in World War II. (Turkey stayed neutral until January 1945 when it joined the victorious Allies.) The countries of the West were too preoccupied in the struggle to pay much attention to Arab hopes, but the Allies did not want another Arab revolt. Hitler and Mussolini had the same enemies as many Arab nationalists, whether in colonial or mandated territories. Throughout the Middle East Arab leaders intensified their demands in the face of the increasing sympathy for Zionism among the free nations. Anthony Eden, the British foreign secretary, issued a statement in February 1942 that endorsed Arab unity throughout northern Africa and the Middle East. In Lebanon, vexed by conflict with the Free French, Christian and Muslim Arabs had already combined in a national movement for independence. General Charles De Gaulle, however, was determined to maintain a French presence in Syria and Lebanon. He went so far as to send Senegalese troops to Beirut in 1945, provoking riots in Damascus and elsewhere. After firm protests by Britain and the United States, France ordered the soldiers back to their barracks.

At the other end of the Arab world Mohammed V, the sultan of Morocco, met with U.S. President Franklin D. Roosevelt at the Casablanca conference of 1943 and was led to believe that America would support Arabs in a postwar confrontation with the French. Many ordinary Egyptians hoped that an Axis victory would rid them of the British, and King Farouk's intimate friends included many Italian fascists. In the summer of 1942, Italian and German forces came close to conquering Egypt, advancing to within forty miles of Alexandria. The British victory at el-Alamein, however, ended the invasion crisis. As Zionists pressed their claims on Palestine, Egypt began an active role in the pan-Arab movement. Jews in Palestine were building a munitions industry, and twenty-seven thousand Jews were trained to serve in British forces. Zionism, however, was counting on its greatest support from the United States.

The Arab League

King Farouk and his government had shown strong sympathy for Lebanese Arabs against the French, and he took a firm anti-Zionist position. In 1944 the prime minister of Egypt, Nahas Pasha, presided over a conference of Arab leaders at Alexandria. When it ended on October 7, the tangled pressures of Egyptian politics forced Farouk to dismiss Nahas Pasha, his personal enemy, but the foundation had been laid for the future Arab League.

During World War II there was another enormous increase in the demand for oil, and there were many technical improvements, notably in laying the pipelines, within the petroleum industry. Oil, however, had not yet become an issue in the Middle East. The most important issue after World War II was Palestine. From their own factories and by stealing from the British, the Jews of Palestine had acquired a vast cache of armaments. With British encouragement, seven Arab states—Egypt, Syria, Lebanon, Iraq, Transjordan, Saudi Arabia, and Yemen—met at Cairo in March 1945 and formed the loose confederation known as the Arab League. (Britain saw the Arabs as potential allies against a Soviet presence in the Middle East.) In August, as the defeated Axis powers lay in ruins, U.S. President Harry S. Truman requested Clement Attlee, the prime minister of Britain, to help with the immediate admission of one hundred thousand Jews into Palestine. In December the U.S. Congress asked for unrestricted immigration of as many Jews as Palestine could accept.

Political Zionism had started in response to persecution by European Christians. Its cause had been aided by Christians who saw historic justice in the return of Jews to the land of the Old Testament. Both these "peoples of the book," Christian and Jew, were fueling the Arab sense of betrayal by the West. At the same time Western money and experts had launched a revolution in the ancient kingdom of King Sa'ud. Another complex factor had entered the modern Arab world.

9.
Independence, Israel, and Oil

The original seven states of the Arab League formed in 1945 were joined by other countries as they became independent: Libya (1953), the Sudan (1956), Tunisia and Morocco (both 1958), Kuwait (1961), Algeria (1962), southern Yemen (later the People's Democratic Republic of Yemen, 1968), Bahrain, Oman, Qatar, and the United Arab Emirates (all in 1971), Mauritania (1973), Somalia (1974), and Djibouti (1977). The Palestine Liberation Organization was granted full membership in 1976. The Arab League gave each member state one vote, and it required unanimous decisions. Needless to say, such a dream of pan-Arabic unity has never been realized across a spectrum as diversified as Arab politics, economics, and geography. In varying degree the countries of the Arab League have the same problems as do Israel, the secular

Afar women in traditional costumes dance at ceremonies marking the independence of Djibouti in 1977.

and technological West, and the undeveloped Third World. The fact that each country serves Islam and its sense of Arab history in its own way remains another potent force for differences in an age of modern evolution.

Outside of the Arab minorities of Israel—Muslim, Christian, and Druze—other Arab communities are found in Chad, Iran, and the Americas. Within the Arab League itself non-Arab minorities include the Kurds and Christian Armenians of Iraq and those Berbers of northern Africa who have never become Arabized. In southern Sudan, many different tribes without a common language are only now coming under the influence and control of Arabs.

The Birth of Israel

The state of Israel—the modern focus of Arab "unity"—came into being on May 14, 1948. The following dawn, units of the armies of Syria, Transjordan, Iraq, and Egypt crossed the Israeli frontier.

Arabs, who played a relatively minor role in World War II, had begun their struggle with the prospects of a future Jewish state in December 1945 when the Arab League declared a boycott of Zionist goods. A futile proposal for Arab-Jewish autonomy within Palestine was worked out in July 1946. Meanwhile, British authorities were beleaguered by unauthorized immigration and by attacks of the radical Zionist underground. Its forces blew up part of the King David Hotel in Jerusalem on July 22, 1946, killing ninety-one occupants and destroying British military offices.

Harassed by all sides—and pressured by U.S. President Harry S. Truman's support of Zionism—Britain referred the Palestine question to a United Nations (UN) commission. In 1947 the commission recommended partition into Arab and Jewish states. With the assent of the United States and the Soviet Union, the UN General Assembly approved. All of the Islamic countries of the Middle East voted against the resolution, questioning the right of the United Nations to divide up the territory against the wishes of its Arab majority. The Zionists approved partition because it would recognize a Jewish state and give fifty-five percent of Palestine—including the Negev, a large desert area in the south—to Jews.

Soon after the UN resolution, fighting intensified in Palestine. Zionists redoubled their efforts to bring in immigrants. As the British administration collapsed and as the United States and the UN weakened their roles in the area, Zionists launched operations Nachshon and Jephtha in April 1948. The success of these offensives coincided with the death of Abdul Kader Husaini, an Arab national hero, in battle on the Jerusalem front and with the massacre of two hundred and fifty Arab civilians in the village of Deir Yasin. The Zionists captured Haifa and Jaffa, and Arab refugees streamed into neighboring countries, where regular Arab troops stood ready to intervene. Toward the end of April the Arab countries—with Egypt the last to concur—decided to take action.

Arab-Israeli Confrontation

On May 14 the British commissioner of Palestine departed. President Truman recognized the new state of Israel within hours, and the first Arab-Israeli war began. Arab forces from Egypt, Transjordan, Iraq, Syria, and Lebanon captured areas of Palestine not inhabited by Jews and the small Jewish quarter of the Old City of Jerusalem. The Israelis captured the main road to Jerusalem through the Judaean Hills and drove off other Arab attacks. In September Zionist terrorists assassinated the UN mediator. Early in 1949 Israelis occupied all of the Negev up to the former Egyptian-Palestinian frontier, except for the Gaza strip. By July, through armistice agreements, Israel had fixed its frontiers.

In September 1951 members of the Arab League were asked to intensify the economic boycott of Israel and shut off its oil supplies. In August 1955, Israeli and Egyptian troops clashed on the Gaza strip. Israel attacked Syrian outposts along the Sea of Galilee in December and was censured by a unanimous vote of the UN Security Council for violating the armistice. In April 1956, UN Secretary General Dag Hammarskjøld effected a cease-fire between Israel and Egypt. Israel invaded the Sinai Peninsula in October 1956, however, after Egypt's President Gamal Abdel Nasser seized the Suez Canal from its European owners. In five days Israelis occupied most of the peninsula east of the canal. After the Anglo-French action against Egypt, a UN emergency force arrived in December. Israeli forces withdrew in March 1957.

On the morning of June 5, 1967, Israeli aircraft struck at nineteen Egyptian airfields and virtually destroyed the air force of the then United Arab Republic (U.A.R.). Air action was accompanied by the advance of Israeli ground troops across the Sinai Desert. In four days of fighting the Israelis reached the Suez Canal, leaving seven shattered U.A.R. divisions in their wake. In almost simultaneous actions, retaliating against artillery bombardments from Jordan and Syria, Israel's ground troops, with almost total air cover, overran the West Bank area of Jordan and crashed through Syria's West Wall of fortifications adjacent to Israel.

The causes of the Six-Day War were complex—heavy incursions of Al Fatah guerrillas from Syria, the Egyptian-Jordanian Defense Pact, an Egyptian army buildup, and the withdrawal of the UN Emergency Force after President Nasser had declared his intention of sending Egyptian ground troops up to the Sinai border with Israel. Behind these events was the increasingly heavy Soviet involvement in the Middle East, with arms shipments to the U.A.R. army and a growing feeling in Israel that combined Arab action was imminent. By the time the UN cease-fire resolution was accepted, however, the Israelis had won a decisive military victory.

Then, after more years of sporadic fighting, Egypt and Syria attacked Israel on October 6, 1973, the Jewish holy day of Yom Kippur. The religious holiday found Israeli reservists at their homes or synagogues and the roads free for mobilization. Arab armies showed an aggressive fighting spirit, and the Israelis suffered heavy casualties. On October 19 the Arabs began to stop oil shipments to the United States. The Israeli army counterattacked, however, pushed into Syria, and also crossed the Suez Canal. A cease-fire agreement was signed in November and a peace plan agreed to on January 18, 1974. Israeli troops withdrew to the Sinai Peninsula, and another UN peacekeeping force arrived. In March the oil embargo was lifted. In May Israel and Syria signed a cease-fire and separated their forces outside a UN buffer zone.

The four major encounters between the Arabs and the Israelis produced perhaps one million Arab refugees—the number is disputed—from the old territory of Palestine and led to the formation of the Palestine Liberation Organization (PLO), originally an underground group of exiled politicians and terrorists. Since 1970 the PLO has been recognized by the Soviet Union and others, particularly in the Third World, as the spokesman for Palestinians. Details of the PLO program have been subject to change. Its thrust, however, has been to restore Palestine as an independent, secular state of Muslims, Christians, and Jews—a goal that usually assumed the destruction of Israel.

The Six-Day War highlighted the larger struggle between Arab nationalism and the West as well as the Cold War between the Western and Communist worlds. Israel allied itself with the West after 1948 and supported U.S. policies in the Third World. Israel profited little, however, from such alliances as the shaky Baghdad Pact of 1955 between Iraq, Turkey, Iran, Pakistan, and Great Britain. (The pact was at once denounced by Egypt as contrary to Arab League security and was moribund by the time it was replaced in 1959 by the Central Treaty Organization with headquarters in Ankara, Turkey.) After Israel's victory in 1967, relations between the Arab countries and the United States reached a low point. The Arab states—even those that accepted Soviet aid and arms—had no reason, however, to turn toward a Soviet alliance. Traditional conservatism and local Arab nationalism were deeply hostile to Soviet Communism.

In February 1966 a bloody coup in Syria—the eighteenth since independence—brought the pro-Communist wing of the Ba'ath Party to power. The coup increased Syrian support of al-Fatah, the Palestine terrorist group organized the year before. After the Six-Day War of 1967, Egypt's defeated forces were rebuilt by the Soviet Union; Jordan's, by the United States. Meanwhile, for ten years—in another typical twist of Middle East politics—the Israeli government had actually supported the Hashemite kingdom of Jordan against Egypt, its chief enemy.

Before and after the Six-Day War "radical" Arab countries such as Egypt and Syria continued in an uneasy alliance with "reactionary" states such as Jordan and Saudi Arabia. In this complex and shifting situation, U.S. companies raised their concessions to Arab oil governments. Despite official U.S. friendship with Israel, the common interests of the United States and local Arab rulers became more obvious. This was dramatized in the fall of 1970 when the Jordanian army crushed the forces of the PLO while Egypt watched in silence and the U.S. Sixth Fleet demonstrated in support of the Jordanian king. Meanwhile, amid rival and often short-lived Arab regimes, neither the Soviet Union nor the United States could count on old-fashioned alliances. One day's foe could be the next day's friend.

With an hour-by-hour necessity for understanding the confused patterns of Arab politics, Israel developed one of the world's toughest and most efficient intelligence systems. Old clandestine organizations—the Haganah, Irgun, and Stern groups—helped provide a nucleus of brave and experienced intelligence officers. Of its five major agencies, the

Shin Bet—along with the Special Investigations Department of the police—became concerned with internal security and terrorist activities. Numerous Israeli secret agents continue to live among Arab peoples. Others live in European capitals, in American cities, or in Cairo itself, served by their long experience as exiles and by skill in the languages and customs of other lands.

Oil Economics and Politics

Besides Israel, the greatest factor in modern Middle East politics has been oil. After World War II the balance of production shifted from North America to Iran and the Arab states. Huge fields were discovered in Saudi Arabia, and new agreements made with U.S., French, Italian, and Japanese interests gave the Saudis a bigger share of the profits. Iraq's production, which was interrupted by Israeli wars, was wholly nationalized in 1972. Between 1949 and 1970, the British Protectorate of Qatar increased its production sixfold under agreements with British and French companies. Algeria took over fifty-one percent of French interests in 1971. Libya, a major postwar producer, has put strong pressure on Esso Standard, the discoverer of the prodigious Zaltan field. In 1971, Libya nationalized British Petroleum, a result of Col. Muammar al-Qaddafi's anger when Britain failed to stop Iran from seizing islands in the Persian Gulf.

By 1950 a fifty-fifty profit-sharing arrangement had been accepted by Middle East producers and foreign companies. Due to oversupply, however, market prices were falling by 1960, and the producing states began to lose revenue. The result was the formation of the Organization of Petroleum Exporting Countries (OPEC)—basically the Middle East and Venezuela—which set its own prices. In 1971 OPEC forced major concessions from the international oil companies by raising prices again, taking fifty-five percent as a minimum share of profits, and adding an annual percentage increase to offset the inflated prices of Western goods the producing countries were importing. These agreements brought a massive rise in revenue to the Arab oil states. During the Yom Kippur War of 1973–74, these states imposed a total ban on oil exports to the United States and other friends of Israel, and later doubled their prices. The embargo was lifted for the United States in March 1974, but it continued against certain other countries for some time.

When an industrial nation has to pay more for Arab oil, its

power costs inevitably go up, and so do the prices of the manufactured goods it sells to Arab nations and in other markets. Arab producers, therefore, have a twofold interest in keeping the price of their oil in balance. First, they want to avoid having to pay increasingly inflated prices for the Western goods that they must import. Second, Arabs want to keep the economies of industrial nations, where Arabs have acquired large investments, from going broke.

Postwar oil profits have brought Western technology and education to certain Arab states and have created an oil-rich group within the Arab League as a counterbalance to the central position and prestige of Egypt. The benefits of oil profits, however, have been less visible than the coups and assassinations that have ripped through the Arab world in the wake of independence. King Farouk, the last of Mohammed 'Ali's line and a gross relic of the colonial past, was thrown out in a coup of July 1952. Other upheavals have ranged from Morocco—where political unrest surfaced in the Casablanca riots of 1965—to Iraq—where King Faisal II was killed in July 1958 along with Prime Minister Nuri as-Said, the conservative pioneer of Arab nationalism who had played a leading role in Iraqi politics for 37 years. As Arabs shook off the last traces of colonial domination amid memories of how they had once beaten Spanish armies and driven off the Crusaders, Egypt took a dominant position.

The Role of Nasser

In June 1956 Colonel Nasser was elected president of Egypt after outwitting his political rivals through years of intrigue. Almost fatally wounded in the 1948 war with Israel, accused of complicity with the Muslim Brotherhood (an extremist group with branches throughout the Arab world), and later having escaped assassination by the group, Nasser became an international figure. When John Foster Dulles, the U.S. secretary of state, refused to honor a pledge for funds to build the Aswan High Dam, Nasser took over the Suez Canal in July 1956 and withstood a combined retaliatory invasion by British, French, and Israeli troops. He obtained a cease-fire and began to build the Aswan Dam with Soviet aid. From these events Nasser emerged with unparalleled prestige in the Arab world. His policies were anti-Israeli and anticolonial and in favor of the developing African countries.

Egypt's efforts at social reform and land redistribution and its association with the Soviet Union were typical of the challenges and choices Arab leadership faced after World War II. Even with all of his prestige, however, Nasser could not rally the basic spirit of Arab unity. Egypt joined Syria in forming the United Arab Republic in 1958 with Nasser as the first president, but Syria withdrew after three years. Radio Cairo broadcast far and wide the Nasser goals of Arab socialism and denounced the personal extravagance of the oil sheikhs. Nasser won over many Arabs of the younger generation, even in Saudi Arabia, but made himself an enemy of the wealthy classes and conservative religious spokesmen.

Instead of oil, Nasser had the power and profits of the canal, which had once been entirely in Western hands. Until Nasser, Egyptians had not been counted solidly as Arabs. Even Egyptian defeat by Israel in the Six-Day War of 1967 was not a complete disaster for Nasser. He managed to improve his relations with the monarchies of Saudi Arabia and Jordan, and the oil countries agreed to compensate Egypt for revenues lost while the canal was closed during the war. Nasser also used the 1967 defeat as a chance to reform the army and the government—risking his life again, provoking riots, and meeting some of the demands for press and political freedoms. With massive popular support, he stipulated at the Khartoum Conference of 1967 that a political solution for "liquidating the consequence of Israeli aggression" would have to be sought on the basis of no negotiations, no recognition, and no peace with Israel—guidelines that are still in effect.

France and the United States had come to be seen as the props of Israel. Many Arabs viewed the United States as the prime enemy, a new addition to the list of "betrayers." Iraq, whose Jewish community of more than one hundred thousand had fled almost en masse to Israel in 1950–51, had oil in such huge quantities as to compel the good will of the West. To keep Egypt preoccupied with Britain and to arouse public opinion in the West against Egypt, Israeli agents attempted in 1955 to blow up British and American information offices in Egypt. This unusual bungle of Israeli covert operations—exposed as the "Lavon affair"—led to greater tension between Egypt and Israel and helped turn Nasser toward the Soviets. A secret meeting between Britain, France, and Israel—recalling the undercover deals of the former colonial powers—led to the 1956 Israeli invasion of Egypt. It was further proof in Arab eyes that Israel and the West were the common enemy.

Arab Disunity

A common enemy, however, did not produce a common Arab response. After combining into the United Arab Republic in 1958, Syria and Egypt found that Nasser socialists and Syrian Ba'ath socialists could not coexist. After an officers' coup in 1961, Syria withdrew from the alliance. Conservative Arabs again had reason to decry "Egyptian imperialism" when Egypt "helped" establish a republic in Yemen after the death in 1962 of Imam Ahmad, its tyrannical ruler.

The PLO became another divisive factor. Following atrocities such as the massacre of Israeli athletes at the 1972 Olympic Games at Munich, PLO terrorists broke into a reception in 1973 at the Saudi Arabian embassy in Khartoum and seized six diplomats as hostages. (The Sudanese later agreed to free the terrorists, although they had murdered two Americans and a Belgian.) At a 1966 meeting of the Islamic World League in Mecca, King Faisal of Saudi Arabia had put great stress on Arab unity as opposed to Arab nationalism, but his pleas continued to be only a vision. After the Six-Day War of 1967 the Arab underground in general could not agree on its actions and remained as fragmented as the legitimate Arab governments it so often opposed.

The surge of anti-Western feeling aroused by Israeli victories in the 1967 war was not abated by unanimous passage of Resolution 242 by the UN Security Council. The resolution guaranteed the integrity of every state in the war area and called for freedom of navigation in the canal, withdrawal of Israeli forces from occupied territories, and a just settlement of the Palestinian refugee problem. (Of the Soviet bloc countries, Rumania alone refused to condemn Israel in the United Nations.) Also in 1967, an Arab Development Fund was established in Algiers, but at an Arab summit in Rabat two years later the Saudis refused to mix oil policy with policy toward Israel. The "oil weapon" was not actually used by Arab producers until the embargo of 1973–74.

There is much evidence that a solid unity among the factions in the Arab world will not be achieved easily. Oil and Israel are the two issues common to many Arabs. But the oil-producing countries do not always agree on strategy, and the separate Arab governments often fail to support one another's position on the question of Israel. In addition, the PLO—itself a divided organization—is not controlled by any single Arab country or faction.

Changing Arab Lands

Beneath the conflicting currents of Arab disunity, swollen as in the past by powerful rhetoric and long memories, a new spirit of objectivity and even of self-criticism has emerged. Whether or not this change has been fortified by Western ideas, it has begun to have a profound effect on Arab education, especially on the position of Arab women. The survival of the harem and the veil, once symbolized by the neon-lit palaces of conservative Saudi oil princes, has come under extreme pressure by the avalanche of Western influences that descended on the Arab world after World War II.

Polygamy has become rare in all Arab lands. In countries such as Libya women do remain restricted by traditional Islamic customs, but the wives of Anwar el-Sadat of Egypt and of Habib Bourguiba of Tunisia have played important roles in their husbands' politics. The University of Riyadh graduates women doctors, even though they find practice difficult among conservative masses outside the urban centers of modern Arab culture. In Algeria and Libya mass conservatism still supports relegation of women to secondary roles. Male politicians in Kuwait still fight against the emancipation of the young generation of women, many of whom have been sent abroad to college. Under the old-fashioned tyranny of Imam Ahmad in Yemen, girls had no education at all; and progress is still hampered there, as elsewhere, by persistent poverty.

The new freedom many Arab women are beginning to enjoy will undoubtedly have an effect on family mores and on politics. As was true of the past—except for the occasional, and sometimes astonishing, glimpses given by Victorian travelers like Sir Richard Burton—there has been no adequate modern research on sexual matters. There is no adequate method today of measuring how the private world of Arabs has been altered by the various policies of "female liberation." It seems almost certain, however, that changes in the status of women may have a more profound effect on the Muslim of tomorrow than rhetoric, weapons, or even oil wells. As in nearly every other aspect of Arab life, the question "How does the Arab woman respond to her new freedom?" must be answered with other questions: Which Arab woman? In what country? Rich or poor? In a city or in a peasant village? About women, as about other matters, there are few generalities in the Arab world.

Many women in Dhofar, the southern province of Oman, still cover their faces with masks in public (above), and schools for girls (opposite) are still a novelty in this conservative Arab country.

When Henry A. Kissinger became U.S. secretary of state in 1973 and began "shuttle diplomacy" in an attempt to be an honest broker between Arabs and Israelis, the United States and the world confronted an Arab League whose members must always be considered separately. It must also be remembered that changes can be sudden and that statistical and other "hard" information is often impossible to obtain. To the traditional intricacies of Middle East politics have been added the strong, competing presences of the United States and the Soviet Union and the constant activities of underground organizations, as well as civil wars and factional coups. (Between 1949 and 1970, Syria alone suffered twenty more or less violent changes of regime, with consequent changes in the country's relationships with Israel, the Arab states, the Soviet Union, Communist China, and the West.) Violence and fanaticism, however, cannot obscure the steady evolution of the Arab world into the new economic and technological structure of the nuclear age. As this process takes place, the Arab genius for rhetoric—heard in an eloquent stream of revolutionary and nationalistic propaganda from major capitals—retains an immense psychological power.

The geographical boundaries and political leaders and the enmities and alliances of many Arab countries can still change as fast as a headline. Nevertheless, an overview of the Arab countries does reveal certain aspects about them that provide some clues to understanding their present situations and prospects.

Morocco

In spite of the European atmosphere of cities such as Casablanca, the Kingdom of Morocco must still be considered an underdeveloped country. Out of a population of more than seventeen million—nearly half under fifteen years of age—more than seventy percent depend on traditional farming and herding. King Hassan II, who traces his line to the Prophet's son-in-law 'Ali, has immense dynastic prestige among his Sunni Muslim subjects—Berber, Arab, and Negro. Many Moroccan Jews have emigrated to Israel, and a number fled after persecution in 1967.

In 1956 France and Spain agreed to the independence of Morocco. The country became a constitutional monarchy in 1962 and elected its first national parliament in the following year. Under a form of democratic kingship—for Hassan an hereditary monarchy is safer than elections—Moroccans enjoy more free speech and personal liberties than many other Arabs. Wide reforms followed an unsuccessful attempt on the king's life at his birthday party in 1971, a coup led by the king's personal adviser.

Morocco supported Algeria in its struggle for freedom against the French, put three battalions under Egyptian command in the 1967 Arab-Israeli war, and sent more troops in 1973. In 1976 King Hassan consolidated his victories in the "lost territory" of the Western (Spanish) Sahara with a formal division of land between Morocco and Mauritania after withdrawal of the last Spanish forces. Fully supported at home by all political parties, Hassan fought off Algerian troops, which supported a Saharan independence movement.

Although Moroccan history since independence has never been without conspiracy and violence—in 1972 the king's airplane was strafed as he returned from France—Hassan is taking steps toward greater self-government at all levels in spite of economic problems. Exports in phosphates, despite the huge resources of the Saharan territory, have been disappointing; and production of vegetables, the second biggest export, has declined. One-third of Morocco's foreign aid comes from Arab states, and the rest comes from the International Bank, the United States, and Western Europe. After President Sadat of Egypt split the Arab world by opening separate negotiations with Israel in late 1977, King Hassan became the first major Arab ruler to encourage the Egyptian initiative. In return, the King has looked to the United States for military support against the Saharan independence movement. Development of Moroccan agriculture, industry, and tourism continues. An explosive population increase, which began after the French introduced modern hygiene in 1947, is a principal factor in the economy.

The national schools teach in both French and Arabic. Arts, science, and law are taught at the University in Rabat, and Casablanca has a medical school. Islamic studies, especially Koranic law, are maintained at Fes and Marrakesh.

Algeria

The Republic of Algeria, Morocco's neighbor to the east, has an area of almost nine hundred thousand square miles. It is the second largest country in Africa and the tenth largest in the world. In the United Nations and on its own continent, Algeria occupies a key position as a leader of the Third World. After its long cultural association with France—Albert Camus, the Nobel laureate writer, was born and educated in Algeria—the former colony now faces the problem of becoming less French and more Arab, while at the same time advancing in a world dominated by Western ideas. By history, customs, language, and religion, Algeria is properly central to the Arab world.

A landmark date for Algerian freedom was May 1945 when a scuffle between Algerian nationalists, who were celebrating the Allied victory in Europe, and French authorities led to not less than 1,800 deaths. Independence was not actually proclaimed until 1962, after years of bitter warfare.

Proclaimed a one-party, socialist, Islamic republic under President Houari Boumédienne, Algeria has a "plague of bureaucracy" that has been blamed for the slowdown of agrarian reform and industrial development. Its government is authoritarian and often restrictive. (Algeria's first president, the popular Ahmed ben Bella, has been imprisoned since Boumédienne's coup of 1965.) Oil was found in 1957, and Algeria ranks fourteenth in world production. Agreements have been made to supply liquefied natural gas to the United States, France, and Belgium. Although the petroleum industry is expanding, agriculture remains predominant.

The growing population of more than seventeen million is almost all Muslim—eighty percent Arab and nineteen percent Berber.The Association of Algerian Ulama, historically an advocate of freedom from France as an independent Islamic nation, has condemned both the influence of European culture and the superstitions common among the Muslim masses. In the 1930s these views aroused the opposition both of French-oriented Algerians and of Sufi brotherhoods. Today, the psychological struggle between European and Islamic influences marks Algeria's progress as a free country.

President Boumédienne's main problem in foreign affairs is his backing of the Saharan nationalists against Morocco. (Mauritania and Morocco broke off relations with Algeria in 1976, and Moroccan residents in Algeria were expelled.) Relations with France are made more difficult by the presence of many Algerian migrants in French cities and by the large Algerian trade debt owed to France. Although Algeria encourages foreign investment from countries, it remains a loud spokesman for underdeveloped countries against the "industrial superpowers," with most of its criticism directed against the United States. Some consider Algeria a radical and even revolutionary country, and it is experimenting with its own form of Islamic socialism. On the streets of Algiers, however, more women—both young and old—still wear the veil than are to be seen in any Arab capital outside of Arabia.

Algeria contains many of the apparent contradictions that are found throughout the Arab world. It maintains ties with its former colonial master, yet it has become a symbol for nationalists and for independence movements. Algeria emphasizes its traditions while trying to become a full partner in the modern industrial world.

Tunisia

As its leaders often repeat, the destiny of Tunisia is both Mediterranean and African. The nearly six million Arab and Berber inhabitants of this small republic, which became independent from France in 1956, have rather meager resources at their disposal. Relations with France were embittered by the Algerian struggle for independence and reached a low point in 1958 when the French bombed a Tunisian village. With considerable aid from the United States, Tunisia now enjoys excellent economic and diplomatic relations with France and most of Western Europe.

Despite support of a unified "Arab west" in northern Africa, Tunisia charged Algeria with complicity in an attempt on the life of President Bourguiba in 1963 and made the same charge against Libya in 1976. Nonetheless, Tunisia and Libya have agreed to exploit offshore oil deposits in the Mediterranean jointly until the International Court of Justice marks out their respective zones. A treaty of friendship with Algeria was signed in 1970. President Bourguiba's proposals in 1965 for a negotiated settlement with Israel met with such hostility from other Arab states that Tunisia boycotted a meeting of the Arab League. In 1967, however, Tunisia sent troops to Nasser, although they could not reach the Israeli front before the war ended.

Domestic political turbulence did not keep Bourguiba, elected president for life in 1974, from becoming a leading personality in the Arab world. Amid student and union outbreaks, treason trials, and economic disorders, for many years he steered a neatly balanced course between the interests of his Arab neighbors and his European friends. Age and illness, however, have stemmed the flow of ideas with which Bourguiba once challenged Arab leadership. Early in 1978 young Tunisian radicals rioted in the worst outbreaks since independence. Many Tunisians believe that they were inspired by Libyan agents. Politicians are divided into cliques centering around Bourguiba's second wife and the son of his first marriage. At age 50, the son himself is in poor health. In this power struggle, military forces are poised against Libyan intervention. Meanwhile, the unspoiled countryside brings more than $100 million annually from tourism.

Libya

Under Qaddafi, the socialist Libyan Arab Republic exports almost two million barrels of premium light crude oil a day, mainly to Japan and Western Europe. Seeking a "third way" between capitalism and communism, Qaddafi has raised many problems for his Arab neighbors since he and a military junta deposed King Idris in a 1969 coup. Among a predominantly Muslim people numbering nearly two and a half million, Qaddafi has governed through "popular committees," while fomenting radical and revolutionary activities abroad. He has even been suspected of sending supplies to the Irish Republican Army. A scheme for the union of Egypt and Libya was cancelled in 1974 when Egypt charged that Qaddafi had conspired in the bombing of an Egyptian presidential palace. In 1976 Libyan agents were accused by Cairo of renewed bombings and of kidnapping fugitive Libyan politicians. The hostilities with Egypt grew into brief warfare in 1977. Many Egyptians working in Libya left the country, leaving Libya acutely short of skilled personnel. In 1976 Libya was also accused by the Sudan of aiding an attempted coup against its president. Libyan involvement in Lebanese hostilities became clear in the spring of 1976, after Qaddafi had long been suspected of secret payments to left-wing groups in Lebanon. In 1977 Qaddafi supported Ethiopia in its border disputes with Somalia and the Sudan. Libya has occupied and claimed a section of northern Chad that has large uranium reserves and has also supported guerrillas fighting against the government of Chad.

Oil has changed Libya from a poor country to one of the richest in the Middle East. Although Qaddafi has tried to use oil revenues to establish a welfare state, violence has erupted at universities, and Libyan students abroad sometimes have been alienated by his policies. (Students were summoned home in 1975 and 1976 and encouraged to celebrate the anniversary of the Qaddafi government.) Qaddafi has announced a five-year economic plan for 1976-80, involving about $20 billion. Agriculture would receive a major share of the subsidies followed by the development of heavy industry, especially iron and steel. Libya has been able to buy an interest in Fiat, the giant Italian automobile firm.

Qaddafi receives huge amounts of arms from the Soviet Union—$1 billion worth in 1975—as well as the help of Soviet technicians. His acts and statements continue to be brutal and extremist, and whether Qaddafi can win Arab support away from more moderate leaders is a major question for the entire Arab world. A fanatic Muslim puritan, Qaddafi apparently considers Communism as such to be hostile to traditional Islam, even though the Soviet Union is his closest ally. He believes in the natural inferiority of women and in the total destruction of Israel.

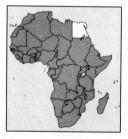

Egypt

The death of Nasser in 1970 marked a turning point in the affairs of the Republic of Egypt. His successor, President Sadat, expelled almost twenty thousand Soviet military advisers in 1972, one year before a Soviet airlift helped in his surprise attack on Israel in the Yom Kippur war. Egypt is the most populous of all Arab states, with more than forty million inhabitants. In the decades after World War II it weathered a series of major crises in its internal and foreign affairs—the 1952 uprising that forced King Farouk to abdicate; continued disturbances from the outlawed Muslim Brotherhood; the Suez crisis of 1956; Nasser's triumph as a leader in Arab politics; and the collapse in 1961 of the ill-fated union of Syria and Egypt. After the 1967 Six-Day War, Egypt broke off relations with the United States, and they were not resumed until 1974. The key position that Egypt occupies as custodian of the Suez Canal and as Israel's on-the-line opponent has colored its volatile relationships with other Arab countries (often mistrustful of Egyptian dominance in the Arab League) and with the Soviet Union, the United States, and the Third World.

In November 1977, Sadat made a dramatic visit to Israel for talks with Menahem Begin, the newly elected Israeli prime minister. An historic event—the first time an Arab government leader had visited the state of Israel—Sadat's "sacred mission" of peace once again threw the Arab world into divided camps. According to the Tunisian foreign minister, Egypt's overtures to Israel made the situation "the most difficult we have ever known." At meetings in Tripoli and Algiers, Palestinians and representatives from Syria, Libya, southern Yemen, and Algeria began to plan strategies to block Sadat's sudden initiative. Egypt recalled its ambassador from the Soviet Union and denounced Sadat's Arab opponents as tools of the Soviets. Diplomatic ties between members of the Arab League were stretched to the breaking point over Sadat's peace proposals. Underground Palestinians were enraged at what they considered a sellout of their interests and resorted again to extremist tactics—including the murder of a "moderate" PLO official in London.

Although no effective Egypt-Israeli dialogue was established in the ensuing months, Palestinian terrorists struck at Israel again on the Sabbath of March 18, 1978. Based in Lebanon, a "suicide squad" in commando boats landed on the coast between Tel Aviv and Haifa. They killed thirty-seven men, women, and children and wounded at least seventy more. (The orgy of violence came on the eve of another visit by Israeli Prime Minister Begin to Washington, where he hoped to reconcile President Carter to his firm position on Israel's occupied territory.) Within a week, Israel raided Palestinian enclaves across the Lebanese border, using arms supplied by the United States. The foundering peace talks, as hard-line Palestinians hoped, were further than ever from fruition.

At home, Egyptians gave their overwhelming support to Sadat. Many Egyptians felt that, while other Arab countries had talked about the wars against Israel, Egyptians had fought them and had suffered the burdens. In some years up to one-third of Egypt's budget has been spent on arms, while the domestic economy has gone from crisis to crisis. (Well aware of his internal difficulties and political opponents, Sadat himself formed the habit of sleeping with a gun under his pillow.) To the Egyptians, however, problems at home have remained paramount.

When Nasser switched on a turbine at Aswan in 1960, the waters of the Nile began flowing through the dam built with Soviet financing and were used for the first time to generate electric power. As Egypt strives to improve education and social conditions, it suffers from the conservatism of farm families who keep children out of school to work on the crops, from a drain of educated specialists toward better pay in other Arab countries and in the West, and from eye disease, hookworm, and other rural afflictions. Progress has been made in stamping out the once endemic diseases of cholera, plague, smallpox, and malaria.

Above all, Egypt must cope with a population increase of one million persons a year, a top-heavy bureaucracy in which a single desk may be manned by four different officials, and massive migration by the poor from the countryside into cities like Cairo and Alexandria. Revenues from canal tolls and development of the Sinai oil fields—given back to Egypt by a 1975 accord with Israel—have not been enough to reform the traditional Egyptian economy. Sadat continues to rely on aid from the United States and the oil states of the Arabian Peninsula and on foreign investments. Aid from the oil states in particular is now linked with developments in Sadat's peace initiative toward Israel. To some Arabs, any peace diplomacy with Israel is equivalent to treason.

President Sadat approved the eventual development of Egypt's single party, the Arab Socialist Union, into a multiparty system. The Young Nasserists, the Muslim Brotherhood, and other dissidents claimed that his plan would not represent their programs or ideologies. In 1977 a military court jailed Muslim sectarians for practicing "sacred terror" and decreed death for their leader, a young agronomist styled as "God's caliph on earth and prince of the faithful." Sadat has silenced left-wing journalists and had political activists arrested. In May 1978, faced by mounting dissension, Sadat announced a referendum on allowing Communists, pro-Soviet politicians, and members of the New Wafd Party to keep their positions. Public strikes and riots have been provoked by rising inflation, overcrowding in the cities, and the visible luxuries of the upper class.

After the Sinai accord with Israel in 1975, Syria, Iraq, and the PLO accused Egypt of putting self-interest ahead of the war with Israel. At conferences of Arab leaders in 1976 at Riyadh and Cairo, Egypt—along with Yasir Arafat, the PLO leader—supported a Syrian peace-keeping force to suppress the civil war in Lebanon. Egypt also announced plans to restore harmony with Syria. Egyptian relations with Libya collapsed after Qaddafi—whom Sadat called "Libya's madman"—was held responsible for bombings in Egyptian cities. Egyptian-Libyan hostilities erupted into brief fighting in 1977. Sadat's claims for aid from other Arab states have been based on Egypt's having shouldered the main burden of the Arab-Israeli wars. This claim has not prevented him from seeking aid in Western Europe, the Soviet Union, the United States, and China. An open-door policy toward foreign investors has bolstered the private sector of the economy.

When he enplaned for Jerusalem and later addressed the Israeli Knesset, Sadat altered forever the relatively moderate role he had formerly played in the crosscurrents of Arab politics. Knowing that the Egyptian people can meet their staggering problems with some chance of success only by avoiding more wars and internal upheavals, he took the enormous risk of launching a unilateral peace program. Like a Bedouin of old seeking to end a blood feud, Sadat made the *sulha*, a visit to the land of the enemy. Whether or not the door he opened with Israel leads to peace, Sadat has changed the course of history for the Arab world.

Sudan

After British and Egyptian troops withdrew in 1956, the Democratic Republic of the Sudan proclaimed its independence. Its population of about eighteen million—Arabs in the north and Negroes of various tribes in the south—is more than seventy percent Muslim. Sudan's impoverished economy is based on dirt farming and nomadic flocks, with limited commercial agriculture and industry in the north. Plagued with political instability, the Sudan has no formal constitution. After eight years of power, President Gaafar al-Nimeiry survived the most serious threat to his regime when two former ministers, who were backed by Libyan arms and money, attempted a coup in 1976. In the wake of this attempt, Nimeiry signed a mutual defense pact with Egypt and began talks with Saudi Arabia—measures aimed at isolating Qaddafi in Libya. In 1977 Nimeiry invited political exiles to return and announced that elections for the national assembly would be held in 1978.

After the Israeli retaliatory attack against Lebanon in March 1978, Nimeiry showed support of Sadat's peace initiative by proposing a new Arab summit meeting to bridge over difference between "moderate" Arab states and "rejectionists" who oppose any settlement with Israel. The Sudan serves as a pipeline for arms for some of its African neighbors and has reached limited agreements with Ethiopia, in spite of the fact that the Sudanese government has supported the Eritrean rebels in Ethiopia.

President Nimeiry's most important domestic problem, like that of his predecessors, is to placate the fears and suspicions of the southern, largely non-Muslim tribes and to end their guerrilla activities. If he succeeds, the Sudan with its mixed population will become a highly visible link between the Arab world and black Africa. The 1972 agreement between Nimeiry and southern leaders of a liberation movement was an important step in this direction. Fired by memories of the Arabs as slave traders, the long hostility between north and south has not disappeared, however, with the signing of papers or with Sudan's membership in the Organization of African States. When pacification does come, the Khartoum government will still have to reckon with the Sudanese Communist party, the most vigorous in the Arab world. The government must also deal with ambitions of the Mahdists, a party led—until he was shot trying to flee to Ethiopia—by the grandson of the leader whose Islamic followers had beaten back the British a century earlier.

Sudanese Muslims often marry Egyptians and study in Egyptian schools. The Nile unites both countries, and if

Sudanese Arabs resent any suggestion of Egyptian domination, they also are bound to their Arab neighbor by their hatred of Israel. With a low literacy rate and few trained college graduates, the Sudan will have much work to do to realize its sound economic potential once its political problems are reduced.

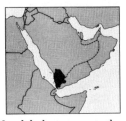

Northern Yemen

Directly across the straits of Bab el-Mandeb that separate the Horn of Africa from Arabia lie northern and southern Yemen. After Turkish defeat in World War I, northern Yemen was ruled in medieval style by Imam Yahya through a generation of frontier quarrels and dynastic intrigue until his assassination in 1948. His sadistic son Ahmad succeeded to the imamate and in 1955 beheaded two of his brothers for conspiring against him. On Ahmad's death in 1962 the palace was bombed, his son fled to the mountains, and, supported by Egypt, the newly appointed chief of staff proclaimed the Yemen Arab Republic. Saudi Arabia supported the exiled ruler and his followers. Chaos continued throughout the 1967 Arab-Israeli war, in which the republicans sided against Israel. In 1970 the republicans and royalists were reconciled, and a constitutional government was established. In 1974 an army coup put the government into the hands of Col. Ibrahim al-Hamdi, who was assassinated with his brother in October 1977. His successor, Col. Ahmed al-Ghashmi, was also assassinated, in June 1978, just two days before the presidential council of southern Yemen, Salem Ali Rubyyi, was ousted in a power struggle with other members of his Marxist regime and then executed with two of his aides.

A population study of this small country produces an "Arab world" in miniature. Of the more than five million inhabitants, more than half belong to Shi'ite sects, the remainder being Sunnis. Mostly peasant farmers and tradesmen, they nearly all fall into four groups. The descendants of the Prophet through the line of Husain form a religious aristocracy. Tribesmen of the original southern Arabian stock form the bulk of the people. In the third group are the merchants, artisans, and craftsmen of the towns. Lastly comes a mixed group, mostly of African descent, that includes former slaves and the "sweeper" class. Added to these are minorities of Indians, Eritreans, Somalis, Turks, Syrians—and recently Egyptians, Chinese, and Russians. It is an astonishingly complex but backward land. Northern Yemen has discovered no oil as yet and has possibly the lowest per capita income in the world. Saudi Arabia supplies financial aid.

The country has received Soviet arms and has discussed buying weapons from both France and the United States. With hopes that the Shell Oil Company will find offshore deposits, relations with southern Yemen have improved despite the usual border incidents commonplace in a peninsula where borders have always been contested. But the prospects of free elections and of unity with southern Yemen were severely set back by the assassinations of 1977 and 1978.

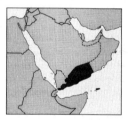

Southern Yemen

Under British protection for over a century, southern Yemen became an independent republic in 1967 after a threat of civil war between rival nationalist groups. In 1970 its name was officially changed to the People's Democratic Republic of Yemen. The capital is Aden, the old "Coalhole of the East" during the imperial age of the British navy. Commerce through this port—more important than the country's threadbare agriculture and a small fishing industry—suffered badly when the Suez Canal was closed from the 1967 war until 1975. Aden also has an oil refinery.

Oriented toward Communist China and the Soviet Union, the country is theoretically a Marxist state. Although Islam is the official religion, the "atheists" of this tiny republic have long been anathema to the Saudi royal family. It is impossible, however, to apply Western political terms, especially in a country that preserves an ancient tribal system and a caste structure reminiscent of India. The sayyids, who claim descent from the Prophet, often own great estates, and some are venerated as saints after death. Together with the sheikhs, also above the tribal structure, sayyids usually live in towns, carry no daggers, and cannot be the subject of blood feuds. A class of black servants is at the bottom.

In 1976 diplomatic relations were established with Saudi Arabia, which provided millions of dollars in aid. A cease-fire also was declared with neighboring Oman, where Yemeni Marxists had been supporting a rebel movement. (The same Marxists are still giving support to Eritrean rebels on the Horn of Africa.) Like Libya, the government of southern Yemen accepts aid from the Soviet Union without endorsing Soviet foreign policy or communizing the country at home. And also like Libya, the independent, unpredictable policies of this republic often infuriate the heads of other Arab states.

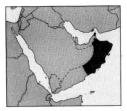

Oman

Next door to the relatively poor inhabitants of southern Yemen, the Sultanate of Oman enjoys oil revenues from production that is expected to yield as much as a million barrels a day by 1979. Because almost half of the national budget is spent on the military, the living standards remain closer to the Middle Ages than to the twentieth century. When Qabus ibn Sa'id overthrew his father in 1970, he freed five hundred of his father's black slaves. The new sultan abolished many of the restrictions of the old regime. The bans on smoking, singing, and the wearing of Western dress were lifted. New projects were announced for the development of the country.

Oman had been a British protectorate since 1798 with a long history of tribal rebellion, court intrigue, and quarrels with Saudi Arabia about borders and oil. In 1960-61 the Arab League and other countries placed the question of Oman before the United Nations. Five years later, after committee investigations and reports, the General Assembly called on

Britain to grant Oman complete independence. The 1970 coup in which Qabus seized power was hailed by many of his subjects, but rebels had begun guerrilla warfare in 1962 and were receiving Soviet and Chinese weapons from southern Yemen.

In 1975 the sultan was able to declare the rebellion virtually finished. He resumed diplomatic relations with Iraq, which had aided the rebellion; and Saudi mediation established a cease-fire between Oman and southern Yemen. Iranian troops, however, were employed by the sultan until 1977 in case of new hostilities. Although handicapped by the suspicion of many Arabs that he is too close to Britain, Qabus has started a program of educational, medical, and commercial improvements that may advance his people from the "romantic" Arab world of the past into a more liberal and modern present.

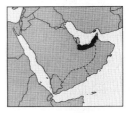

United Arab Emirates

In 1971 the seven states of Trucial Oman—Abu Dhabi, Ajman, Dubai, Fujairah, Ras al-Khaimah, Sharjah, and Umm al-Qaiwain—merged to form the United Arab Emirates, which stretch inland from the Persian Gulf toward indefinable boundaries with Saudi Arabia. Beginning in 1892, these states had a special relationship with Great Britain, but the old treaties have been replaced with a treaty of friendship. The discovery of enormous oil deposits in Abu Dhabi and Dubai began to attract U.S. interests, which were fully nationalized in 1975. Port Rashid, under construction in the 1970s, is likely to become the largest port in the Middle East. With a small population of less than a quarter million persons and huge annual revenues from oil, the inhabitants of the United Arab Emirates enjoy one of the world's highest per capita incomes. Abu Dhabi has the highest per capita income in the world. Petroleum production ranks ninth in the world. The country followed Saudi Arabia's lead in 1977 by limiting its oil price increase to five percent.

Internal disagreements have hampered economic development, but recent projects include natural gas exploitation at Abu Dhabi, along with a new oil refinery and an aluminum smelter in Dubai. As a major financial power, the United Arab Emirates' aid is sought by other Arab countries, especially Egypt. The armed forces consist of about thirty thousand troops, of which a few are said to serve on the Israeli-Lebanese frontier. The new Hilton Hotel in Abu Dhabi reminds the visitor of the power of oil, while boats of the pearl gatherers and fishermen of the gulf are a reminder of the timeless Arab past. The oil sheikhs of this small corner of the peninsula are emerging from that past with shattering economic impact.

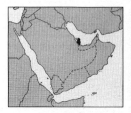

Qatar

The State of Qatar, just west of the United Arab Emirates and the smallest of Arab countries, has been independent since 1971. The discovery of rich oil fields in the 1940s and the advent of Western technology have catapulted this tiny territory from a feudal backwater into a modern monarchy with roads, hotels, modern government buildings, an international airport, and a television network. Industry now includes a fertilizer plant, a cement factory, and a motorized fishing fleet. The former British protectorate has no exact land borders with Abu Dhabi and Saudi Arabia.

With oil revenues of about $2 billion a year, Qatar has undertaken nationalization of all petroleum interests once held by foreign companies, paying the former owners a royalty in return for continued technical services. All Qataris enjoy educational and state welfare benefits under the rule of Khalifah ibn Hamad al-Thani, who deposed his cousin without bloodshed in 1972. (In 1977 Khalifah appointed his son as crown prince.) Oil wealth has been used not only for diversified industrial developments but also for gardening, and Qatar is self-sufficient in vegetables. At the other extreme, in 1976 an earth satellite communications station was installed by the Nippon Electric Company of Japan. Like their Saudi neighbors, most Qataris belong to the Wahhabi sect. But for a 1916 agreement with Great Britain, Qatar might have been absorbed into Saudi Arabia instead of achieving independence.

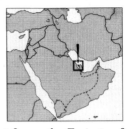

Bahrain

Like Qatar, the group of islands that forms the Emirate of Bahrain became independent from Great Britain in the treaty negotiations of 1971. Oil was discovered in 1932, but relatively little is now produced. The country's present prosperity is due to its central position in the Persian Gulf, its development as a financial center, and an airport that can accommodate the supersonic Concorde airliner.

The ruling Emir dissolved the national assembly in 1975 and faces political unrest, inflation, and diminishing oil reserves. In recent times Bahrain has had to resist annexation by Iran, while its own demands have made federation with other Arab states of the Gulf impossible to accomplish. Many of the people are of Iranian origin, with the Muslim majority divided between the Sunni and Shi'ite branches.

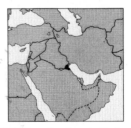

Kuwait

At the upper corner of the Persian Gulf lies the desert Emirate of Kuwait. At its peak in the early 1970s, Kuwait was the fourth largest oil producer in the world after the United

States, the Soviet Union, and Venezuela. In oil reserves Kuwait ranks high among producing countries. Its enormous revenues—more than $7 billion estimated in 1977—make the Kuwait Fund for Arab Economic Development and other aid programs of supreme importance for Kuwait's friends in the Arab world and in underdeveloped countries.

Britain established its official protectorate over Kuwait in 1914 and recognized the sheikh's independence in 1961. Iraq renounced its claims to Kuwait two years later. After thirteen years of parliamentary rule, the national assembly was dissolved in 1976, and press curbs were imposed. The country has been disturbed by repercussions of the Lebanese civil war—especially among the Palestinians in its population, who are estimated to number nearly three hundred thousand —and there have been incidents of bombings and sabotage. The government has maintained a neutral stand in Arab affairs and has joined with Saudi Arabia in mediation between Egypt and Syria. After the death in January 1978 of Sabah al-Salim, the ruling sheikh, power passed smoothly to his successor, Crown Prince Jabir. The new ruler was expected to continue moderate policies and to avoid military showdowns in the Palestinian-Arab-Israeli confrontation. Kuwait has purchased weapons from the Soviet Union, the United States, Britain, and France.

Kuwaitis drink distilled seawater, an expensive necessity, and live and work in air-conditioned surroundings. The old city of Kuwait was bounded until 1954 by a mud wall with gates that led only to an endless desert. It is now a center of schools, hospitals, and office buildings. Engineers, doctors, contractors, and merchants from every corner of the world are busy planning expansion for an already booming metropolis. A large influx of migrants has made the country one of ethnic contrasts—Arabs from neighboring states, Indians, Pakistanis, Iranians, Britons, and Americans. Under British, American, European, and Japanese concessions, oil production has produced a per capita annual income of about $10,-000 and a complete welfare state without taxes. A French company has contracted to build an ice-skating arena, with 2,100 square yards for men, and a separate rink, half the size, for women. Another Kuwaiti diversion will be an amusement park in al-Doga, estimated to cost $172 million. The new generation of Kuwaiti women enjoys a somewhat liberated life-style, despite the large conservative bloc that once dominated the government.

Kuwait was the first Arab country to have abundant revenues left over for investment abroad and may be the first to see its oil reserves run out—something that could happen, according to one report, by 2005. In that event, Kuwait could become the first Arab state to live off its shares in foreign industries. It is a prospect that colors every relationship between oil-producing Arab countries and the industrial countries that are their customers today but may be, in a sense, their investment portfolios tomorrow.

Saudi Arabia

Occupying four-fifths of the Arabian Peninsula—and three times the size of Texas—the Kingdom of Saudi Arabia has matched its size and wealth with its leadership in Arab affairs. By the time of his death in 1953 the patriarchal ibn Sa'ud had launched his country's first medical, irrigation, and flood control programs and had built new roads, ports, and the 300-mile Dammam-Riyadh railway. An airforce was in training, a radio network was in operation, and the schools were partly secularized. Ibn Sa'ud had virtually created Saudi Arabia, but his strict Wahhabi faith remained at odds with the flood of oil wealth that Americanized the life-style and lowered moral standards. The country had been changed beyond all recognition.

Of his sons, Prince Sa'ud ibn Abdul, the eldest, shared his father's simple desert conservatism. His brother Faisal, raised in cities and abroad, stood for the new century. In 1958, after a long rivalry, Sa'ud transferred his powers to Faisal. In 1964, Sa'ud was finally deposed, and Faisal was declared king.

Saudi Arabia has remained pro-West and anti-Communist, despite intervals of disagreement with Western powers. (The Suez crisis of 1956, for example, caused a seven-year break in Saudi-British relations.) Ancient hatreds such as the hostility toward the Hashemite monarchs of Jordan and Iraq have been forgotten in an effort to create a conservative, pro-Western Arab front. Slavery was abolished in 1962. Relations with Egypt often have been strained, since Nasser represented the "left wing" of the Arab world. In 1958 Nasser even accused the Saudis of plotting his assassination.

As Saudi Arabia has continued to become richer and more modernized in recent years, the paradox of the land of Mecca and Medina as the Arab country with the closest ties to the West can be seen in every area of Saudi life. Under Koranic or Saudi tribal law, murderers still lose their heads to the sword. At the same time, television is a major medium not only for entertainment but also for education. Literacy centers abound throughout the kingdom, and by royal decree girls have gone to school since 1960. Saudi students by the thousand attend U.S. colleges.

Billions of dollars are spent on defense, and the more modern Saudi troops are posted in the northwest along the strategic invasion route from Israel. The fierce anti-Israeli attitude of the Saudis was softened in November 1977, however, to allow the first Israeli Muslims in a generation to make the pilgrimage from Jerusalem to Mecca. The token delegation of four men was obliged to travel on Jordanian passports.

Sitting on the world's largest oil reserves and ranking third in production, Saudi Arabia's power is felt from the Persian Gulf to the ends of the earth, wherever oil is used or money is sought for development. Under King Khalid—who succeeded to the throne after the assassination of Faisal by a nephew—Sheikh Ahmad Zaki Yamani has served as the Saudi oil minister and has held down prices. At the same time, he has warned the industrial West that "appreciation" is expected in return for a stable oil market. Appreciation is seen in some quarters as meaning less Western support for Israel. The U.S. Congress is caught between its normally pro-Israel policy and the desire to maintain friendship with Saudi Arabia as a source of oil and as a pro-Western influence in the Arab world.

In uncertain health, King Khalid has allowed Crown Prince Fahd wide powers as deputy prime minister. (Behind the scenes, decisive power at the highest level is wielded by members of the "Inner Six," a council of heads of the six chief branches of the Saud royal family.) Fahd has the usual domestic problems that huge budgets and new programs bring with them. Inflation, profiteering, port congestion, bureaucratic delays and inefficiencies, and shortages in labor and housing are all a thorny part of the current $142 billion five-year development plan. Construction and development continue in every possibly sphere. New sports arenas are planned for Riyadh, Jidda, Dammam, and Mecca at a cost of some $440 million, and another $50 million is to be spent on raising the standard of Saudi soccer teams. A complete take-over, with compensation, of American oil concessions was completed in 1977. Such a move can only accelerate the scope of westernization and the confrontation, or concilia-tion, of the birthplace of Islam with the twentieth century.

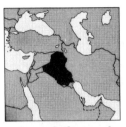

Iraq

Important racial and cultural differences mark the peoples of the Republic of Iraq. Arabs here, a notably homogeneous group, have lived in the central area and in the west and south since very early times. The Kurds, racially akin to Iranians, are located mainly north and east. Together with the kindred Yezidis and Assyrians, Kurds form about eight-een percent of the population. Most of the Arabs and about half of the Kurds are Shi'ite Muslims, but a minority of Sunni Muslims have long held political dominance. Most tribal chiefs and politicians are Sunnis, a chief factor in the uneasy nature of politics in the country that ranks sixth in world oil production. Often independent of other Arab nations, Iraq refused to sign a truce with Israel after the 1948 war.

In 1953 young King Faisal II took the throne after the last British troops had left Iraq, and parliamentary elections were held for the first time. In July 1958 in an army coup the king, the crown prince, and almost all of the royal family were assassinated, and a republic was proclaimed. In its turbulent history since World War II, Iraq has unsuccessfully attempt-ed federation with Jordan and with the United Arab Republic (Egypt and Syria) and has rejected all compromises in deal-ing with Israel. At home the government has been shaken by a series of coups, some led by "Nasserite" officers, and by a virtual civil war against the Kurds.

In the 1967 Israeli war, Iraq threatened to nationalize Western oil companies and did break off relations with Britain and the United States and shut off oil shipments to the West. The Arab defeat intensified Iraq's problems, and in 1968 a coalition group took control in a bloodless coup. This unstable group made wholesale arrests and executions of its political enemies—including "pro-Jewish" spies—and deported large numbers of Iranians. Public executions in 1970 inflamed world opinion and forced the government into yet another round of negotiations with the Kurds. In 1972 Iraq nationalized the oil industry and signed a friendship treaty with the Soviet Union.

In 1975 an Iraqi-Iranian agreement resulted in the collapse of the Kurdish rebellion and the establishment of a long-delayed autonomous Kurdish territory in the north. Kurdish unrest continued, however, and only the future will tell if the Kurds can live peacefully with this settlement or if Iraq can live peacefully with its neighbor Iran. Meanwhile, Iraq has started to invest almost a third of its petroleum revenues and has borrowed huge sums from Japan in return for oil. An almost continuous state of political emergency has prevented Iraq from developing social programs. Students and union leaders are preoccupied with doctrinaire politics. Teaching at the University of Baghdad tends to be dry and abstract rather than practical, and many Iraqi students complete their studies abroad. With a large-scale agriculture potential in addition to its oil, Iraq awaits a full solution to the Kurdish problem and a measure of internal stability before the five-year development plan of 1977 can be realized with any confidence.

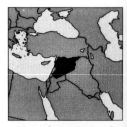

Syria

A great surplus of agriculture resources, its location in the heart of the old Fertile Crescent, and a central position on trade routes have given the Republic of Syria favorable omens for its future. But since independence in 1946, Syrian politics and widespread corruption have prevented the development of Syrian prosperity. After the 1967 war, Israel occupied the Golan Heights, more than four hundred square miles of territory in southwest Syria. About $1 million a day of the budget continues to be used to maintain Syrian troops in the Arab peacekeeping force in Lebanon.

Fundamental to Syrian politics is the presence of ethnic, religious, social, and economic blocs whose efforts to form a workable administration have seldom been successful. Among the Muslims are Alawites (who profess the divinity of 'Ali, the Prophet's son-in-law), Isma'ilis, and Sunnis, the latter including an Arab majority as well as a Kurdish minority. There are Druze communities and large groups of Greek Orthodox Christians. The population is divided among town, farm, and desert tribal people whose goals have little in common. Neither the rich class of landowners and businessmen nor the socialists of the Ba'ath party and its allies—often military officers—have been able to forge a unified structure.

As veteran pan-Arabists, the Ba'aths supported the 1958-61 union of Syria and Egypt until a coup of "rightist" army officers made Syria independent again. U.S. President Dwight D. Eisenhower officially brought the Middle East into the Cold War in 1957 with his "doctrine," ratified by the U.S. Senate, that American troops would resist Soviet aggression in Syria and elsewhere. Interference by pro-Western Iraq in Syrian affairs turned Syrian politicians toward union with Nasser's Egypt and to friendly relations with the Communist world. Egypt paved the way for Syrian rejection of the United Arab Republic, however, by its high-handed dealings with Syrian officials, treating them almost like colonial subjects.

Under the recent government of President Gen. Hafez al-Assad, Syria has won the sympathy of Jordan for its attempt at peacekeeping in Lebanon—a grim situation in which any move Syrian forces make is almost certain to provoke the hostility of the PLO and its friends in the rest of the Arab states. Sadat's visit to Jerusalem provoked Syrian fears of being left in isolation if Egypt made a separate peace with Israel. Although its other Arab relationships—particularly with Iraq—have been shaky, Syria now receives about $1 billion a year from the oil states in return for its adamant opposition to Israel, which only recently began to soften. Jordan and Syria have developed close social and economic cooperation in recent years. Despite friction with the Soviet

Union, Syria is supplied with large quantities of Soviet arms.

Against the day when Middle East oil runs out and water once again becomes the most precious Arab resource, Syria is developing dams and irrigation. The first woman in Syrian history was recently appointed as minister for culture and national guidance. Culture, antiquities, and ruins—and the tourism they can attract to a beautiful countryside—may be another of Syria's most important assets if it can achieve stability with Israel, with other Arabs, and with itself.

Lebanon

Affairs in the Republic of Lebanon provide another dramatic, if tragic, example of the futility of seeing Arab politics in conventional Western terms of "right" and "left." The sources of the civil war that has turned the country into a battlefield do not lie entirely in the presence of some four hundred thousand Palestinian refugees. The conflicts spring more deeply from religious and communal differences within the native population of Sunnis, Shi'ites, and Maronite Christians. Long known as the most literate of Arab peoples with a tradition of free debate on all issues and asylum for dissident minorities, Lebanon approved the secret ballot in 1960 while maintaining a ratio of six Christians to every five Muslims in its national parliament. The country was without an official state religion, but a pact between Christians and Muslims maintained an uneasy balance of sectarian power in the government. In 1958 the pro-Western government of President Camille Chamoun was rocked by Muslim riots in Beirut and Tripoli, allegedly provoked by Syria and Egypt. President Eisenhower landed ten thousand U.S. Marines near Beirut, a coalition government took office with U.S. approval, and in 1961 a coup was crushed and unity temporarily restored. Good relations were maintained with the West and with the other Arabs.

In December 1968 Israeli commandos raided the Beirut airport in reprisal for an attack on an Israeli airliner at Athens, said to have been made by terrorists from a Palestinian camp in Lebanon. The Lebanese government was criticized for its inability to resist Israeli aggression and for attempting to suppress PLO guerrilla movements. Demonstrators clashed with police, and the government resigned. More Palestinians arrived and were met by the Lebanese army, itself split along sectarian lines. The Palestinians were able to establish guerrilla bases from which they launched raids against Israel. As these raids drew renewed Israeli reprisals, Lebanese factions demonstrated for and against the Palestinian commandos.

A new Lebanese government reached an agreement with the PLO, allowing it to attack Israel from specified camps. Five years of attacks and reprisals culminated in a massacre by Christian Lebanese militia of Palestinian bus riders in 1975. Christian Lebanese blocked Palestinian refugee camps, and Palestinian forces attacked Lebanese Christian villages.

In the hope of preventing a partition of the country, Syria intervened in 1976 by allowing PLO forces under its control to enter Lebanon and then by sending in Syrian troops, which opposed the extreme Palestinians and supported the Christian faction. (Other Arab countries had meanwhile supplied arms to groups on both sides.) Casualties mounted into the tens of thousands; Beirut was besieged, stormed, and divided. Efforts of the Arab League to find a peaceful settlement have been frustrated by the divisions within the country itself. Until his assassination in 1977, the so-called Muslim left was led by Kamal Jumblatt, a Druze of an apparently Kurdish family that had been prominent in sectarian Lebanese politics for centuries. The Phalangist right-wing Christian forces have been aided by Israel, and an indication of the complications of the situation is the fact that in many "leftist" guerrilla organizations Arab Christians predominate.

In southern Lebanon Christians have been receiving Israeli military aid since 1976, and some have crossed the border for medical services or to find jobs. When Israel retaliated against the PLO guerrilla raid of March 1978 civilian casualties sent thousands of refugees once more into the Lebanese countryside. Israeli forces, nonetheless, were supported by Lebanese Christians as they occupied a six-mile strip of territory south of the Litani river. A UN peace-keeping force arrived almost at once, although the PLO refused to acknowledge the UN cease-fire. Factions in the battle-scarred area became increasingly hostile and embittered as Israeli soldiers began to withdraw.

More than half a million Lebanese have fled this continuing internal bloodshed and live in exile. Their country is occupied by UN forces, by whatever PLO enclaves were not "cleaned out" in the Israeli reprisal, and by an Arab League peace army of thirty thousand troops, mostly Syrian, posted over more than half of its territory.

Despite the presence of the Arab force, sporadic fighting has continued. If Lebanon must be divided as the condition of a truce between the combatants, it will be difficult to draw boundaries in a country so bitterly divided on ethnic, religious, and political lines.

Lebanese merchants and entrepreneurs have begun the long struggle to rebuild Beirut's businesses and have even restored some of the city's formerly dazzling night life. Dory Chamoun, the son of the former president and himself a leader of the "right wing" National Liberal Party, has demanded total withdrawal of all Palestinian refugees. Lebanon has more refugees than any other Arab state, and Chamoun has declared that his country will not accept permanent Palestinian settlements as the price to pay for the mistakes and plots of other Arabs.

Whatever the outcome, one tragedy is that the intellectual freedom of old Lebanon, which gave the world a literature of Arab nationalism and served as an anvil for new ideas, may take so long to be restored. Banking, tourism, textiles, goods and services—the elements of a precarious but once prosperous economy—meanwhile lie like Beirut in a shambles.

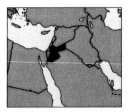

Jordan

The Lebanese catastrophe brought the transfer of much Arab business and a small economic boom to Amman, the capital of the Hashemite Kingdom of Jordan. Within the nominal framework of a constitutional monarchy—with a cabinet and a two-house national parliament—King Hussein I rules a country spare in economic resources but abounding in all the varied political and ideological divisions of the Arab world.

Jordan is not only the neighbor of Syria and Israel but also has become a refuge for thousands of Arabs who have left their homes in the Israeli wars. Its native Arabs, mainly Sunni Muslims with some Christians, are divided along the traditional lines of Qays (northerners) and Yemeni (southerners) and between the Bedouin nomads east of the railway and the settled inhabitants to the west.

Jordan is rich in the most ancient archaeological artifacts and religious associations. Economic aid came first from Britain and later from the United States; more recently aid has come from the oil states of Kuwait, Libya, and Saudi Arabia.

In 1948 British-trained Jordanian troops captured areas of central Palestine including part of Jerusalem, the so-called West Bank of the Jordan River. This action added to the population large numbers of Palestinian refugees hostile to the Hashemite dynasty. Most of the Arab League protested the annexation of Arab Palestine into Jordan. In 1951 King Abdullah was assassinated, his son was deposed because of mental illness, and in 1952 his grandson Hussein was proclaimed king by the parliament. After the Six-Day War of 1967, Israel took over all of the Jordanian territory on the West Bank including the sector of Jerusalem—only about six percent of Jordan's total area but about half of its agricultural land and half of its population.

Internally, Jordanian politics have veered between pro-Nasser, anti-Western cabinets and moderates more aligned to the king's generally pro-Western position. After a wave of anti-British riots, however, Hussein dismissed Sir John Glubb as commander of his troops in 1956. A brief attempt at union with Iraq in 1958 lasted five months.

Border clashes between Israel and Palestine commandos in Jordan were marked by several Israeli attacks in 1965 as reprisals against those places that Israel claimed had supported the underground Palestinian terrorist organization known as al Fatah. The old hostility of many Arabs toward the Hashemite family, radical political shifts within Arab League nations, and King Hussein's policy of trying to restrain PLO guerrillas inside his borders won him the hostility of Palestinians as well as of Syrians and Egyptians, whose radio propaganda urged the king's elimination. It was a cruel position for a monarch who saw himself as symbolizing the Arab revolution for independence and who was a firm advocate of Arab unity.

After talks between the king and the Palestinians broke down in 1970, the Popular Front for the Liberation of Palestine, a Marxist guerrilla group, hijacked three airliners with hostages to an airstrip near Amman. Hussein made concessions to Arafat, the group's leader, after ten days of civil war between refugees and the Jordanian army. Tension continued, however, and Hussein destroyed guerrilla strongholds.

In revenge the so-called Black September group of terrorists killed the Jordanian prime minister outside a Cairo hotel and tried to kill Hussein's ambassador in London. In this period of turmoil, Syria supported the Palestinians against Jordan.

In the 1973 war against Israel, Hussein sent troops to help Syria, but his own borders remained neutral. Despite Jordan's moderate policies, Israel has made no move toward diplomatic discussion of the West Bank. In October 1974, Jordan agreed with other Arab states to recognize the PLO as the official representative of the West Bank Arabs, whom King Hussein—despite years of agitation and terrorism—had so long claimed to be under his own protection.

In the face of another outbreak of war with Israel, Jordan has moved into a limited alliance with Syria and has supported Syrian intervention in the Lebanese civil war. In the aftermath of Sadat's 1977 peace initiative, the king remained silent about prospects of an Israeli agreement but was said to feel extremely pessimistic about the lack of progress.

Hussein has exchanged diplomatic visits with the Soviet Union but has retained his ties with the West, insisting on U.S. participation in a solution to the Arab impasse with Israel. After various interruptions, aid continues from the Arab oil states and the West.

The sole Jordanian port of Aqaba is doubling its trade volume, and billions of dollars are earmarked for a five-year development plan. The fact that Hussein's Jordan—so often isolated and buffeted by the changing fortunes of Arab affairs and torn by its own internal battles—can survive as a moderate force is witness to some ray of hope in the tangled future of the Middle East.

Mauritania

Among the most recent members of the Arab League, the Islamic Republic of Mauritania at the western tip of the Arab world in Africa has been renowned throughout the Muslim world for centuries as a center of learning and culture. Independent of France since 1960, it has resisted Morocco's claims to sovereignty, although some groups in northern Mauritania have supported these claims. In 1976 both countries opposed the establishment of an independent Arab republic in the former Western (Spanish) Sahara, while Algeria recognized the new state. The Arab League and the Organization of African States have attempted mediation.

Meanwhile, in an agreement with Morocco, Mauritania has added a Saharan sector rich in phosphates to its territories, in spite of continuing harrassment by an Algerian-backed Saharan independence movement. President Moktar Ould Daddah has a small population and a weak economy to support his campaign against the Saharan nationalists, the Polisario Party. The government has been forced to spend one-quarter of its budget on arms, with severe economic consequences. With France looking over his shoulder at the valuable phosphates of the Saharan region, President Daddah has continued to be an ally of royalist Morocco against socialist Algeria and the Polisario guerrillas. Mauritania received aid from both China and the United States after the drought of 1973–74. The country has continued to be heavily dependent on French aid and the French air force.

With important mineral reserves, Mauritania may be able to improve its economic situation. Economic progress will depend, however, on a number of factors, including peace and the further development of education. Although Mauritanians have justly maintained pride in their traditional Arabic and Islamic heritages, the government has begun to promote technical education. It is one of the compromises necessary for Mauritania to become a stronger country.

Somalia

On the Horn of Africa jutting into the Arabian Sea, the Somali Democratic Republic (popularly known as Somalia) still suffers from the effects of drought and famine in 1974–75. The Somalis, whose handsome African features suggest an Arab or Semitic strain, have long traded with Arabia, and Islam is the state religion. From 1900 to 1920 British colonial forces were kept at bay by the dervish followers of Mohammed bin Abdullah Hassan, a learned and aggressive Islamic reformist sheikh who was derided by the British as "the Mad Mullah of Somaliland." Somali territories were later contested between Britain, Italy, and Ethiopia; in 1960 the two Italian and British protectorates were united as an independent republic. A political group seized power in 1969 and dissolved the assembly. Somali, spoken by the majority, became the official language. After internal political upheavals, the Revolutionary Socialist Party took over in a bloodless coup planned by the army and the police.

Having inherited boundary disputes originating in colonial times, the government has continued to be enmeshed in border wars with Ethiopia and the newly formed state of Djibouti. Many nomadic Somalis have continued to live in Kenya or Ethiopia. Cooperatives have been set up for destitute former herdsmen and farmers. The foreign aid essential to the impoverished country has come from Britain, Italy, the United States, and the Soviet Union.

The Soviet Union had formerly supplied arms to the Somalis, but in the late 1970's shifted its support to the radical government in Ethiopia. Some of the jet fighters of the Ethiopian air force were made in the United States and are still serviced by Israeli mechanics. They have been supplemented and partly replaced by a huge arsenal sent by the Soviet Union. An estimated 1,000 Russians and a force of more than 7,000 Cuban pilots and ground troops also supported the Ethiopians.

Faced by such massive opposition, Somali President Mohammed Siad Barre was forced to pull his troops out of the disputed territory of Ogaden after a crushing enemy assault in March 1978. The Ethiopian victory brought active hostilities to a momentary conclusion. The Somali army, all but ruined, blamed defeat on the intervention of the U.S.S.R. and Cuba. (In fact, Soviet generals had to restrain Ethiopian troops from pressing further into Somali territory.)

In this complicated struggle, according to the charter of the Organization of African Unity, the Somalis are nominally the aggressors. After its defeat of Somalia, Ethiopia launched an offensive in May 1978 to retain control of Eritrean dissidents on the Red Sea and to avoid a totally landlocked future. Besides having Israeli support, Ethiopia is also backed by Libya and the Marxists of southern Yemen. The "leftist" governments of Syria and Iraq and the anti-Communist governments of Egypt and the Sudan agree in their support of Somalia. With the Soviet Union participating and the United States watching, the struggle on the Horn of Africa has long-term international significance. At the end of 1977, Somalia expelled all Soviet advisors, doctors, and technicians and gave Cuban diplomats forty-eight hours to close their embassy. After the Ogaden defeat the following year, foreigners in the streets of Mogadishu, the Somali capital, were liable to be stoned if they looked like Soviets. The United States issued a cautious word of praise for President Barre's withdrawal from the Ogaden region.

Republic of Djibouti

Formerly the French Territory of the Afars and Issas—but for many years known as French Somaliland—Djibouti became an independent republic in 1977. A popular referendum had overwhelmingly approved independence from France. Djibouti is a small country of less than 9,000 square miles and less than a quarter of a million people. About sixty percent of the people belong to the two African groups of Afars and Issas. There are much smaller groups of Arabs and Europeans. Djibouti is predominately Muslim, however, and in 1977 it became the newest member of the Arab League. Hassan Gouled Aptidon, a leader of the independence movement, was elected the country's first president. He appointed a government that preserved Djibouti's ethnic and political divisions. Terrorism during 1977 was blamed on an Afar movement, and four Afar government officials resigned in December.

Djibouti lies just south of the straits of Bab el-Mandeb at the entrance of the Red Sea—an immensely strategic location. Commerce through the port of Djibouti is perhaps the country's greatest potential for economic development. In 1977 the war in Ethiopia severely affected the Djibouti economy. Rail traffic with Ethiopia was stopped, and the port dues of Djibouti dropped fifty percent. Both Ethiopia and Somalia are interested in the vital port facilities of Djibouti, and the two neighbors' rivalry has created uncertainty and unrest in Djibouti in recent years. In 1977 Djibouti signed cooperative agreements with France, and a small French force remained in the country to train Djibouti soldiers. Because it is located in an area of unrest and because it has a weak economy, Djibouti is likely to retain close ties to France for many years.

The Palestine Liberation Organization

The decision to admit the PLO to the Arab League was taken at a meeting of league foreign ministers in Cairo as PLO leaders were urging the Arab states to halt the fighting in Lebanon. The original Palestine National Congress convened in the Arab sector of Jerusalem in 1963. It proclaimed a Palestinian National Charter, organized camps to train refugee Palestinian boys, and formed the PLO. (As many as ten Palestinian underground groups, divided by politics and tactics, have since joined in commando and terrorist activities against Israel and those suspected of Israeli friendship.) At a 1969 meeting of Palestine guerrilla (or fedayeen) leaders, Arafat was made PLO chairman. The radical Popular Front for the Liberation of Palestine, the Marxist group, withheld its cooperation.

Although originally a sponsor of terrorist raids, Arafat—in contrast to his more extreme associates, many of whom are

Beirut's Holiday Inn was one of the casualties in the Lebanese civil war that began in 1976.

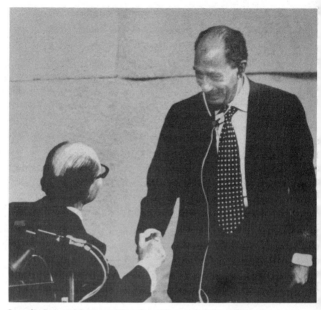

Israel's Prime Minister Menahem Begin (left) and Egypt's President Anwar el-Sadat shake hands after Begin responded to Sadat's address to the Israeli Knesset in November 1977.

dedicated to the destruction of Israel—has taken a comparatively moderate position in stressing Palestinian territorial claims. Using the United Nations as a forum, he has walked a difficult tightrope between the extremists of his own party and Arab leaders like King Hussein, who have found being host to the Palestinians a dangerous form of hospitality. In 1974 the United Nations invited the PLO to take part in a debate on the Palestine question—over the lonely opposition of Israel, the United States, Bolivia, and the Dominican Republic. Arafat told the UN General Assembly, "I have come bearing an olive branch and a freedom fighter's gun."

Although many nations have met with or recognized the PLO, the position of the United States as a leading supporter of Israel remains crucial. Efforts to ease tension between Israel and one or another of the Arab countries—seen in the diplomacy of Kissinger after the 1973 war—have not been welcomed by the PLO. Al-Fatah, Arafat's own guerrilla group, attacked Tel Aviv in 1975 in order to make the United States and the world aware again that no diplomacy in the Middle East could succeed without PLO assent. The Lebanese-PLO crisis split Arab leadership as Arafat attempted to reach a settlement in 1976. Saudi Arabia, with its vast economic power, has done its best to find means of accommodation, mainly by increasing the Arab peacekeeping force in Lebanon to thirty thousand men.

At the onset of Sadat's personal negotiations with Israel in 1977, the question of the Palestinians again revealed divisions within the Arab states. History shows, however, no reason why Arab governments should share identical views any more than do the governments of Europe. The path to another full conference on the problems of the Middle East, including the future of the Palestinians, might best be prepared for by head-to-head bargaining in the style of Sadat. After the Palestinian terrorist raid of March 1978 and the Israeli reprisal attack on Lebanon, Arafat showed a hard line toward UN peace-keeping forces. Hardly a month later, however, he claimed that Israel would have nothing to fear from the creation of a Palestine homeland on its western border. Despite fears that the Soviet-supported PLO would be a constant source of future trouble in a Palestinian state, Arafat argued that the new country would have to "start from zero" and would be too busy getting on its feet to be a threat to a "realistic settlement" with Israel. Israelis were unconvinced.

The Heritage and the Future

Arabs today live in every kind of culture, from "backward" to "advanced." There is no "average Arab," any more than there is an "average European." In the common tradition of a great heritage, however, there is much that Arabs can use in solving the problems they share with the rest of the modern world—to say nothing of the question of Israel and of mutual Arab conflicts.

The riches of Islamic history can be a source of fraternity as well as hostility, of wisdom as well as of destructive pride. Whether Arabs can find common roads toward their difficult goals is an awesome question for the coming generations.

10.
Today and Tomorrow

From Dammam on the Persian Gulf a refurbished stainless steel train carries passengers three hundred and fifty miles across Saudi Arabia to the terminal at Riyadh. The tracks were laid down for King Sa'ud by the Arabian American Oil Company and run through some of the kingdom's richest oil fields. The diesel-electric engines are built to withstand the sun and sandstorms; the dining cars have microwave ovens. It is the only operating Saudi railway, for after guerrilla raids during World War I, the old Medina line was never repaired. Especially popular with Arabs during the pilgrim season, the line carries a hundred and seventy thousand passengers a year. Tickets are actually cheaper than they were in 1936 when the trains, known as Burlington Zephyrs, were on their original run between Denver and Chicago. The air-conditioned ride is more luxurious today than it was in the past.

Even closets are air-conditioned in the modular housing units supplied to American workers by their employers in Saudi Arabia. Americans cannot buy land outright from Saudis—when Americans drill for water they sometimes strike oil—but the Saudi who leases his land can quickly get a fifty percent return on his investment. In the next two decades perhaps fifty thousand more of these prefabricated houses will be shipped to the Arabian Peninsula. An Arab buyer need only add a guest bath and an extra wall for his women's privacy in order to preserve the custom of the Prophet. If there is any conflict between an air-conditioned technology and the ancient practice of Islam, it has not noticeably inhibited the astute dealings of Saudi princes and their family friends with Western businessmen.

The Impact of the West

While luxuries, innovations, and industry and technology arrive day after day in the ports of rich Arab countries, relatively poor nations like Tunisia and Morocco must import basic necessities, including weapons, from the *jinni* of the West. (The time, a thousand years ago, when Arab goods surpassed anything manufactured in Europe has vanished into fable.) In colonial days the *jinni* demanded a high price—exploitation or even submission—for their wares. Today the sophisticated middlemen who negotiate with Westerners on behalf of their Arab superiors can bargain with confidence over any table. No matter how great their skill, however, they cannot control the invisible exchange that still rules the marketplace of ideas. The conflict between Islam and Christendom may never end, as many Arab nationalists believe, but if Islam is to survive such a struggle, it must avail itself of Western ideas as well as Western machines.

The Arabic poet who writes on contemporary themes must graft Western expressions onto desert traditions—a process long since begun with the Arabic literary revival and with modern Arab nationalism. The Saudis, conservators of the heart of Islam, realize that they cannot confiscate Western ideas at the customs office. The French government's Radio Monte Carlo has one of the most powerful Arabic transmitters in the Middle East, heard clearly along the Mediterranean and audible from Baghdad to Libya. Its news broadcasts and pop music—all in Arabic—are peppered with commercials for cameras, radios, watches, and household goods. (Japanese sponsors buy nearly all of the advertising time.) The station's most serious competitor for listeners is the British Broadcasting Corporation's transmitter in Cyprus. The British programming reflects an increasing Arab appetite for Western culture, an invisible export of far greater impact than a few British troops and tea tables along the Gulf of Aden. Among the rich but still largely uneducated populations of Bahrain and Kuwait, almost every household has a television set, and a score of local advertising agencies produce commercials for imports like English toiletries, Australian beef, and Japanese automobiles. After an interval of more than ten years, an Arabic *Reader's Digest* has resumed publication and circulates in twenty-two countries.

The westernizing of Arab music, literature, and art is not drastically new—it could be noted as early as the 1900s—but modern communications have speeded the pace. The Arab painter who seeks to work in today's idioms must make a break with the Arab past. If human figures are painted or sculpted, it is a break with tradition, even though the Omayyad caliphs broke the same tradition long ago. A modern Arab writer speaking to his own generation must forge ahead, either adapting Western forms or creating a new Arabic style of his own. For an Arab artist loyal to his own culture—in which the mosque tradition of a scholar surrounded by his disciples retains a powerful position—innovation often carries with it a certain sense of uneasiness regarding the West, the prime source of novelty for the modern Arab. It was only yesterday that most Arabs were educated in the rote learning and medieval attitudes of the *ulama* schools. Some modern Arabs have begun to value separation of the *ulama* and the state—the creation of a secular society—as a benefit equal to modern technology itself. In fact, the psychological difference between what is professed and what is believed is probably now as much a part of ordinary Islam as of ordinary Christianity. Many Arabs must, however, still fight the old battle between reason and revelation. Such a battle easily assumes the appearance of the West against Islam and leaves numbers of Arab intellectuals anti-Western in politics but pro-Western in a cultural sense.

At heart, even an Arab most at home in the streets of London or most advanced in the study of American medicine can feel that the West is the eternal foe of his race. Western values, insidious and invisible imports, are seen as the cause of any or all Arab grievances. Even the devoted and sympathetic scholarship of Western Arabists is suspect—another skein in a web that could ultimately destroy Islam. The fear exists despite efforts of Western Arabists to rid themselves of the prejudices of an earlier generation of scholars, all too quick to invoke some mysterious and irrational "oriental" quality in the Arab soul or to see the romantic Bedouin of the desert as typical of all Arabs.

Conflicts among Arabs

An educated Arab today is, however, likely to have parents or grandparents brought up in the Bedouin tradition. Besides speaking a European language, the modern educated Arab can be acutely aware of the difference between his own language, close to classical Arabic, and the local dialect of his community. To the split between the West and Islam is added a cultural split between the educated elite and an uneducated majority, evident at once in the spoken tongue. (Many Arab leaders look forward to developing a "middle language" between the classical Arabic of the Koran and dialects of ordinary conversation—a pan-Arabic dialect of the future.)

Quite obviously, the cultural conflict between a literate minority and the illiterate masses is not one that affects most Arabs. No longer nomadic in their daily habits—about ninety percent of today's Arabs live in towns or villages—many Arabs are in danger of losing the spirit of ancient Islam as they become urbanized. In the age of their decline, most Arabs forgot that they had a royal past. Now the problem arises again, not from defeat and poverty, but from schools and education. One modern observer has warned that Arabs, the most nostalgic of all Muslim peoples, might lose the splendors of their oral tradition once preserved in tenacious memories as their children depend more and more on the printed word.

The Israeli Presence

Another psychological conflict is created by Israel, that highly visible symbol of the West close to the heart of the Arab world. Interrupted only by the open hostilities of 1967 and 1973, the business of tourism between Israel and its Arab neighbors continues. The "open bridges" policy of the Israeli government is a typical enigma of the Middle East. By the hundreds of thousands, especially during summer, students and families from Arab countries visit the Jewish republic. Signs of the West—of its institutions, science, and industry—are everywhere to be seen. They are overwhelming evidence of Israel's success as a state. Besides seeing Israel at firsthand, many Arabs read translations of Israeli books and listen to broadcasts from Jerusalem, Tel Aviv, and Haifa.

Israeli politicians, both left and right, engage in passionate debate on every topic, including Prime Minister Menahem Begin's personal diplomacy with Egyptian President Anwar el-Sadat. In April 1978 members of Israeli's "Peace Now" movement were able to demonstrate by the thousand, in complete freedom, against Begin's "uncompromising" foreign policy. Although new Jewish settlements in the occupied West Bank and in the Sinai Peninsula continued at the risk of stern disapproval from the United States, the settlements remained a highly visible sign of Israeli confidence. In occupied territory at the tip of the Sinai Peninsula, Israeli engineers started oil production in defiance of official American advice against exploitation of offshore resources. When in 1976 Palestinian highjackers forced an Air France jet with Jewish passengers as hostages to land in Uganda, the dramatic rescue by Israeli commandos at the airport at Entebbe won worldwide admiration.

As much as a Hilton hotel built on an oasis in the United Arab Emirates, the Israeli life-style exemplifies the Western notion of progress. The idea runs directly counter to the old Islamic doctrines of predestination and fatalism that are said

Modern high-rise buildings stand along the age-old trading routes of Kuwait. Although cities in the Middle East are rapidly being modernized, land transportation is still often difficult because of the lack of adequate roads.

to impede Arab planning and Arab progress. Contentment with the blessings of the day and tranquillity in the face of hardship are part of the gift of Islam. Suicide is rare. The Protestant work ethic, with its ulcers and materialist ambitions, has not been one of the imports from the West or from Israel. Like a Bedouin in the days of the Prophet, many Arabs find manual and farm labor degrading, one of the trials of the human condition not unlike God's curse upon Adam. If work with the hands is something to be left to subject races, slaves, and inferior beings, however, it is all the more difficult to get an automobile engine repaired or to maintain a refinery. Tomorrow's technology will depend on skills that do not yet seem desirable as such to the Arab workman, skillful though he may be in other respects. Here again, Israel provides a sharp and irritating contrast.

Another contrast is evident in the position of women, even

as it changes for the better. (Although Western philosophic works are available in Arabic, the only writing of the nineteenth-century German philosopher Arthur Schopenhauer translated so far is his diatribe against females.) The time may be past when an Arab male would refuse to sit with women at a social function. But like the manual worker, women will have to rise to a higher level in Arab society before the average Arab himself rises to the level of the progress he sees in Israel and the West. Old convictions of masculine superiority and old bonds of male friendships, the nostalgic sexual isolation of the desert warrior, are still a striking anachronism compared with the everyday life of Israel and with the life that Arab men and women enjoy abroad. Many conservative Arabs, however, even those whose wives and daughters are educated, see modern reforms in the role of women as a virtual threat to their honor. Muslim women, even those who most desire liberation, instinctively feel that such changes are a threat to the security of their Islamic heritage. In caring for male patients in a modern hospital, for example, a female Arab nurse faces cultural problems for which there are no easy remedies.

The Arab Sense of Honor

Wajh, the Arab sense of honor so often concentrated in the purity of a man's female relatives, has been compared to the Japanese notion of "face." (Although both the Japanese and the Arab historically went to extremes to regain lost honor, the Japanese often killed himself; the Arab, somebody else.) In a culture in which so many points of honor rest upon female virginity and family kinships, where memory survives of northern opposed to southern tribes, where family authority is patriarchal, the relaxed ways of Western education and society can have a disturbing impact. The father figure is reflected in authoritarian systems of government, and kinship loyalties show themselves in political parties. These patterns are hardly unique to Arab society but are inevitable among peoples whose worst insult involves a charge of mixed blood and who can still trace whole tribes back to a single ancestor.

Electoral politics are not easy in any culture in which the loser's relatives are willing to use arms to avenge a defeat at the polls. The very notion of defeat is intolerable if it means loss of face for a family, a clan, a tribe, or a nation. More than most politicians, the Arab leader must be able to promise victory next time—even if victory means nothing more than vengeance at the price of national or party unity. Confronting this mixture of face, kinship, ancestral memories, and politics, few nations are in a position to judge the Arabs harshly. The advance of republican government is an even greater achievement where the sense of history itself can be a handicap.

The Arab Mind

In the modern political world, the ideal of pan-Arabism itself —as opposed to the religious mystique of Islam—is hardly two generations old. As seductive as always, Arab rhetoric remains rooted in tribal rivalries. Its emotive power, its force of exaggeration, its ease of blending wish and reality—all help resist the impact of Western uniformity, the view of reality that links causes with effects to create a precise technology. The tide of Arab rhetoric carries the listener from one individual moment to another. (The intricate, isolated sections of Arab music, without the climaxes and finales that give coherence to a Western symphony, illustrate the same trait.) Such an absorption in particular moments—a great help to Arab scientists in taking their experiments far beyond what was achieved in Greece and Rome—leads at the same time to a lack of overall unity. In much Islamic art and Arab politics, the parts are seen as separate entities although the design of the whole may be less evident.

The absence of a unified vision has been termed "atomism" by H. A. R. Gibb, the distinguished twentieth-century British Arabist. Atomism cannot, of course, be said to be characteristic of every Arab mind, but it is a key psychological feature of Arab culture. As such, atomism not only makes the rhetoric of politicians less "rational" in the Western sense but also must be reckoned with in Arab attempts to balance political unity against local loyalties.

Open Conflict

Islam itself has proven to be no more a unifying political force for the Arabs than has Christianity or Buddhism for other parts of the world. Muslim Iran, for example, presses claims along the Persian Gulf and against the United Arab Emirates and provokes hostility as far away as Libya. The memory of their own Saladin, who founded the Ayyubid dynasty in the twelfth century, is stronger than the voice of the Prophet when non-Arab Kurds confront their Iraqi neighbors. Mohammed Iqbal of Pakistan, the great modern prophet of Islamic unity, died in 1938 after having acknowledged the impossibility of his ideal. (The 1971 civil war between the Muslims of West and East Pakistan confirmed his pessimism. Algeria, Libya, Saudi Arabia, and Jordan declared Islamic solidarity with West Pakistan against the Bengali Muslims of Bangladesh in the east.)

No less than did President Gamal Abdel Nasser of Egypt, Col. Muammar Qaddafi of Libya has proclaimed a vision of Islamic-Arab unity under the rule and justice of the Prophet, but this led to open hostilities with Egypt after Nasser's death. At the same time, Libya encouraged Muslim guerrillas in the Philippines and served as a mediator on behalf of the Moro National Liberation Front. Qaddafi's pan-Islamic program seems to call for worldwide revolution. His anti-Egyptian tactics, meanwhile, have been denounced as a setback to Arab solidarity by the Arab League. Yet Qaddafi and the league played an effective role as mediators when northern and southern Yemen were on the verge of war in 1972. The historic gift of the Arabs for mediation and arbitration has failed to bring Iraq solidly into the framework of Arab states. The historic "tribal democracy" practiced in true Koranic spirit by King Faisal of Saudi Arabia could not save him from the fatal attack of a nephew. Like the Irish, the "nation of Arabs" has not yet found a way out of fraternal strife. Arab unity remains in the tactical stage.

Despite centuries of cultural coexistence—Syrians in the town of Maloula still speak the Aramaic of Christ—certain minorities like the Palestinians of Kuwait turn to bombs and sabotage. In Lebanon students on the Beirut University campus seem split more than ever into Christian and Muslim factions, even as Beirut shopkeepers attempt to restore normal trade amid the ruins of shellfire. Nearly all of the large hotels that were used as bases by Muslim or Christian factions were reduced to rubble. Although half an hour away on the Bay of Jounieh the gambling tables at the Casino du Liban were miraculously undamaged and although jet flights have resumed to Beirut's airport, the troubled city has a long way to go before recovery. After dark, customers go to the movies and sit in cafes. Few, however, dare cross the invisible border between Christian and Muslim sectors. As in so many conflicts of the Middle East, the streets of Beirut will probably not be safe until outside intervention is at an end. The solution will require cooperation among the bordering Arab states and among the moderate Palestinian factions.

Militant Muslim extremists—whether political, like the Egyptian students who rioted against Sadat in 1973, or religious, like the terrorists who were tried in Cairo in 1977—continue to threaten Islamic and Arab unity. Disunity among opponents can actually be welcomed at times by Arab leaders. King Hussein of Jordan, for example, was not unhappy when radical Ba'ath politicians failed to achieve union between Syria, Iraq, and Egypt in 1963. While not on the wane, extremism and faction have not been able to prevent today's useful understanding between Egypt and Saudi Arabia. Leaders of the Arab League see much to be gained in a balance of Egyptian military power and the economic power of Saudi oil. Economic cooperation is a prime Arab objective, often discussed and often advanced at Arab summit meetings. The same leaders have little difficulty in seeing the ancient model of Arab arbitration as more sensible than the overkill strategies of the West and the Soviets.

Nonetheless, weapons constantly pour into the Arab world, supplied by the United States and Europe or by the Soviet Union, according to the exasperating shifts of alliance that have characterized the Cold War's presence in the Middle East. After prolonged debate, and against Begin's persistent appeals, the U.S. Senate narrowly approved President Carter's package plan to sell the most advanced American jet fighter planes to Saudi Arabia and Egypt as well as to Israel. This action, in the spring of 1978, came as another blow to the Israeli prime minister, whose opponents have accused him not only of bungling President Sadat's peace overture but of eroding the traditional ties between Israel and Washington. The future of peace in the Middle East still depends on Soviet strategy and American domestic politics as well as on the Arabs' own progress toward unity and toward negotiations with Israel. On an even broader scale, detente between the United States and the Soviet Union is seen by some Arabs as a threat to the tactic of playing off capitalist against communist in the Middle East, and in the underdeveloped Third World with which most Arabs are allied. Even such an unpredictable Muslim ally as President Idi Amin of Uganda is said to receive a vital flow of arms and cash from Saudi Arabia, Libya, Kuwait, and the United Arab Emirates. (Another black ruler, Jean-Bedel Bokassa of the Central African Empire, converted to Islam in 1976 in the hope of receiving Libyan aid. When the aid did not arrive, he crowned himself Emperor Bokassa I in December 1977 in an extravagant ceremony that included a Roman Catholic high mass.)

Marxism, Capitalism, and Socialism

Although the Soviet Union is still the leading exporter of weapons to Arab governments, its failure to export Marxism to any degree is significant for the future. After World War II, Marxist Arabs tried to identify their cause with Arab nationalism. They hoped to propagandize the war against Israel as a popular struggle leading to a general revolution. Israel's victory in 1967 was blamed on Arab failure to follow the doctrines of Marxist thought. Such arguments, however, ran counter to Muslim tradition—"backward" and "stagnant" in one view or, in another, rooted too deeply in the Islamic past to accept the atheistic message of Communism. The People's Democratic Republic of Yemen rests on theoretical Marxist foundations, but the fact remains that few Arabs are Marxists or Communists, no matter what their relationship may be with China, the Soviet Union, and Eastern Europe.

Marxist radicals and rebels may be found in Arab capitals, but they are Arabs first and Marxists second. Even conservative Arab leaders took a dim view of Qabus of Oman when he used British troops against Marxist guerrillas who, after all, were Arabs. Conservatives in the Saudi government are also Arabs first and capitalists second. They have not reached the point of invoking a Soviet alliance as a counterpart to U.S. aid to Israel. They do, however, see the westernization of their country, largely American in tone, as a threat to the puritan style of their faith.

More important than modern ideologies, and perhaps as important as Islamic tradition, are the hard economic factors of Arab life. The non-Marxist Yemen Arab Republic can round up fewer than a hundred camels. The country has fewer than three thousand students in higher education, and many of its people chew the kat leaf as a narcotic against poverty. In this situation Yemeni leaders are less interested in theoretical politics than in where their countrymen are going to find a helping hand. There is no ideological reason to prevent Yemenis from buying arms from France, the Soviet Union, and the United States, from announcing their intention of unifying the republic with the Yemeni Marxists, or from accepting aid from conservative Saudi Arabia.

Given this kind of practical economic necessity—and taking into account factors such as overpopulation, malnutrition, and disease—it is difficult to envision a textbook line of development in the Arab world, whether the text is by Marxists or capitalists. Where would a Marxist class war begin in the Arab world? With the legendary peasant farmer—eternally oppressed, religiously fanatical, and fatalistic? It is difficult for a Marxist to find weapons against capitalism in any part of the Islamic legacy, including the Koran or the traditions derived from Mohammed. Nonetheless, some Arab Marxists believe that economic factors alone will prevail, that a class war will take place, and that revolution will bring down all the trappings of the old Arab world, including Islam.

Against this prediction of Marxist triumph, other observers see some type of socialism in the Arab future. Predictions range from the paternal socialism of a welfare state that is also a kingdom or dictatorship to democratic socialism along Scandinavian lines. If socialism does develop in the Arab world, however, it is unlikely to be a classic textbook socialism that repudiates Islam and chooses friends and foes according to ideology. Whatever name Arab socialists might choose to adopt, their policies would probably be Islamic and, almost certainly, Arabic.

Petrodollars

Arab oil knows no ideology, and for the moment the petrodollar makes its own rules. (As shown at the Organization of Petroleum Exporting Countries [OPEC] meeting at Qatar in December 1976, however, Arab oil states can be deadlocked over just what these rules should be.) The Arab Monetary Fund—a counterpart to the International Monetary Fund—uses oil revenues to capitalize new Arab developments and hence determines the flow of both skilled and unskilled migratory workers between Muslim lands as far away as Morocco and Malaysia. Persian Gulf oil provides cheap power that makes possible the use of raw materials too low-grade, like the aluminum of Bahrain, to be profitably exploited elsewhere. Cheap power pays for extracting magnesium, sodium, and chlorine from coastal lagoons and can eventually help pay for solar-powered desalination plants to provide supplies of fresh water. The bill is ultimately passed along to the oil-consuming nations, headed by the Western industrial countries and Japan.

Petrodollars have also given Arabs a huge stake in Western banking systems, with about $50 billion deposited in U.S. banks alone. Whether Arab leaders try to use these reserves to influence Western policies depends on whether an immediate tactic seems more important than the general prosperity of the Western countries in which Arabs are building up large investments. Arab politicians are aware that some day their oil will run out and that not much more major exploration remains to be done in Arab countries. (Israeli oil exploration in the occupied Sinai Peninsula is off to a promising start and is considered to be a negotiating chip for Israeli diplomats.) Meanwhile, Arab buying from the West and from the Soviet Union, Japan, and China goes on at such a pace that some economists estimate that, far from holding a massive balance of the world's capital reserves, the Arab oil states may drastically drain their petrodollar holdings by 1980.

Modern Problems

As is the case everywhere in the Third World, economic development in Arab countries can be a mixed blessing. The Aswan Dam brings snails carrying intestinal parasites, along with floods of fertile Nile water, but some nomadic tribes along the widened riverbanks have had their way of life destroyed forever. Conservationists often oppose projects such as swamp drainage in the Sudan, which would decrease rainfall and spell disaster for adjacent Dinka tribesmen. It is no easier to divert the progress of technology in Arab lands, however, than it is on the shores of Lake Michigan.

The military weapons Arabs buy cost huge sums of money, but the damage these weapons do adds another cost—repairs. Rebuilding Beirut, for example, will cost almost $1 billion, according to a new master plan. Some of the expense will be covered by European and American aid, but much will have to come from Arab sources. Reconstruction in all of Lebanon may cost as much as $5 billion.

In war or peace, most Arab countries have population problems. Not necessarily on the scale of Mexico, the problems are nonetheless acute in some areas. If, as statistics predict, Egypt doubles its population in the next generation, neither the Aswan Dam nor any other current project will be sufficient to prevent an increase in poverty and an exhausted country. The *ulama* have given official approval to birth control—Islam forbids abortion—but conservative village sheikhs reflect the attitude of farming peoples everywhere in Arab countries. They may pass along what government and religious leaders say about the need for birth limitation then and add bitterly, "God forgive them!" Like the specter of war itself, the birthrate for Egypt and other countries is a potential time bomb in the Middle East.

Economic Weapons

The shock once predicted if Arab governments nationalized foreign oil companies has not materialized. The minds that historically kept business flourishing in Cairo, Aleppo, and Damascus have proved capable of taking over the oil refineries. Iraq, Kuwait, Saudi Arabia, and Iran have successfully taken this revolutionary step. Nationalization has been of immense leverage not only in setting prices but also in maintaining the Arab boycott of unfriendly powers—a weapon first used after the establishment of the state of Israel in 1948 but not employed effectively until the oil embargo of 1973. Individual companies, especially in the United States, have been boycotted on a selective basis, along with entire small countries like Denmark and the Netherlands.

The Arab League empowers a commissioner general to blacklist foreign businesses trading with Israel and has recently added "all raw materials"—presumably phosphate, manganese, cotton, and natural gas—as subject to the same embargo as oil. Arab economic weaponry has created intense problems for American businessmen. They may wish to support Israel, but they must act in the overall interests of their companies. In its effort to find an antiboycott law that would limit American compliance with Arab demands, the U.S. Congress has been pressured both by pro-Arab oil companies and pro-Israel businessmen. The imprecise bill that was passed in 1977 required "the judgment of Solomon" from companies dealing with Israel and the Arabs. Revised regulations adopted in January 1978 were somewhat more tolerable.

Dealing with Israel

Another form of attack on Israel has been the Arab effort to condemn Zionism as a Jewish brand of racism. In 1975 the UN General Assembly voted to denounce Zionism as "a form of racism and racial discrimination." (Some delegates who supported the resolution privately apologized for their action.) Arabs have also raised the Zionist issue as part of the United Nations' "Decade Against Racism," a program begun in 1973. The notorious *Protocols of the Learned Elders of Zion,* first printed in Russia in 1903 and exposed as a forgery in 1921, is still circulated by Arabs as proof of a Jewish

Members of a Jewish settlement on the West Bank of the Jordan River prepare to begin a new life, while an Israeli soldier stands guard nearby.

conspiracy to destroy Christian civilization and to turn the world over to Zionists and Freemasons. On the thirtieth anniversary of the state of Israel, the Soviet press in May 1978 scathingly characterized Zionism as imperialist, racist, and reactionary—"the enemy of the whole of mankind." Israeli settlements in occupied territory on the West Bank are seen as further proof of Israeli imperialist ambitions. Saudis seem especially vigorous in the cause of anti-Semitism.

Free elections recently allowed West Bank Palestinians to throw out their old-fashioned mayors and councilmen and to elect more radical anti-Israeli politicians. The Arab minority living in Israel, although many enjoy a better standard of life than Arabs elsewhere, consider themselves as second-class citizens at best. Israel's war victories make it a country of ten thousand square miles at present, as opposed to the five million square miles of Arab territories. The Yom Kippur war of 1973, however, showed that Israelis still commanded battlefield superiority, even when caught by surprise and opposed by effective Egyptian forces. Arabs have no illusions about Israeli arms, which remain well-stocked, up-to-date, and dominant in the area. President Carter's policy of selling F-15 and F-16 fighter planes to Saudi Arabia and Egypt, in addition to the number already promised to Israel, has been seen as tilting the former balance, despite any "safeguards" attached to the sale agreements, and the problems of maintenance and training that always come in the same package as the planes.

Paradoxically, however, the zealous Zionist spirit of the 1948 generation—the Zionism so bitterly denounced by Arabs—has given way to an equally staunch but less emotional attitude today. A population becoming more mixed between Sephardic and Oriental (or North African) Jews and European Jews is producing younger leaders, more attuned to Israel's essential vulnerability and to practical politics than to Old Testament geography. Their voice will be heard in future cabinets and parliaments and has already been heard in the anti-Begin protests of 1978.

The young Jewish families in more than one hundred West Bank settlements, however, have hardly forgotten their religion and origins. They are aware that neither the Vatican, the United States, nor most foreign powers recognize Jerusalem as their official capital. They are aware of the UN resolution —passed with the United States abstaining—that "strongly deplores" the settlements. These Israelis do not mingle easily with their Arab neighbors, and life in the "administered area" resembles life under a military occupation, despite the relaxed border policy with Jordan. Local Palestinians feel a blunt Israeli presence in every aspect of their day-to-day existence.

Some observers contrast outspoken Israeli manners with traditional Arab etiquette, just as Jewish "practicality" is contrasted with Arab "rhetoric" and "style." As long as emotion predominates, neither tradition seems likely to contribute to a solution of the Palestinian problem. In addition, oriental Jews who were driven from their former homes in Arab countries do not feel indebted to their Palestinian neighbors. And, despite increasingly more mixed marriages, Orientals account for more than half of Israel's population.

While Israel undergoes a form of abrupt cultural evolution at home, Israeli attitudes arouse conflicting passions among Jewish intellectuals abroad. Debates and divisions are not uncommon in the pages of Western literary journals. Israeli militancy on the Palestine question is not universally supported. Few Jews, however, can forget the original Palestine Liberation Organization (PLO) premise that Israel must be driven into the sea or forget the atrocities committed by Palestinian terrorists. To the question of whether Israel should negotiate at the same table with PLO leaders, the reply has often been, "Would you talk with a person who says you must die at the end of the conversation?" If Yasir Arafat indicates a more moderate stance, Israelis have been taught by experience to wait for other Palestinian leaders to follow the new line—or counter it with renewed terrorism.

Mediation

Whether an American secretary of state or any other diplomat can mediate between the two sides today depends on some understanding of the historic associations between Arabs and Jews that go back to biblical times and show as many parallels as confrontations. Both peoples have suffered at the hands of Christians and the West, and both have emerged from periods of decline. Despite inflammatory rhetoric and uncompromising statements headlined day after day in the press, neither culture is a stranger to the process of mediation. Even if the Prophet himself failed to arbitrate matters between Jews and Arabs at Medina, his failure did not prevent the coexistence of the two peoples in the Great Age of Islam. Both the Arab historian and his Jewish colleague can find treasures in the medieval documents buried for a thousand years and then rediscovered in the 1890s in the *geniza*, or "storage room," of an ancient Cairo synagogue. Their histories are intertwined.

Whatever peace may eventually come to the Middle East, it will, like many other agreements, be exposed to accusations of sellout and treachery by politicians on every side. Marxists of the People's Democratic Republic of Yemen opposed admission of their newly independent Gulf neighbors into either the Arab League or the United Nations, and they are unlikely to compromise their devout, independent anti-imperialism in favor of an accommodation with Israel. One should keep in mind, however, that nothing is really impossible—even a fragile peace or productive stalemate—in the politics of the Middle East.

The Problem of the Palestinians

Now scattered between Libya, Syria, and the Persian Gulf,

The bitterness and frustration of thirty years of conflict is reflected in the faces of these Arab women of the West Bank.

Palestinians seek a recognized geographical homeland even if it means only a mark of national identity. Many would not want to leave their present homes to move to the West Bank, where there is not room in any event for the more than two million Palestinians living abroad. As a PLO leader has declared, the existence of a Palestinian homeland would not mean that all Palestinians would live there. Those Palestinians still in refugee camps—whose Arab support comes not from the rich oil states but from Syria, Jordan, Lebanon, and Egypt—would, however, presumably welcome a permanent place to live. The tireless diplomacy of U.S. Secretary of State Henry A. Kissinger as a broker between Israelis and Arabs brought this problem no nearer to agreement.

The peace conference convened at Geneva in December 1973 by the United Nations lasted only two days. Called to order under the joint chairmanship of the United States and the Soviet Union, it was recessed to allow Israel to hold elections and then faded into the background as Kissinger began a diplomatic shuttle between Syria, Israel, and Egypt. The principal issues, however, did not fade away. Who are the Palestinians? Now living as refugees, are they exiles or established newcomers in various Arab lands? Who represents the Palestinians—the PLO or more radical groups? Why cannot the rich Arab states assume responsibility for refugee Palestinians? Did Palestinians not leave their home-land temporarily at the specific request of the Arab League to make way for the 1948 invasion of Israel? Should a new Palestine be an autonomous nation or should it be attached to Jordan? Will Cuba, whose troops helped defeat one Arab League nation, join the Soviets in backing another member? Questions like these are made no easier by Israeli extremists. The problems are certainly not made easier by extremist groups like the Popular Front for the Liberation of Palestine (not the PLO), which threatened during talks in 1977 to "act against" any Arab leader who recognized Israel. In a general denunciation of terrorism, U.S. Secretary of State Cyrus R. Vance publicly accused Libya, Iraq, southern Yemen, and Somalia of aiding international air terrorists.

Global Politics

If the eyes of the world are now more than ever on the Middle East—to the point of causing a dramatic rise in Islamic and Egyptian art prices after a slump of several decades—Arab eyes turn more often to global landscapes. Saudi Arabia's vast wealth and wide investments make its leaders think in terms of geopolitics, of Australian oil rigs in the Bass Strait off Victoria, of leftist victories in France, and of solar energy in the United States. Against these horizons, Israel seems less like the major problem. Egypt, whose Suez victories in 1973 gave Arabs their first large-scale victory over Western arms since the Crusades, can look away from Israel to Soviet interests in Ethiopia, to Islamic strategy along the vital Horn of Africa, and to relations between Arab and black peoples.

The power that Arabs now have and the possibility of being a fertile link between developed and undeveloped countries reduce the temptation for Arabs to dwell on a past golden age. Today, more than one hundred million Arabs live in contiguous territory as a potential "Arab nation," with cultural and economic resources far more vital than demagogic and nostalgic oratory. (It may be that Arab rhetoric has been softened by Israeli victories and that Israelis are more vulnerable than before to their own orators.) A new sense of realism can be detected in the traditional Arab outlook, replacing the illusions and enthusiasms that vanished in the Six-Day War of 1967. Another sign of realism is found in recent Arabic scholarship, which has begun for the first time to examine the romance of Arab history with the tools of modern research.

Realism and Romance

Can realism ever be more attractive than romance and rhetoric? Can the "atomistic" Arab mind come to terms with Western "logic"? The sophisticated techniques that Arab oil ministers use in a complex world market provide substantial evidence that the Arab world can indeed deal with the West. If the industrial West can be accommodated by the Arab world, is there reason to believe that Israel, which Arabs see as a Western transplant, can be accommodated someday?

The struggle of realism against rhetoric has hardly begun. Recalling that the war of 1967 was won on the radio and lost on the battlefield, educated Arabs have become skeptical of political propaganda. Political sophistication even among the educated, however, is hindered by the Arab need for scientists and technicians, leaving students of the social sciences, history, and the humanities with far fewer job opportunities. The majority of Arabs probably continue to remain susceptible to rhetoric — weak in calling for unity, strong in preaching disunity. Iraqi radio urges the people of Syria to overthrow their leaders, and Syrian radio sends the same message to Iraq. Broadcasts from Baghdad — the "Voice of the Masses" — loudly denounce other Arab governments for stupidity in the face of "imperialist-Zionist machinations."

Increasing familiarity with the West, of course, does not necessarily make an Arab pro-Western. It is more likely to produce an informed anti-Western attitude, easily confirmed by general anti-Arab prejudices found in Europe and the United States. Although U.S. President Jimmy Carter has defended human rights in other countries and American editorials have denounced oppression of such rights in Tunisia, occupants of a Park Avenue building in New York City can publicly refuse to sell an apartment to a Saudi prince. Ethnic jokes about Arabs are as common today in London or Hollywood as Arab jokes once were about races subject to the caliph.

Arabs do not have to resolve their conflicting feelings about the West in order to bring their own masses up to a Western standard of life. Tunisia, oppressive or not, is part of an Africa that is making its first serious and effective effort against the scourges of disease and poverty. A middle class is slowly filling the gap between the poor and the westernized rich. The urban poor, however, are often unskilled and often out of work, and they remain a prey to revolutionary and religious propaganda in Arab countries. It will need more than memories of the Arab past and more than an injection of Western technology here and there to deal with urban frustrations. Problems in the Arab world require a true liberation of Arab intellectual and psychological energy.

The Past and the Future

Certain urban plagues of the West such as high crime rates have been discouraged by the severity of Islamic law. Although the Saudi tribes still preserve their ancient desert social democracy, the loosening of tribal ties in urban populations and the growing emancipation of women have produced profound reforms in legal practice. Under the Fatimids of Cairo, jewelers had no need to lock up their shops, and in most Islamic lands today crime has continued to be comparatively rare. The Arab League has recently reported an across-the-board increase in crime, however, especially in the oil states. Much of the increase is blamed on Western movies and TV and on the flood of new money.

Traditional punishments may have less deterrent value today than they seemed to have in the past. Rapists in Saudi Arabia, however, are beheaded, and thieves have their hands chopped off as the Koran prescribes. Adulterers have been buried to the waist in sand and stoned to death by modern Saudi mobs. One Saudi judge ordered that a German girl who had been raped be flogged for having helped incite the crime. (Not all Arab countries enforce basic Koranic law—even the puritanical regime of Libya jails thieves without amputating hands.) Such highly visible manifestations of Islamic justice have seemed primitive and horrible to Western critics, while the routine laws of marriage and divorce, as well as Islamic trial procedures, have been quietly modernized.

The most urgent social issues in Arab countries remain beyond the reach of any law. Birthrates soar while water supplies are scarce and oil revenues move toward their inevitable decline. Casablanca, Cairo, and Kuwait each has its special problems, but every Arab country will face the need for new economic resources. (Edward Teller, the U.S. atomic physicist, says that nuclear energy will become essential for *all* emerging nations; Israel is already the world's leading per capita user of solar energy.) If Syria can become the Middle Eastern California of tomorrow, equally dramatic solutions will be required for the rest of the Arab world. The visitor to Syria's future tourist, agricultural, and other wonders, however, will still find a culture defined in its own Arab terms.

In the streets of Cairo, where Egyptian humor has been famous for centuries, the latest jokes will continue to reflect an essentially Arab psychology. Arab folklore and language will continue to absorb new ideas as it did in the days of the conquests. The finest of modern Arab poets continue to write lyrics for the masses—a phenomenon unknown in the West. When the hypnotic Umm Kalthoum—the greatest Arab popular singer—died in 1975, she was wildly mourned not only by crowds in Cairo but also by millions of Arabs everywhere. She was succeeded as the popular favorite by Abdel Halim Hafez, known as "the tan nightingale"; and when he died two years later, the prime minister of Egypt led tens of thousands in the funeral procession. Like humor, poetry, and song, other Arab traditions will not easily be silenced in a technological future. The history of the Arabs lives as a treasury of romance and adventure, and their schoolchildren are not likely to forget the past splendor of great Arab courts or the victories of Arab heroes over the Crusaders. But traditional wisdom is always a more difficult lesson than patriotic romance. In the ninth century, a brave and innovative scholar called al-Jahiz, "the goggle-eyed," was recognized as a master of Arabic prose. Among the riches he left after his death, one short anecdote can testify to his prophetic genius:

> Ghailan son of Kharasha said to Ahnaf, "What will preserve the Arabs from decline?" He replied, "All will go well if they keep their swords on their shoulders and their turbans on their heads and ride horseback and do not fall prey to the fool's sense of honor." "And what is the fool's sense of honor?" "That they regard forgiving one another as a wrong."

Few races or nations have attempted to practice the wisdom of al-Jahiz, to forgive one another. As Arabs take up the difficult tasks of healing their own wounds and of building bridges between themselves and their neighbors in Africa and the emerging new countries, they may also find the bridge between themselves and Israel. These efforts will certainly mean more to the Arab future than the oil reserves that will one day be no more than a memory. Mecca and Medina have outlived all the glories of imperial Baghdad. If today's Arabs renew the wisdom as well as the chivalry of their tradition, the world will learn from them again.

BIBLIOGRAPHY

The New Encyclopaedia Britannica (15th Edition)

Propaedia: This one-volume Outline of Knowledge is organized as a ten-part Circle of Learning, enabling the reader to carry out an orderly plan of study in any field. Its Table of Contents—consisting of 10 parts, 42 divisions, and 189 sections—is an easy topical guide to the *Macropaedia*.

Micropaedia: If interested in a particular subject, the reader can locate it in this ten-volume, alphabetically arranged Ready Reference of brief entries and Index to the *Macropaedia*, where subjects are treated at greater length or in broader contexts.

Macropaedia: These nineteen volumes of Knowledge in Depth contain extended treatments of all the fields of human learning. For information on *The Arabs: People and Power*, for example, consult: Afars and Issas; Algeria; Anatolian Cultures; Arabia, History of; Arabian Desert; Arabian Religions; Arabian Sea; Baghdad; Baha'i Faith; Bahrain; Caliphate, Empire of the; Calligraphy; Córdoba; Crusades; Damascas; Druzes; Egypt, Arab Republic of; Egypt, History of; Fatimids; Hadith; Hamito-Semitic Languages; Iran, History of; Iraq; Islam; Islam, History of; Islamic Law; Islamic Mysticism; Islamic Myth and Legend; Islamic Peoples, Arts of; Islamic Theology and Philosophy; Israel; Istanbul; Jordan; Kuwait; Lebanon; Libya; Maghrib, Cultures of the; Mamluks; Mashriq, Cultures of the; Mauritania; Mecca; Medicine, History of; Mesopotamia and Iraq, History of; Middle Eastern and North African Peoples and Cultures; Morocco; Muhammad; North Africa, History of; Oman; Ottoman Empire and Turkey, History of the; Qur'an; Saudi Arabia; Seljuqs; Seville; Somalia; Sudan, The; Syria; Syria and Palestine, History of; Tunisia; United Arab Emirates; Yemen (Aden); Yemen (San'a'). For additional biographical and geographic entries, check individual names.

Other Publications:

Association of Arab-American University Graduates. *The Arab World from Nationalism to Revolution.* Edited by Abdeen Jabara and Janice Terry. Wilmette, Ill.: Medina University Press International, 1971.

Gibb, Hamilton A. R.; and Kramers, J. H., eds. *Shorter Encyclopaedia of Islam.* Edited on behalf of the Royal Netherlands Academy. Ithaca, N.Y.: Cornell University Press, 1953; reprint ed., Leiden: E. J. Brill, 1974.

Glubb, John Bagot. *A Short History of the Arab Peoples.* New York: Stein and Day, 1969.

Goitein, Solomon Dob. *Jews and Arabs: Their Contacts through the Ages.* 3d rev. ed. New York: Schocken Books, 1974.

Guillaume, Alfred. *Islam.* Harmondsworth, Middlesex: Penguin Books, 1954.

Hitti, Philip Khûri. *History of the Arabs from the Earliest Times to the Present.* 10th ed. New York: St. Martin's Press, 1970.

Hodgson, Marshall G. S. *The Venture of Islam: Conscience and History in a World Civilization.* 3 vols. Chicago: University of Chicago Press, 1974.

Holt, Peter M.; Lambton, Ann K. S.; and Lewis, Bernard. *The Cambridge History of Islam.* 2 vols. Cambridge: Cambridge University Press, 1970.

Hudson, Michael C. *Arab Politics: The Search for Legitimacy.* New Haven, Conn.: Yale University Press, 1977.

Lewis, Bernard. *The Arabs in History.* 4th ed. London: Hutchinson, 1966.

Lewis, Bernard, et al. *Islam and the Arab World: Faith, People, Culture.* New

York: Alfred A. Knopf, 1976. British ed. published under title: *The World of Islam*. London: Thames and Hudson, 1976.

Lewis, Bernard, ed. and trans. *Islam from the Prophet Muhammed to the Capture of Constantinople*. 2 vols. New York: Harper & Row, 1974. Vol. 1: *Politics and War*. Vol. 2: *Religion and Society*.

Mansfield, Peter. *The Arab World: A Comprehensive History*. New York: T. Y. Crowell, 1976.

Picture Credits

Key to abbreviations used to indicate location of pictures on page: t.—top; b.—bottom; *—courtesy. Abbreviations are combined to indicate unusual placement.

Page 8 Alain Nogues—Sygma -20 *Exxon Corporation -21 (t.) Staatliche Museen, Berlin -21 (b.) The Oriental Institute, University of Chicago -22 H. Roger Viollet -35 *The Chester Beatty Library, Dublin -46 Alain Nogues—Sygma -48 Middle East Features—Black Star -71 Klaus D. Francke—Peter Arnold, Inc. -87 Pier Gorgio Sclarandis —Black Star -95 Jean Dieuzaide—Rapho/Photo Researchers -115 George Holton—Photo Researchers -124 Jean Dieuzaide—Rapho/ Photo Researchers -129 The Metropolitan Museum of Art. The Cora Timken Burnett collection of Persian Miniatures and other Persian art objects. Bequest of Cora Timken Burnett, 1957 -175 Claude Salhani—Sygma -184 Sipa Press—Black Star -194, 195 Camera Press—Photo Trends -227 Claude Salhani—Sygma -228 UPI Compix -234 Sven Simon—Katherine Young -243 William Karel—Sygma -246 Sipa Press—Black Star

Index

a

The Inquisitive Mind

Bantam/Britannica Books were created for those with a desire to learn. Compacted from the vast Britannica files, each book gives an in depth treatment of a particular facet of science, world events, or politics. These accessible, introductory volumes are ideal for the student and for the intellectually curious who want to know more about the world around them.

☐ 12486 **THE ARABS:**
      People and Power $2.50
☐ 12487 **DISASTER:**
      When Nature Strikes Back
                                     $2.50
☐ 12488 **THE OCEAN:**
      Mankind's Last Frontier $2.50
☐ 12485 **THE U.S. GOVERNMENT:**
      How and Why It Works $2.50

The world
at your
fingertips

Leading historians, sociologists, political
scientists, economists, and anthropologists
offer personal and political analyses of the
world's developing lands.

☐ 11199   **QUESTIONS AND ANSWERS ABOUT ARABS AND JEWS** $1.95
           Ira Hirschmann

☐ 2884   **JAPAN YESTERDAY AND TODAY** $1.50
           Edited by Ray F. Downs

☐ 7473   **INDIA YESTERDAY AND TODAY** $1.50
           Edited by Clark D. Moore & David Eldredge

☐ 6426   **A DOCUMENTARY HISTORY OF THE MEXICAN** $1.50
           AMERICANS   Wayne Moquin

☐ 11068   **CHINA YESTERDAY AND TODAY** $1.95
           Edited by Molly Joel Coye & Jon Livingston

Buy them at your local bookstore or use this handy coupon:

Bantam Book Catalog

Here's your up-to-the-minute listing of over 1,400 titles by your favorite authors.

This illustrated, large format catalog gives a description of each title. For your convenience, it is divided into categories in fiction and non-fiction—gothics, science fiction, westerns, mysteries, cookbooks, mysticism and occult, biographies, history, family living, health, psychology, art.

So don't delay—take advantage of this special opportunity to increase your reading pleasure.

Just send us your name and address and 50¢ (to help defray postage and handling costs).